Abiding
in Christ

Abiding in Christ

Studies in John 15

James E. Rosscup

Wipf and Stock Publishers
EUGENE, OREGON

Wipf and Stock Publishers
199 West 8th Avenue, Suite 3
Eugene, Oregon 97401

Abiding in Christ
Studies in John 15
By Rosscup, James E.
Copyright© January, 1973 by Rosscup, James E.
ISBN: 1-59244-254-4
Publication date: June, 2003
Previously published by Zondervan Publishing House, January, 1973

*To some very dear people who are,
with me, among the many branches
in the True Vine:
My wife,* MILDRED;
my daughters, DIANNE *and* CAROLYN;
and my mother, MRS. LOLA ROSSCUP

Contents

Preface 9

1. The Meaning of the Vine to Us 13
2. What Suggested the Illustration? 20
3. Why Christ Calls Himself the "True" Vine . . . 29
4. The Father Is the Husbandman 38
5. The Pruning of Branches That Bear Fruit . . . 43
6. What Is So Important About Fruit? 64
7. Things That Sometimes Pass for Fruit 70
8. What God Labels as Fruit 78
9. Are Good Works Fruit? 91
10. What Makes a Good Work? 101
11. Things Involved in Abiding 106
12. Living Where God's Action Is 127
13. Abiding — With or Without Effort? 146
14. Let's Put It All Together 171
15. God's Judgment on a Professing Believer . . . 185
16. The Man Who Does Not Abide 211
17. Does the Father "Lift Up" Branches? 238
18. John 15:1-6 in a Nutshell 246

Preface

When John R. Mott was only about ten years old, his mother said to him one day, "The greatest chapter in the whole Bible is the fifteenth chapter of John." The boy grew up to become a great leader in the Student Volunteer Movement in the cause of Christ. John 15 became very meaningful and had its part in molding his life. While we do not need to claim that John 15 is the greatest chapter in the Bible, where there are many great chapters, we do recognize that it is very strategic. Because of its significance, there is much reason to devote a book even to the first six verses alone. I believe these first six verses are important to consider in detail for at least five reasons.

First, all the spiritual-life teaching which our Lord gave in the gospel of John and the upper room discourse reaches its apex in the illustration of the vine and branches. Christ taught other choice lessons, as when He spoke of His followers as servants who should wash one another's dirty feet and as friends who would do whatever He has commanded. But in the figure of the vine the intimacy of the Savior and His people is deepest. We immediately sense that our spiritual life itself flows from Him who tells us, "I am the vine, ye are the branches."

Second, most of the crucial aspects at the heart of the Christian life appear here. In Christ's words "I am," we are immediately involved with who He is. Then we see the Father's loving care, our own suffering, and our being cleansed by the Word of God. The life of abiding makes its compelling appeal to our hearts with a mysterious power of attraction. Vine branches richly loaded with the most lush and pleasing fruits flash before our eyes. Then comes a solemn note about judgment, and after this a brighter note on the sweet hour of prayer. In our meditation, it is not long before we realize that a serious look at John 15 involves us in the whole of the New Testament and, indeed, the entire Bible. What Christ tells us here is the heart of it all.

Third, I have been surprised to discover how little, apart from commentaries, seems to have been written specifically on the vine and the branches. Although there are several special books on Paul's concept of the body of Christ and the words "in Christ," it is not so with the vine. Andrew Murray has written more that bears directly on the subject than have others, especially in his books *The True Vine* and *Abide in Me* (1860). These, of course, were written a long time ago. There are, to be sure, books on certain subjects such as fruit and fruit bearing, but these do not seriously deal with John 15 per se. Most of them simply explain and apply the nine virtues in the fruit of the Spirit (Gal. 5:22, 23). For example, there are works like George W. Bethune's *The Fruit of the Spirit* (1839), H. B. Jeffery's *The Fruit of the Spirit* (1940), John E. Brown's *The Fruit of the Spirit* (ca. 1930's), William Barclay's *Flesh and Spirit* (1962), Charles Hembree's *The Fruits of the Spirit* (1971), and John W. Sanderson's *The Fruit of the Spirit* (1972).

None of these books explore many questions which I have found Bible classes often asking. They discuss Galatians 5 and not John 15. Murray's writings are to some degree an exception, since he writes on John 15 and seeks to explain the verses there. Yet he, also, does not consider many aspects of the passage, such as the full meaning of "fruit" as related to the New Testament concept as a whole. Nor does he relate "abiding" to other terms in the New Testament that speak of the Christian life.

Fourth, it is also important to study the allegory of the vine to decide what specific points we are justified in drawing from it and what points our Lord did not actually intend to teach by the illustration. Some make the allegory teach far too much in relation to the Christian. But Christ would not have us misuse His vital words and draw points from them that He did not mean to teach. One example may serve to illustrate the need for carefulness. One writer has said that the tiny particles of matter in the soil mean believers who are incorporated into the vine by the roots. Then he feels also that every cell of the vine represents a believer, each with a different function, as in the figure of the body of Christ (1 Cor. 12). At the same time, he says that each branch is a believer. [1] Two of these inter-pretations miss the point of Christ — that it is the branches that represent believers.

Fifth, it is significant to devote serious attention to the meaning of special problem verses such as two (the first part) and six. These have been much debated. However, apart from brief discussions of a line, a paragraph, or a page in commentaries, works on theology, and books for and against eternal security, it is a rarity to find anything in print that grapples with the identity of the branch which is taken away and the man who is "cast forth."

As I have faced the issues of this passage and the New Testament as carefully and objectively as I know how, I have had to decide against certain interpretations of men I greatly appreciate. It is not pleasant to differ with friends or decide against their views which have some appealing features. I sincerely believe that the views I have taken can be more solidly defended than others, and from more lines of evidence, in the final analysis. For example, this book does not agree with those who say that the person with no fruit (v. 2a) is saved. In the interest of his being saved and eternally secure, some have argued heavily on the fact that our salvation depends upon grace, not merit or fruit. But this logic does not prove that a *saved* person is in view in the first part of verse two. It misunderstands some of the issues, or fails to correlate different facets of the problem. Certainly the Bible teaches that salvation is on the basis of grace (100 percent) and not on the basis of fruit, and certainly it shows that a truly saved person is saved forever. But if we say this and only this, we are not really giving the full impression of the New Testament. We must also responsibly emphasize that it is only those in whom grace manifests the fruit of life (at least *some* fruit!) who have been genuinely saved. Biblical truth should be taught in biblical perspective. It seems to me that the emphasis against which I am reacting, while appearing on the surface to serve eternal security by grace, becomes warped on that one line of thought, doing injustice to the

---

[1] M. Eugene Boylan, *The Mystical Body, The Foundation of the Spiritual Life* (Westminster, Maryland: The Newman Bookshop, 1948), chap. 1, "Christ the Vine."

equally vital doctrine of the perseverance of the saints. True grace fosters perseverance with its fruit, as J. F. Strombeck has so capably reminded us in his book, *Disciplined by Grace*. [2] When I say, therefore, that fruit is a valid evidence that a person has been genuinely saved, and view the man with no fruit in 15:2 as evidently one who only professes to believe, I am by no means slighting the truth that salvation is altogether by grace. I am simply recognizing that "without [holiness] no man shall see the Lord," that "faith without works is dead," and that those actually justified bring forth "fruit unto holiness" (Heb. 12:14; James 2:20; Rom. 6:22). One of the purposes of chapter fifteen of this present book is to develop this concept.

This book seeks its justification, then, in contributing to the five areas just mentioned.

In order to be helpful in these areas, I have devoted the first fourteen chapters to matters of background, exposition, and issues in the Christian life. These chapters will be easier to read for most readers, as they keep the attention on our Lord's main thrust in the passage: abiding in Him and bearing fruit. Chapters fifteen through seventeen are geared more for those who wish to delve into serious study of difficulties in the passage. Since the verses have been explained in so many divergent ways, yet few appear to have searched into the issues very deeply, I have tackled the problem of interpretation in earnest. Pastors, teachers, students, and Christians in general who desire rich involvement in Bible study should find the discussion thought-provoking and profitable. Whether they agree with my convictions or not, they will have to face the issues. The final chapter is a review synthesizing the message of John 15.

My own response will be one of great gladness as a sharer of truth if the Lord is pleased to use this book to bless and build up other Christians. We together are simply branches in the One who told us, "I am the vine, the true one. . . . Abide in me, and I in you. . . . In this is my Father glorified, that you bear much fruit."

JAMES E. ROSSCUP

2 Chicago: Moody Press, 1946.

Abiding in Christ

THE MEANING OF
THE VINE TO US

I am the vine . . . (John 15:1).

A person who studies his Bible thoughtfully will ask,
"Why does Christ compare Himself to a vine? What points
of truth would He have me learn in this illustration about
Himself and believers?" In answer to this inquiry, it may
be said that the vine is an apt figure to teach us several
lessons. Let us consider suggestions about what Christ
wants us to see in the picture.

Lowliness. To some, the vine is an appropriate symbol
to convey the thought of the lowliness and humility of
Christ. The analogy would be this: just as a natural vine
is planted in the earth itself, so God the Father planted
Christ in His incarnation to be "a root out of a dry ground"
(Isa. 53:2). Though from eternity Christ was ever highly
exalted in majesty as God, in great humiliation He "became
flesh and dwelt among us" (John 1:14). He involved Himself with us in our environment, on the earth, and in this
aspect He is like a vine rooted in the earth.

There is nothing in this interpretation that is inconsistent
with what is true of Christ and men. But if this particular
point was in Christ's thoughts at all, it was, at best, only
a lesser point. The emphasis of the context is on other
lessons He intends to have us learn, and there is no focus
upon this idea of lowliness, even though Christ was truly
"lowly in heart" (Matt. 11:29).

Outreach. Macmillan and others have proposed that
Christ used the figure of the vine because a vine has the tendency to spread its branches far and wide. [1] This fits with

[1] Hugh Macmillan, *Bible Teachings in Nature* (New York: D. Appleton
and Company, 1867), pp. 174-177.

His purpose in the Gospel to extend His relationship to persons (branches!) to the ends of the .earth (Matt. 28:19, 20; Acts 1:8). If this lesson is intended here, it is in some sense, seemingly, comparable to His illustration of the mustard seed growing up into a tree to picture the magnification of Christ's kingdom reaching out in the world to embrace peoples from afar (Matt. 13:31, 32). This would relate to the fact that the branches of a tree, when used in Scripture, often picture a kingdom's far-flung influence. In such a way the Bible portrays Nebuchadnezzar's Babylonian empire (Dan. 4:10-27), the Assyrian empire (Ezek. 31:3ff), and even Messiah's future kingdom outreach to many peoples (Ezek. 17:22, 23). Young points to various passages in the writings of Herodotus, the Greek historian of the fifth century B.C., which employ the image of a tree.

> Thus, Her. 7:19 relates a dream of Xerxes, who, ready to set out against Greece, beholds himself crowned with an olive shoot, the branches of which stretch out over all the earth, but afterward the crown disappears; in 6:37 Croesus says that he will destroy the men of Lampascus "like a fir" since this tree when cut down, sends forth no fresh shoots, but dies outright; in 1:108 Astyages the Mede dreamed of a vine which grew from the womb of Mandane, his daughter, and spread over the entirety of Asia, the vine being Cyrus. [2]

The Roman historian Pliny, who lived near the time our Lord visited this earth, emphasized at length the remarkable spreading of vines. [3] He described how people in his day could ascend to the roof of the temple honoring the goddess Diana at Ephesus by a staircase formed from a single vine transported from Cyprus. He also wrote of entire country houses intertwined by shoots and tendrils of one vine. Sometimes he had seen the branches of vines embracing the limbs of poplar trees as though taking them as brides and rising even above their tops. One man, hired to gather the vintage of such high-reaching vines, was filled

---

[2] Edward J. Young, *The Prophecy of Daniel, A Commentary* (Grand Rapids: Wm. B. Eerdmans Publishing Company, 1949), pp. 101, 102.

[3] Pliny, *Natural History*, in Loeb Classical Library series (Cambridge, Mass.: Harvard University Press, 1952), vol. IV, bk. XIV. iii 12 ~ ¹⁰⁵

with awe at the sheer risk of climbing so far to bring down
all the grape clusters. So, in his contract, he made sure the
owner was responsible to pay the bill for his funeral and
grave should he suffer a fatal fall! Macmillan felt that
Christ capitalized on this characteristic of vines to spread,
depicting by it His passion for the outreach of His wit-
nesses among all nations. In this spirit we sing today, "My
gracious Master and my God, assist me to proclaim, to
spread through all the earth abroad the honors of Thy
name."

When we evaluate this idea of spreading in relation to
John 15, again we agree that the concept itself is true.
Christ said, "I will build my church," and this includes not
only the spiritual but also the geographical and numerical
aspects of the Church as His servants are mingled among
all nations. In that sense, it is possible to see the vine illustration as consistent at this point, too. Yet the clear-cut
emphasis in John 15 is not on *magnification,* as it is in the
parable of the mustard seed where there is *growth* from
a small seed to a fully developed tree. The more central
truths our Lord concentrates on in John 15 are union, communion, and fruit of the branches, not their tendency to
spread. The best conclusion seems to be, then, that the
vine branch picture is appropriate for, and consistent with,
the outreach of His people, but this is an attendant fact,
not the main emphasis.

Likeness. Macmillan also described how the vine pictures
the resemblance between Christ and His spiritual branches
and among the branches themselves. [4] There is a general
sense, he feels, in which the branches all show forth a similar
pattern, all reflecting the same "vineness." In the spiritual
realm, each believer displays to some degree the rare ex-
cellencies of Christ who has called him into His marvelous
light (1 Peter 2:9). This likeness may be weak and indis-
tinct now, but in normal spiritual growth Christians will
become more like their Lord. Finally, in glorification, they
will be wholly conformed to His image (Rom. 8:29; 1 John
3:2). In this likeness to God their Father, the children of

---

[4] Macmillan, *Bible Teachings in Nature,* pp. 182-186.

God are manifest (1 John 3:10). But, at the same time, this *general* resemblance allows for the *specific* individualities of branches in a vine and of persons in Christ. No two are exactly alike in every way. As Macmillan says of Christians:

> They have each some special divergence from the general type to prove their individuality. . . . In one, Christian reverence predominates; in another, hope; in another, faith; in another, love: the piety of one is retiring, that of another is bold and aggressive. Each one illustrates some special virtue. The manifold grace of God works in no two of them alike. The characters which God's people exhibit; the experiences through which they pass; the circumstances in which they are placed, are in no two cases precisely similar. And this diversity in unity presents in the Christian Church, as it does in the field of nature, the charm of a consistent variety, — each part relieving, heightening, and setting off the rest, and contributing to the harmony and beauty of the whole. [5]

How shall we evaluate this idea of likeness as a possible lesson our Lord may have intended in His illustration? Again, the concept is true to much Scripture and consistent with the nature of a vine. Since the very life of Christ is to be lived in the spiritual branches, and their fruit reflects Him, it would seem to be a valid lesson to draw from the passage. We shall see more of this a little later in the emphasis upon fruit.

Union and communion. The vine as a living organism beautifully illustrates the closeness of Christ's union and communion in life with those related to Him. *Union* is in view in His words "Every branch in me," and *communion* is seen in the words "Abide in Me, and I in you." The many branches in a real vine are a picture of believers sharing the same quality of life in the same source, Christ. Christ also used bread, water, and light to illustrate Himself, yet these are not living things and so are not as ideal as the vine to picture the continuous sharing of His very life essence with His own. Even the very close relationship a shepherd may have with his sheep (note the rich lessons

---

[5] *Ibid.*, pp. 185, 186.

we learn from such a passage as the twenty-third Psalm) does not convey the idea of deep, inner life union constantly enjoyed. Not even in the image of a father and a son is there the same illustration of life flow that is essential to life. A son may live distantly from a father. And so Christ's picture of the vine here serves the thought of union and communion in a very intimate way. It is similar to Paul's figure of believers united as a body with Christ the Head and living vitally by His very life (Eph. 4:12-16; Col. 2:19).

Relating closely with the idea of communion is that of *dependence*. It is a part of true communion. Branches in a natural vine can bear fruit only by virtue of the life they receive from the vine, and similarly those united with Christ must learn to depend upon Him. Adam Philip once said, "The object of Christ is not to make us independent of Him, but to make us dependent in everything."[6] Without Him we can do nothing (v. 5), but by His adequacy we can bear fruit, more fruit, and much fruit. It is significant to notice the way John 14 flows into John 15. As chapter 14 ends, we see the fruitfulness of Christ Himself as He was so perfectly in communion with, and depending upon, the Father for all things. Negatively, the "prince of this world," the devil, had nothing in Him, since the Father had everything. As such a fruit-bearer Himself, He then says, "I am the true vine, and my Father is the husbandman," and pictures by the vine how He is prepared to bear fruit through each person who lives in dependence upon Him for sufficiency.

Fruit. The vine is also ideal to illustrate that people united with Christ bear fruit that reflects Him. In a literal vine, the branches are not there just to decorate or to benefit themselves only. This is true of spiritual branches, too. God has not saved us so that we may make a stunning appearance in this world by showing off flashy personalities and the latest fads in fashions. These may be neutral in themselves; however, they are detracting if they draw attention

---

[6] Adam Philip, *Lingering in the Sanctuary, Notes on John, Chapters XIV-XVII* (London: James Clarke & Co., Ltd., 1936), p. 87.

primarily to ourselves rather than to the beauties of Christ. If we emphasize them for our own personal prestige, that is, with selfish motives, they are sinful, and, sadly, the lives of some are basically oriented around such outward things that will pass away. But it is possible to be "sharp" in personality and dress to the glory of God. We simply need to be pure in our motives and wise with regard to the image we project as Christ's branches, always seeking to show forth *His* likeness (1 Peter 2:9). In this proper sense, we certainly adorn His cause, shining as lights and drawing attention to His Word (Phil. 2:15). As branches, we "adorn" or "decorate" the doctrine we say has captivated our lives (Titus 2:10). Interestingly, Paul's word for "adorn" is the same as the word that describes the temple being adorned with beautiful gifts (2 Macc. 9:16), of a woman being adorned with a gentle and quiet spirit of godly submission (1 Peter 3:3-5, noun form), and even of trees adorned with fruit (Arndt-Gingrich). In this right sense, God desires branches adorned with spiritual fruit that glorifies Him.

Our Lord is honored when one of His own exults in glad testimony, "I am so happy I trusted in Christ, for He has done so much for me," for he is exalting God who "daily loads us with benefits" (Ps. 68:19). Such praise is *one* vital element of spiritual fruit (Heb. 13:15), yet the fruit for which God looks in our lives is "a many-splendored thing," much broader than thanksgiving for benefits alone.

Do you see how Christ continues to speak of this "fruit" for which His heart yearns? Have you noticed the emphasis of the passage? First, the word "fruit" occurs eight times (three times in verse two, twice in verse sixteen, and once in each of the verses four, five, and eight). Then a second feature spotlights fruit. Christ says in verse one: "I am the vine, the true one, and my father is the husbandman." Right at this point we might think it natural for Him to finish out the complete figure with the words, "and you are the branches." If such were the case, the words we find in verse two could then follow quite smoothly. But this is not the way He says it! After the words of verse one, He jumps right past all else and comes immediately to the thought of fruit! It is not until verse five that He rounds out the whole picture, adding "ye are the branches." Where there is union (a branch "in me"), our Lord's heart-passion is for fruit. And so it is also with the Father. The work in which Christ says He is engaged (v. 2) is in regard to fruit, either *no* fruit or *some* fruit. Later, He says, "In this is my Father glorified, that you bear much fruit" (v. 8; cf. also v. 5). This is also the desire of the Holy Spirit, though not specifically stated here, for later we are told of "the fruit of the Spirit," that which it is His business and pleasure to produce in believers (Gal. 5:22, 23).

These, then, are lessons Christ could have intended when He said, "I am the vine, the true one." And in giving these lessons, He is doing what He loves to do. He is visualizing what He is to those who trust Him by using a comparison God had already given to His people. For example, when He says of His relationship to men, "I am the bread of life" (John 6:35), His illustration relates to the manna in the desert (Exod. 16; cf. John 6:31, 32). In His words, "I am the light of the world" (John 8:12), He is evidently thinking of such passages as Isaiah 9 and 60. When He claims, "I am the good shepherd" (John 10:11), the rich background of His words is in such passages as Psalm 23 and Ezekiel 34:23. So His words in John 15 relate to God likening His people Israel to a vine belonging to Him (Ps. 80: 8-16; Isa. 5:1-7; Jer. 2:21; Ezek. 15; 19:10-14; Hosea 10:1). We see, therefore, that all of the important lessons of the vine were related to them. The Lord had planted them in the earth among the nations as His vineyard, as He later planted Christ and the members of His Church as a vine; He had desired that they spread His greatness and light by the very lives they lived; He had emphasized that they were united to Him; He had desired sweet communion with them and a spirit of dependence in them; and He had looked for them to bring forth good fruit showing His own likeness.

All that the Lord was to Israel He is prepared to be to us. Are we prepared to look to Him for this and live as branches related to Him?

WHAT SUGGESTED THE ILLUSTRATION?

I am the vine . . . ye are the branches (John 15:5).

It is constantly intriguing in Bible study to discover some dash of local color that makes the words spring to life for us. We feel as if we are CBS cameramen right there on the spot. Those who have studied John 15 in depth have proposed a wide variety of objects at hand to which our Lord might conceivably have pointed to illustrate His words. It is fascinating to relive those golden moments and ask what may have been before Christ's eyes and mind to prompt the words, "I am the true vine . . . ye are the branches." Here are the main possibilities.

The cup of wine. Christ looked down at the cup during the Last Supper and took His object lesson from "the fruit of the vine," for the wine suggested the vine from which it came (cf. Matt. 26:26-29; Mark 14:22-25; Luke 22:14-20). It was "a glance at the wine cup" that led to the picture, according to H. A. W. Meyer. [1] This is possible, but the connection does not appear to be a direct, immediate, and natural one. Luthardt finds in the proposal the problem

---

[1] H. A. W. Meyer, *Critical and Exegetical Hand-Book to the Gospel of John* (New York: Funk & Wagnalls, Publishers, 1891; cf. also J. H. Bernard, *A Critical and Exegetical Commentary on the Gospel According to St. John.* 2 vols. International Critical Commentary. Edinburgh: T. & T. Clark, 1928).

that the allegory specifically "speaks of the vine, not of the wine." [2] The living organism, not a product somewhat removed from it, is more likely in view.

The closeness of the disciples. The idea of a vine could have flashed into Christ's thoughts as He simply took in the scene about Him in the upper room. [3] His idea would be: "As you now stand around Me, hanging on Me in belief and love — I am the vine, you are the branches." Again, however, the connection would not be so immediately apparent as to prompt the specific figure of the vine.

A branch in the window. Tholuck, among others, sees Christ gesturing to a vine protruding past a window of the room where He was assembled with His disciples. [4] This point of reference, he says, launched the illustration. Some object to this on the basis that no vines grew inside Jerusalem itself, climbing the walls of buildings. But this is uncertain. The conjecture is at least possible.

A vine in the moonlight. This view, like certain others, is joined with the belief that the words following 14:31 must have been spoken after the exit from the upper room. [5] Christ said, "Arise, let us go from here." He could have stopped the party along the way to look at a vine. Others oppose this on the assumption that an address (chs. 15, 16) and even a prayer so intimate (ch. 17) would not have been spoken as likely along the way as in the privacy of the upper room itself. During Passover season, the city was teeming with people. Almost any street or pathway was likely to be busy with traffic.

The vine on the temple gate. Many, including Jerome, have been inclined to this setting. Rosenmuller supposes that Christ paused with His disciples to look up at the beau-

---

[2] C. E. Luthardt, *St. John's Gospel* (Edinburgh: T. & T. Clark, 1878), 3:140.

[3] *Ibid.*

[4] Augustus Tholuck, *Commentary on the Gospel of John* (Edinburgh: T. & T. Clark, 1860), p. 343.

[5] F. L. Godet, *Commentary on the Gospel of John* (Grand Rapids: Zondervan Publishing House, reprint n.d.), 2:293.

tiful filigree adorning the entrance of the Temple of
Herod. [6] Perhaps He even especially made His way to
the Temple to have one last, lingering view of it before
facing the events of His passion which He knew would
transpire so soon and so rapidly. There are some things in
favor of this scene. If our Lord had any particular vine
in view, this would be the most conspicuous one nearby to
arrest the group's attention along the way to the Kidron
Valley and the Garden of Gethsemane. It had been placed
on the gate specifically as a national emblem of Israel, the
nation whose people filled His thoughts as He pictured
Himself as the true vine. But there are also objections to
this view. Schaff says, "Christ would scarcely set Himself
over against a dead image of man's workmanship." [7]

In other words, this vine, though emblematic, was a *dead*
image in itself. Lange's objection is in essence the same.
The temple vine is only "artificial," not "lively." [8] And
Trench calls it "that dead work of man's art and device." [9]
However, one who favors the suggestion could answer that
such objections strain at a gnat, so to speak, since Christ
could have had in view the *life reality* which the filigree
itself only represented. But still another difficulty with the
idea of a discourse at the Temple gate is that the bustling
activity of crowds in the area during Passover time would
make such an intimate disclosure unfitting. Again this is not
conclusive. A group of people carefully concentrating may
form a little island of privacy among themselves even
though a sea of activity flows ceaselessly around them.
Nevertheless, the view does not appear really convincing
or likely.

The pruning fires of Kidron.   Certain eminent scholars
such as Lange and Westcott have felt that Christ caught

---

    [6] "Vine," *Calmet's Dictionary of the Holy Bible* (Charles Taylor, 1861),
pp. 876-879.

    [7] Philip Schaff, ed., "The Gospel According to John," in vol. 9, Lange's
Commentary (Grand Rapids: Zondervan Publishing House), p. 461.

    [8] J. P. Lange, *The Life of the Lord Jesus Christ* (Grand Rapids: Zon-
dervan Publishing House. 1958 reprint of 1872 edition), 3:158.

    [9] R. C. Trench, *Studies in the Gospels* (New York: Charles Scribner &
Co., 1896), p. 274.

sight of fires in the Kidron Valley east of Jerusalem as His party passed through on their way to the Mount of Olives. There, they suppose, laborers in the vineyards were burning the dead branches of the vines they had pruned. [10] This natural, on-the-spot scene prompted Him to draw a picture to fit with what He had said about intimate union in chapter fourteen ("you in Me, and I in you," v. 20). Lange thinks this background reasonable on several bases. One is that our Lord refers *first* to unfruitful branches, which are taken away (v. 2a). This would be natural if the most prominent spectacle immediately before the eyes of the disciples was that of the burning of such branches. Christ could later go back to what might have been. Also, Christ's present tenses in the last three verbs of verse six depict the actual process as though it was right then transpiring before their very eyes: "They are gathering them, and casting them into the fire, and it is (or they are) being burned." Lange bolsters this with the argument that it was the right time of the year for this type of burning. Engel rejects this setting with the contention that Christ spoke the words of John 15 in the springtime, whereas the vinedressers pruned their vines in the autumn or winter. [11] Engel's objection is not valid, however, since it is too limited in its understanding of pruning times in Palestine. It is true that the general grape harvest came in October and the pruning of the vines down to the stocks followed. But earlier prunings during the process of the growing season preceded that final pruning. One writer tells us:

> In March, after the vine has produced the first clusters, they cut away from the fruit that wood which is barren. In April a new shoot, bearing fruit, springs from the branch that was left in March, which is also lopped; this shoots forth again in May, loaded with the latter grapes. Those clusters which blossomed in March, come to maturity and are fit to be gathered in August; those which blossomed

---

[10] Lange, *The Gospel According to John*, Vol. 9 in Lange's Commentary. 12 vols. (Grand Rapids: Zondervan Publishing House), pp. 461-464; B. F. Westcott, *The Gospel According to St. John* (London: John Murray, 1882), pp. 216-218.

[11] F. G. Engel, "The Ways of Vines," *The Expository Times*, 60:111.

in April, are gathered in September; and those which blossomed in May, must be gathered in October. [12]

The noncommittal attitude.   Some agree with A. B. Bruce, who avoided hazarding even a guess: "For, after all, what does it matter how a metaphor is suggested (a thing which even the person employing the metaphor often does not know), providing it be in itself apt to the purpose to which it is applied?" [13] He is safe and also right in his emphasis, in a sense. Our Lord's point, not the setting, is the essential thing. However, it is still a matter of responsible study to decide, if we can, whether Christ was lingering in the upper room or was somewhere outside. The statements of 14:31 and 18:1 are involved, and we should seek to come to a decision about them. Also, is it not a part of the total essence of the meaning if the particular vine suggesting the figure is itself vitally related to the understanding of the allegory here?

The nation of Israel.   Some believe, and this is the best explanation, that Christ spoke the words of chapters fifteen to seventeen while yet in the upper room. He did not need an object directly at hand as a point of reference. Moreover, it is best to say that the specific suggestion for the figure He used was the fact that His people Israel had been described as God's vine. The basic setting makes the vine an ideal image to illustrate His relationship to the Church when the particular nation of Israel is set aside in this new age. We can see this, in the first place, by showing that it is more likely that Christ was still in the upper room and second by tracing the natural relation of the vine to Israel.

First, then, there are definite reasons supporting the belief that our Lord spoke the words about the vine in the upper room itself.

(1) The statement in 14:31 seems to suggest that they would go out immediately. But this is not a necessary inference. The verse does not say that they *did* go. The next statement about what Christ actually did is in 18:1,

12 "Vine," *Calmet's Dictionary,* p. 876.
13 A. B. Bruce, *The Training of the Twelve,* 5th ed. rev. (New York: George H. Doran Co., n.d.), p. 412.

and it does say unequivocally, after the words of chapters fifteen to seventeen, that Jesus and His disciples went forth. It appears best, from the little that the passage itself gives us to decide from, to understand 18:1 as meaning that they finally went forth *from the upper room.* As Lyman Abbott has said, 18:1 plainly implies that Christ did not go out from the room until the end of the conversation and prayer. [14]

(2) It would be quite natural for Christ to go on to say more after 14:31 before really leaving. All of the words of the following three chapters could have been spoken in a short time and, as Tholuck has suggested, "in the very intent of going, it happened, as is wont with persons about to depart, the impulse to communicate more still detained the Saviour in the room." [15] We ourselves know what this is in everyday life. When we have been visiting friends and say that we must be going, we do not go rushing out the door. Usually we linger a bit longer before leaving, exchanging our last words. This natural possibility fits with 18:1.

(3) The privacy would be greater in the upper room for chapters fifteen and sixteen and even more so for the prayer of chapter seventeen.

(4) Christ did not *need* an object visible at the moment as a springboard for His words. It is true, of course, that He frequently did use things at hand as take-off points for some analogous truths about Himself and men. There are examples such as those of the water at the well (John 4), the bread (John 6), and the death of Lazarus which occasioned His words "I am the resurrection and the life" (John 11). The same could be true in 15:1. But on the other hand, our Lord often illustrated freely and yet graphically from objects present only to the mind's eye at the moment. Think, for instance, of His likening the lifting up of Himself to Moses' lifting up the serpent in the wilderness (John 3:14).

Second, the very background of Israel as the vine in Old Testament, intertestamental, and Gospel times in itself made

[14] Lyman Abbott, *An Illustrated Commentary on the Gospel According to St. John* (New York: A. S. Barnes & Co., 1888), p. 185.
[15] Tholuck, *Commentary on the Gospel of John,* p. 343.

the figure of a vine instantly relevant to each disciple. Christ would not need the wine cup or a real vine to arouse His imagination or theirs. We have already referred to passages comparing Israel to a vine. The imagery of Israel is varied, of course, and so sometimes the symbol of fruitfulness is, variously, a fig tree (Luke 13:6-9), an olive (Jer. 11:16; Rom. 11:16-24), a fir or cypress tree (Hosea 14:8), a palm (1 Kings 6:29; 7:36; Ps. 92:12; Ezek. 40:16; 41:18), or a cedar (Ps. 92:12; Ezek. 17:22, 23). But the vine was the most notable of all the symbols from plant life.

A vine so fittingly pictured the idea of fruitfulness for Israel that the psalm writer uses the figure of a vine to describe the wife of a man of Israel (Ps. 128:3).

That Israel should be called a vine was richly appropriate and meaningful to a people who could see all around them illustrations of the law of bearing fruit. Their God had established this order in creation itself. Each plant was to bring forth seed "after its kind" (Gen. 1:11), and God had said to man, "Be fruitful, and multiply, and replenish the earth" (Gen. 1:28). The word "fruit" had come to designate the product of plants, animals, and people. Used metaphorically, it meant even the product of a person's thoughts, words, or acts.

Isaiah tells us that God had made Israel His vineyard with the supreme desire that she bear fruit to the glory of His great name. But despite His faithful care and all the advantages He had given her, Israel had brought forth stinking, worthless fruit (Isa. 5:4). Isaiah goes on in the passage to particularize what this bad fruit was. Where God had looked for the fruit of equity, He found inequity, and where He sought for righteousness He saw riot (v. 7). Greedy property owners heartlessly manipulated the weaker to rob them of their homes and lands (v. 8). Life for many had dwindled to the pitiful spectacle of a drinking debauch from morning to evening (vv. 11, 22). Worship of idols was rampant as men escorted their gods along in little carts (v. 18). Men whose values were all twisted came to evaluate their evil acts as good and appraised true good as evil

(v. 20). For example, it was common for a judge to hand down a decision getting a wicked man off the hook and condemning an innocent man in return for a bribe (v. 23). So God did not find in Israel, His vineyard, the true fruit for which He looked, but He found false fruit instead.

The Lord freshly emphasized His desire for good fruit in His vine, Israel, during the ministry of Christ and His forerunner, John the Baptist. This is portrayed in the parable of the wicked husbandmen, whose wrongs against God finally led them to put even His Son to death (Matt. 21: 33-41). The idea of fruitfulness also occurs in the figure of a tree which is similar to a vine. Indeed, as Pliny tells us, a vine could sometimes grow to such proportions that the ancients classified it as a tree. When John spotted spiritually dead religious authorities showing up at His baptisms, he called upon them to bring forth fruit consistent with genuine repentance (Matt. 3:8). Christ concluded His Sermon on the Mount with three striking illustrations depicting the saved and the lost. One of these featured a good tree bearing good fruit and a bad tree bearing bad fruit (Matt. 7:15-20). Our Lord frequently appealed to the imagery of plants when He wanted to picture the fruitfulness which He desired in His people (Matt. 12:33; 15:13; 21: 33-41).

It is natural, also, in the light of the Old Testament background relating Israel to a vine, that the people of Israel during the age between the Testaments chose to have the image of a vine on certain of their coins. This was an emblem of Israel. And in the Temple of Herod in Jerusalem, rising as an ornamental border above and around the gate leading from the porch to the holy place to the height of more than a hundred feet, was a richly wrought vine. Again, it stood for Israel. Its branches, tendrils, and leaves were of fine gold and its grape-clusters of precious jewels. Jewish men of wealth, inspired by pride in their nation, had added to the decorative luster at various times either a grape, a leaf, or some other feature of costly material. Some are reputed, though possibly with some exaggeration, to have valued that vine's cost at more than $12,000,000. [16]

It is easy to see, then, that when Christ chose the symbol of a vine in John 15, He was using one of the main images dear to Israelites. Some of their prophets, Isaiah (27:6) and Hosea (14:8), had even conceived for the nation a glorious future in terms of bearing fruit, which had largely failed to bear in the past. And an apocryphal book of the first century A.D., 2 Baruch 39:7, pictures Israel's future Messiah as a vine.

This background of Israel, and the lessons in it that also apply spiritually to Christ's body, the Church, in this age, which is in His thoughts in John 13-17, richly explains why He used the image of the vine at this time.

---

[16] "Vine," *Calmet's Dictionary*, p. 877. Cf. also Stewart Perowne, *The Life and Times of Herod the Great* (London: Hodder and Stoughton, 1957), p. 140; for ancient accounts, cf. Josephus, *Antiquities of the Jews*, xv. 11, 3, and *Wars of the Jews*, v. 5, 4, in William Whiston, trans., *Josephus, Complete Works* (Grand Rapids: Kregel Publications, 1960).

WHY CHRIST CALLS HIMSELF THE "TRUE" VINE

I am the vine, the true one . . . (John 15:1).

Have you ever noticed that when Christ says, "I am the vine" (v. 5), He has first specified (in a literal translation): "I am the vine, the true one"? We wonder immediately, if we are really thinking about our Lord's words, what is the shade of meaning He intends in the word "true"? Our English term translates the Greek word *alethinos.* We may discover the idea He invests in it by inquiring along two lines. First, we may simply pursue a word study of what it means in other passages. Second, we may look at the way this meaning harmonizes with the background of God's vine, which we have already traced.

The meaning of "true." Different shades of meaning are attached to *alethinos* in the Bible. It can speak of being true in the sense of that which is genuine, trustworthy, or faithful as distinguished from the false or spurious. So the Christian is to serve God with "a genuine" or "a faithful heart" (Heb. 10:22). In accord with this meaning, the word is even used of the genuine or "true God" in contrast to the empty delusion of false gods or idols (Isa. 65:16; 1 Thess. 1:9). The word in the Greek translation of the Old Testament corresponds with the Hebrew word *emeth* which is used, for instance, to denote "the true God" of Israel (2 Chron. 15:3). It comes from the root word *amen,* "to fix, establish," and, when used of God, represents Him as possessing firmness, stability, trustworthiness. He has this, of course, to the infinite degree. Idols do not. They are only the false objects of devotion in a heart diseased by sin and its delusions.

But this word *alethinos* in John 15:1 can also mean true in the sense of that which is eternal, heavenly, divine reality as distinguished from human and earthly reality only. It signifies the highest, most ultimate realization, the complete in contrast to the incomplete, the adequate as over against the inadequate, the perfect as distinct from the imperfect. It is the ultimate realization answering to a type. In the book of Hebrews this connotation comes out very clearly. Christ as our High Priest has entered into the "true tabernacle" in the heavens (Heb. 8:2), in contrast to the earthly tabernacle in the wilderness where the Jewish priests ministered. This does not imply falseness in the Old Testament tabernacle, which was made in obedience to God according to the very pattern He showed (Exod. 25). It means, rather, that it was only an imperfect earthly model of the ultimate reality already conceived in heaven. The Old Testament ordinances and ministries were "the example (i.e., copy) and shadow of heavenly things" (Heb. 8:5; 10:1) while, as Trench says, "the so filling up of these outlines that they should be bulk and body, and not shadow any more, was of Christ (Col. 2:17)." [1]

In the same way, John's frequent use of "true" in the sense of a perfect or ideal realization establishes an immediate context to help us define what Christ means in 15:1. Christ is the "true light" (John 1:9; cf. 1 John 2:8), which is the same as "the light of life" (John 8:12). [2] He is spiritually the highest quality or essence of light in distinction from human, earthly light; from physical, astral bodies He created; from John as a burning and shining light (John 5:35); and from other believers who serve Him as lights in the world (Phil. 2:15; Matt. 5:14). All of these are truly lights, but only He is the true light. Similarly, He

---

[1] R. C. Trench, *Studies in the Gospels* (New York: Charles Scribner & Co., 1867), p. 28.

[2] Gerhard Kittel, ed., *Theological Dictionary of the New Testament,* article on "Alethinos" (Grand Rapids: Wm. B. Eerdmans Publishing Company, 1964), 1: 250.

is "the true bread out of heaven" (John 6:32), the "bread of life" (John 6:35, 48), as the perfect ideal in contrast to the physical bread from heaven (Ps. 105:40) which God gave to Moses and his people. The Old Testament manna was truly bread, but it was not the true bread, or highest realization. It was only a physical and temporarily satisfying sustenance which pointed ahead to Christ, the bread which meets man's highest need spiritually and eternally. Also in John, the "true worshippers" (4:23) are this in the sense that they live in the sphere in which they enjoy contact with God's gift of the higher, divine life and are permeated by it.

In this sense, then, Christ is claiming to be "the true vine." He is saying, in effect: "I am the finest realization of the relationship which the Father had intended that a vine might bear to Himself. I will fulfill to the superlative degree and to the uttermost what the Father desires in a vine. I credit to myself an essence or spiritual quality that is heavenly and eternal, and not simply on the plane of earthly and temporary quality. As such, I am the resource beyond all resources, sufficient for the highest, deepest, and most ultimate longings of men."

This prepares us for the second phase of our consideration.

The relation of "true" to the background.   Christ's claim to be "the true vine" fits beautifully with the background in which God had planted *Israel* as a vine, and second with *natural* vines in the earth.

First, it fits with Israel. When we see the progressive development of revelation from the Old Testament into the New, several aspects of the relationship between Israel (the nation) and Christ merge. What God has said of the nation comes true in the individual person of her Messiah. Israel is God's son (Exod. 4:22; Hosea 11:1), and so is Christ (Matt. 2:15). Israel is seed which will enjoy the blessing of the covenant made with Abraham (Gen. 13:15; cf. 12:1-3), and Christ is the individual, singular seed par excellence (Gal. 3:16). Israel is corporately the Lord's servant (Isa. 41:8; 42:19, 20; 43:10; 44:1, 2, 21; 45:4), and Christ is the ideal, perfect Servant (Isa. 42:1-7; 49:1-12;

50:1-11; 52:13 - 53:12; cf. also 61:1-3). In a sense like this, then, Israel is the vine of the Lord (Isa. 5:1-7), and Christ is the ideal or true vine (John 15). The Old Testament even distinguishes the Messiah as the individual "Israel" (Isa. 49:3, 6). He is the true Israel, the perfect realization of all that God had intended that Israel could be, and the One through whom all of God's purposes for Israel might finally be realized.

Second, the true vine fits with natural vines in the earth. Christ must have had in His mind some thought of the natural vine. It is unrealistic and unnecessary to deny this, as some do (Trench), simply to establish that He was thinking of Himself primarily as distinguished from *Israel* as the vine. The symbol of a "vine" which had long been attached to Israel was itself derived from the natural plant which grew all about as an object lesson in the daily life of the people of Israel. God has a wonderfully organized plan in which things relate and correlate in the world He created. In His great love for men, He has designed that even things like plants can teach lessons about persons, the kingdom of nature is a picture of the kingdom of redemption, and physical laws often illustrate spiritual laws. The infinitely perfect ideals which He has conceived in heaven He has chosen to reflect on the earth in copies or pictures. These point man beyond himself to the revelation of the ultimate things. God made the vine, with its features, and He made spiritual relationships which it so aptly illustrates. Now this vine did come to be a well-known emblem for Israel, and Christ did have Israel in view in 15:1. But at the same time, the image of the natural vine itself is undoubtedly also in the background as an associated picture. It must have flashed quite spontaneously into the disciples' minds as it does into ours.

Now, consider that Christ claims to be the vine. He is a distinct person, an individual, yet it is also true that as the vine He is the collective whole of those who are organically in union with Him. This is similar to the corporate conception of Christ and His own as a body, "the fulness of Him that filleth all in all" (Eph. 1:23). Godet aptly says that the word "vine" here includes the stock and the branches, as the term "Christ" in 1 Corinthians 12:12 designates Christ and His Church. [3] Commenting on that same verse, Robertson and Plummer agree: "From one point of view Christ is the Head, but that is not the thought here. Here He is the whole Body, as being that which unites the members and makes them an organic whole." [4] In light of this, Hastings says, "Thus we see Jesus the Incarnate Son, a new stock of humanity, planted of God and in the earth, able to expand His own life over others, and so to include their lives in His own, and (if we may use the language here suggested) to ramify Himself in them." [5] Davies says of this conception:

> Such a statement can only be understood in the light of what is called the idea of "corporate personality" in the Old Testament and Judaism. The whole of life was regarded as one bundle. Each was bound to each. What one did affected all others. Thus, when a single member of a tribe sinned, all sinned; each was in all and all in each. One member could *represent* or *be* the whole tribe. It is such ideas that inform the notion of Jesus as the true vine; he is the true Israel. [6]

In line with this conception, when the high priest of Israel went into the Most Holy Place of the tabernacle on the great day of atonement, he represented the entire nation and was, in a sense, the nation there before God (Lev. 16).

How does this truth apply to the life of the Christian today? Hudson Taylor, founder of the China Inland Mission (now the Overseas Missionary Fellowship), tells how a similar insight into his *oneness* with Christ as portrayed

---

[3] F. L. Godet, *Commentary on the Gospel of John* (Grand Rapids: Zondervan Publishing House. Reprint), 2:293.

[4] Archibald Robertson and Alfred Plummer, *A Critical and Exegetical Commentary on the First Epistle of St. Paul to the Corinthians*, in The International Critical Commentary (Edinburgh: T. & T. Clark, 1958), p. 271.

[5] James Hastings, *The Great Texts of the Bible* (New York: Charles Scribner's Sons, 1912), 12:184, 185.

[6] W. D. Davies, *Invitation to the New Testament* (New York: Doubleday, 1966), pp. 477-478; George Johnston, "The Allegory of the Vine: an exposition of John 15:1-17," *Canadian Journal of Theology*, vol. 3, no. 3, July, 1957, pp. 152, 153.

especially in John 15, flooded his life with the joy of trustful rest. This replaced a fretful striving in which he had been depending too much upon his own sufficiency of effort.

> . . . As I thought of the Vine and the Branches, what light the blessed Spirit poured direct into my soul. . . . I saw not only that Jesus would never leave me, but that I was a member of His body, of His flesh, and of His bones. The Vine, now I see, is not the root merely, but all — root, stem, branches, twigs, leaves, flowers, fruit; and Jesus is not only that: He is soil and sunshine, air and showers, and ten thousand times more than we have ever dreamed, wished for, or needed. Oh! the joy of seeing this truth. [7]

If Christ is in some sense the whole vine, He is closely related to every believer in some particular sense. We must not misunderstand that sense. What is the sense, then? He, the true vine, expresses the characteristics of His "vineness" to and through the branches (persons) related to Him. He is "in" every believer in a vital union (John 14:20; Col. 1:27), and so He is everywhere His people are in the sense of this indwelling reality. To the extent that a branch lives by Him, He expresses Himself through that branch as the "true vine," in that place and at that time, even as He, living always by the Father, expressed Him in every place and at all times. He could say, "He that hath seen me hath seen the Father" (John 14:9). Christ, then, is *individually* His fruit-bearing self today in terms of each person who is in Him and *corporately* in terms of the total number of branches throughout the earth and also through the many generations. The truth becomes very personal to me in this way. I represent Him in my sphere of life, opportunity, and influence, with the gifts He has given to me. In my secret life and outwardly to the people I meet, Christ is what I receive Him to be and reflect of Him. In a sense, I am a little of Christ, and the combined life-manifestation of all true believers makes a comprehensive outreach of His heart as expressed in this world today.

---

[7] Cited by F. J. Huegel, *Bone of His Bone* (Grand Rapids: Zondervan Publishing House, 1959), p. 105.

We may draw an appropriate application from Pliny's words long ago about vines in Italy: "When the vine is in blossom all over the country, it gives a scent that surpasses any other in fragrance." [8] Now relate this description to John 15. Christ as the vine has a fragrance above all fragrances that appeal to men in the world. Let us who are branches in the vine give forth His freshness in place of our staleness, His sweetness in place of our stench, His life in place of our deadness, His fragrance in place of our foulness.

But in ourselves we find so much that is stale, stinking, dead, and foul. We have a sin nature, and corruption still permeates our lives to some extent day by day (Rom. 7: 14-25). Every true Christian should realize that as a fruit-bearing branch his appropriation of and reflection of Christ is not yet absolutely perfect. He needs daily cleansing (John 13:10, 11; 15:2b; 1 John 1:9; 2:2; 3:3). He must yet go on to a greater capacity for reflecting Christ by "more fruit" and "much fruit." Even if he is in the category of "much fruit," he finds that it is dynamic and not static. We may be ever abounding more and more within this classification as we go on growing in Him. Whatever is of self and does not have in it the quality and essence of His imparted life ("vineness") from above, the "true life" of the "true vine," is not His fruit. It is in another category, our own "nothing" (v. 5), and so is a sorry contradiction of His life that is in a specific realm — a branch which inconsistently reverts back to the self-sufficiency of the life before salvation and bears "of itself . . . without me" (vv. 4, 5).

Many other applications also begin to dawn upon the Christian. For example, it is not his bank account, or the concept in education that "knowledge is power" (in itself), or the satisfaction oriented to and deriving from sex, that is to become the "vine" in which he lives, the center of his life. As he learns well the new lessons waiting for him in the Word of Christ (cf. Col. 3:16), he sees that he is never to place an improper emphasis upon the limelight of popu-

---

[8] Pliny, *Natural History*, Book XIV, ii.1-9, in Loeb Classical Library (Cambridge, Mass.: Harvard University Press, 1952), p. 191.

larity, fame, or "connections." He must not tolerate becoming absorbed just with "things," as though they are the
be-all and end-all of life for him (married to his work,
inordinately given to food, being a bookworm who craves
romance stories and indentification by imagination, and on
and on). He learns to discern and judge within himself
any relationship, or person, or ambition, or project, or organization that becomes to him, in the final analysis, the "vine."

Take, for example, this situation that often happens. A
Christian girl "falls in love" with a Christian fellow (or
vice versa). She knows that he loves Christ, has a rich
devotional life in the Word, and delights in talking about
Him when they are together. She tunes in to his wave-
length, begins to have times of personal devotions in the
Word, and tries to enter into the conversation. But it just
isn't real to her somehow, since she is only going through
the outward motions, acting a part. Eventually, the fellow
senses this, and as they talk together about the matter, he
realizes that she has actually been orienting her life around
him, not Christ. She has done everything chiefly for his
sake, to win his approval, and not as a "branch" living in
vital relationship with the true vine, Christ.

The church may even be a false vine, believe it or not.
Some churches virtually claim to be a vine, giving people
the idea that their vital life is in the organization and the
activity per se, whereas the emphasis must ever be unmistakably upon Jesus Christ. *He* is the vine, the true one.
And even a regular meeting with other Christians can itself grow into the status of a vine, substituted subtly for
Christ Himself. A believer can keep going back to that
weekly fellowship supper (and he ought to be there if he
can be!), and somehow depend upon that, letting it take
the place of a direct, immediate reliance upon the Lord
Himself that is branchlike. Or, he can hear a captivating
speaker on spiritual life and be carried away with the idea
that if he can only get his notebook crammed with enough
"fabulous" thoughts, he can simply live on these. But if he
traffics only in secondhand truth, or an experience "borrowed" from another, it soon leaves him as stale as yester-

day's toast. He can allow a subtle substitution of another Christian's blessing to be, in effect, his "vine." Even more subtly, he can let his own blessing become a "vine," rather than looking to the One from whom the blessing comes. Again, it may be that his skill or ability looms in his life as a type of "vine." He can become intoxicated with his own prowess as an athlete, living on the deceit that this will carry him through. Or it may be a beautiful singing voice, or great skill in oratory. If so, he must judge within himself that false vine and say by simple faith: "Christ alone is the *true* vine, and He is *my* vine!" For he sees that if Christ is the highest realization of what a vine can be in His relation to men, then all other values in life pale before the value of being rightly oriented to Him.

THE FATHER IS THE HUSBANDMAN

Behold, the husbandman waits
for the precious fruit (James 5:7).

The thoughtful person finds right at the beginning of chapter fifteen a phenomenon that may strike him as strange. Christ pictures Himself as a *plant* but the Father as a *person* who tends the vineyard. This is a good example of the fact that no one image in the Bible is designed to teach *all* details of truth. There is always some main emphasis or point within an allegory, parable, or any figurative literary device. Look for that. Do not demand that the image be perfectly consistent in all facets — that it speak on everything at the same time. In Christ's illustration here, then, His relation to the Father is that of a plant to a person. He pictures His relation to men as that of a plant to its parts, one of close, deep, inner intimacy, just as a branch relates to a vine: "Abide in me and I in you." The fact that He presents the Father as only a vinedresser might disturb some. After all, a vinedresser, even though he works with branches, has no deep, inner relationship with them. He is somewhat removed. We might ask, "But doesn't the Father as God also dwell within the believer? And is His relation to the Christian *less intimate* than that of Christ?"

In response to the first question, certainly the Father does dwell within the true believer (John 14:23; Eph. 4:3). In answer to the second, the Father does have an intimate relationship to the Christian. Christ's illustration is not inconsistent with such a reality which the Bible clearly teaches in other places. Here it is not His concern to include all the technical aspects of the full doctrine of indwelling in one image, but to focus on only certain aspects of truth about Himself and the Father as they relate to believers. If we are to put together a full picture of truth, we must draw from the total expanse of God's Word, correlating all details into one immense and magnificent design.

We see, then, that many different associations may be true at the same time in a beautiful balance. For example, the Father *dwells* within the saved person, yet He also *cares* for him, so that it is fitting to liken Him to a husbandman. But the truth of nearness is not lacking even in the figure of the husbandman. Christ shows this by concentrating specifically on actions the husbandman can do only when he is very close to a branch. He must be near to cleanse a branch. F. E. Marsh once said, "Do not forget that the branch of the vine is never so near the husbandman's hand as when he prunes it." [1]

Just what is a husbandman? The word Christ used in the Greek is *georgos*. It is made up of two words, *ge* (the earth) and *ergo* (to work). Literally, it refers to a worker in the earth, and it came to be used in two ways. First, it meant a tiller of the ground or farmer in general, whatever his product (2 Tim. 2:6; James 5:7). A related form, *georgion*, means "tillage" or "cultivated land," [2] and is applied metaphorically to believers comprising the Church. They are God's field, which He works (1 Cor. 3:9). Paul thought of himself as a co-worker with God in tilling the field of believers so that fruit might be produced in them. Second, the work was applied to a farmer of vineyards, a specialized crop. He was called a husbandman (Matt. 21:33-41; John 15:1). According to some authorities in Greek, *georgos* can mean the proprietor or lord of a farm as distinguished from *ampelourgos*. The latter word occurs only in Luke 13:7 and seems to mean a person in a subordinate capacity

[1] F. E. Marsh, *Fully Furnished* (London: Pickering and Inglis, n.d.), p. 103.

[2] Wm. F. Arndt and F. W. Gingrich, *A Greek-English Lexicon of the New Testament and Other Early Christian Literature* (Chicago: University of Chicago Press, 1957), p. 156.

as a vinedresser. [3] In that verse, the owner of the vineyard issued orders to the *ampelourgos* to cut down the fig tree that was not producing fruit. This worker, in turn, addressed the owner as "lord." That *georgos* can mean the proprietor is also attested by passages from the Old Testament. In the Greek Old Testament, or Septuagint, it is applied to Judah's King Uzziah (2 Chron. 26:10) and also to Noah (Gen. 9:20). The plural form of the word, *georgoi*, translated "husbandmen," occurs in Matthew 21:33-41, where Christ was referring to the chiefs and leaders among the Jews. The *georgos*, as proprietor, could do his work by the hand of others or he could do or share in it himself. When we apply this to God our Father, we recognize that "the earth is the LORD's, and the fulness thereof" (Ps. 24:1). As proprietor over all, He may work directly with His vine and branches, or deal with them through the instrumentality of others who in various capacities carry out His will.

What does Christ mean to teach when He identifies the Father as the husbandman while He is Himself the vine? He explains this immediately in verse two. He sets forth two specific things a husbandman does with branches in the physical realm, and these represent two analogous things that God does with persons in the realm of spiritual reality.

In His explanation, He is not concerned to relate the Father's activity as husbandman toward Himself as a Person but to the branches (persons) in Him. We shall look at this at length in just a moment. But before leaving the matter, how does the Father as husbandman relate to Christ *personally* as the vine?

The Father's relationship to Christ. We may see this in two aspects.

(1) As a husbandman cares for His vineyard, and as God had cared for His own Old Testament vineyard, so He cared for His true vine which He planted in the earth in the

---

[3] R. C. Trench, *Studies in the Gospels* (New York: Charles Scribner and Co., 1867), p. 276; Marvin Vincent, *Word Studies in the New Testament* (Grand Rapids: Wm. B. Eerdmans Publishing Co., 1946), 2:249.

fulness of time to fulfill His purpose for fruit. He brought forth His servant, the BRANCH (Zech. 3:8; 6:12), His "fruit of the earth," Messiah Himself (Isa. 4:2). Christ tells us clearly that He does nothing of Himself apart from the Father (John 8:28; 10:32, 37, 38), that He does the things of the Father (John 5:19), and that He always does the things that please Him (John 8:29). In fact, "the Father abiding in Me does His works" (John 14:10). As husbandman, God the Father watched over Christ

> so as to develop by His providence the true glory of the Humanity. He does not seek to make the manhood of Christ fruitful in any way contrary to the nature of man. Christ's human nature was fitted to germinate in every form of humanity. It possessed the virtues necessary for every individual character, so that His righteousness might really be adequate to all the needs of all times and all ages. The new regenerate Humanity should derive its completeness from the moral nature of Christ, cherished by the providence of God as the great Husbandman. [4]

(2) The Father also cares for Christ the vine by giving believers to Him to be branches (John 6:37; 10:29; 17:6, 12). Under a slightly different figure in the plant world, the Father has planted believers (Matt. 15:13). In Paul's vivid figure from plant life, they are "grown together" or "ingrafted" in the likeness of Christ's death and shall be also in the likeness of His resurrection (Rom. 6:5).

Blessed in the care of the great Husbandman, Christ fulfills His role as vine in two aspects. He brings forth fruit in His own obedient response to the will of the Father. Many agree that Psalm 1:2, 3 is, in the final analysis, a picture of Him, the perfect model of a fruit-bearing tree nourished by the rivers of water. Second, He also lives out His vine life in regard to bearing fruit through others who relate to Him as branches. Paul could say, "Christ liveth in me." This He ever continues to do.

The Father's relationship to believers. As we have said, the emphasis in John 15 is upon the Father's ministry toward *believers.* Christ introduces the believer as a "branch"

---

[4] R. M. Benson, *The Final Passover* (London: J. T. Hayes, 1884-95), 2:6.

and explains how the husbandman works with two kinds of branches. There is the branch that bears no fruit (v. 2a) and the branch that bears fruit (v. 2b).

At this point we will merely summarize briefly the type of persons Christ was referring to by this contrast. First, there is the phrase "every branch in me that beareth not fruit. . . ." This refers to every person who professes a relationship to Christ and is seemingly a follower but who has not actually been saved. That which is a continuing characteristic of his life, the fact that he does not bear (present tense) any fruit at all, is a giveaway of his actual status. The consequence for such a person, who is apparently but not authentically in Christ, is that the Father takes him away. This means that He takes him away in judgment. Christ vividly develops more about this type of person in verse six. Since the meaning of verses two and six is a much debated question and there are many views and facets to consider, we are reserving this for a special, expanded discussion in chapters fifteen to seventeen. Second, we have Christ's reference to "every branch that beareth fruit." The Father's action toward this person is different. He finds in this one some of the precious fruit for which He patiently waits as Husbandman (cf. James 5:7), and knows him to be not merely a professor at heart but really a possessor. He goes on pruning or cleansing (present tense) his life so that, without certain hindrances and with a fuller responsiveness to divine life, he may bear even more fruit. Hence, in the life of this person, who is saved by grace, there is at least *some* fruit showing forth the fact that God's grace has truly touched him. And there is growth which begins and continues with a genuine experience with the Word of God (vv. 3, 7; cf. John 14:21; 17:17; 1 Peter 1:23; 2:2, 3; 2 Peter 3:18, et al.). This is the process within the Christian which we call sanctification, or a life of bearing "fruit unto holiness" (Rom. 6:22).

THE PRUNING OF BRANCHES
THAT BEAR FRUIT

. . . and every branch that beareth
fruit he purgeth it, that it might
bring forth more fruit (John 15:2b).

A congregation was caught up in awe as a scintillating Bible teacher climaxed his conference series with another stirring message. He pictured the believer's privileges in Christ with flowing beauty of argument, sparkling phrases, and vivid illustrations in which all seemed ideal. Then the series ended, and God's people departed in many directions. There had been some dazzling messages, but somehow the speaker had not often touched earth with the shoe-leather realism that most of us have to face in the workaday world as it is. His omission was not intentional, yet his overall presentation was so one-sided that it conveyed a misleading impression that the Christian life is a comfortable luxury ride on Pink Cloud Number Nine.

So, what happened to those who heard? Well, of course, those with spiritual discernment and levelheadedness that comes with maturity inhaled the messages as rarified alpine air. They went back to their daily tasks refreshed and encouraged to live more than ever in the all-sufficiency of Christ. But they fully expected to do this in a context of troubles! And they were not disappointed. Yet they found that Christ actually is completely faithful whatever the circumstances. Other believers, however, had a different experience. They heard the messages without getting them in balance with that total perspective of the Christian life that the speaker should have communicated. They went away with stars in their eyes. Their thoughts were filled with romantic notions about their adequacy in Christ. They took no long, sober account of the rough, tough, and sometimes stormy context in which they would have to face the "acid test" of applying these beautiful concepts. Somehow they expected life to be a comfortable breeze now, not a strong headwind. And then some harsh circumstance slapped at their life as a treacherous wave smashes against a boat on the Sea of Galilee during a storm. They were spiritually dazed and bewildered. Their glamorized idea of life in Christ, so one-sided as to be simply unrealistic, burst like a pricked bubble. They were not prepared to see this abundant Christian life run into a storm. As they compared their notes on the speaker's description of life with their own rugged experience of it, an inward sob arose out of their confusion: "I don't understand it. If God wants me to know the lavish fullness of His life, in an experience that is glorious even now, *why this terrible experience?*"

God voices His answer to this sob frequently throughout His Word, though it might not find its way into a brief series of messages at a Bible conference. Those just beginning in the Lord may not yet realize that the seemingly harsh situations of life must be understood as compatible with, and even as an integral part of, the plan of a God who is love. But any Christian, whether he be a scarred old soldier of many battles or a baby in the "diaper stage" of spiritual living, can receive blessed comfort as Christ briefs him on what to expect: "And every branch that beareth fruit, he (the Father) purgeth it, that it may bring forth more fruit" (John 15:2b). In these words and those that follow in verse 3, Christ speaks particularly in four ways about the Christian's sufferings. [1] He speaks of (1) the *individuals* who are pruned — "every branch that bears fruit"; (2) the *idea* of the pruning — "he purgeth it"; (3) the *intent* of the pruning — "that it may bring forth more fruit";

[1] C. K. Barrett, *The Gospel According to St. John* (New York: The Macmillan Co., 1955), p. 395.

and (4) the *instrument* for pruning — "the word which I have spoken unto you." Let us consider these in order.

The individuals who are pruned. In our Lord's words "every branch that beareth fruit" there are two very encouraging details for the Christian. (Actually, the word "branch" is not repeated in the second half of verse two, but it is plainly understood in the translation because it appears in the preceding phrase.)

First, Christ spotlights the attention upon branches that *bear fruit.* This, in itself, is a blessed comfort to the child of God. The presence of fruit — *some* fruit at least — is an indication that one has actually been begotten unto life eternal. The life of Christ the vine in a branch issues in the product of life — fruit. There are yet possibilities for increase in "more fruit" and even "much fruit," and even "more" for those bearing "much," but it is in order here to dwell upon the fact that *life with its fruit has begun.* One who belongs to Christ in reality may have had heartbroken misgivings about times of emptiness and failure because of sin, yet in the light of God's Word his evaluation can also discern some fruit and a child's desire to do the Father's will. It is true that one may possess salvation but be without *assurance.* Although this may stem from his tolerating and being unrepentant about sin, it may also result from a type of teaching that misconstrues certain verses or from one's own fearful misconceptions about what the Bible says in its total witness on the subject. But it is also true that any branch to whom the Father extends His care of 15:2b can *know* he has eternal life as a present-tense actuality. In 1 John 5:13, John says that we may know. This is because our fruit meets the tests he has given, and we have the "fruit unto holiness" or "fruit of righteousness" to which Paul refers (Rom. 6:21, 22; Phil. 1:11). With T. C. Hammond, we may regard this as a valid and vital evidence. Two cases, those of Dick and Marty, stand as examples.

Dick says that he is a Christian and, in terms of the analogy here, would think of himself as a branch in Christ. He has had his ups and downs, his ins and outs, as far as sweet, experiential fellowship with Christ is concerned. He knows something of the Scriptural concept that fruit is the essence of Christ living in the Christian, and he is sure that Christ has produced some fruit in him. However, he sadly realizes that for the past several days his inward life has been a miserable failure. How could Dick see himself in 15:2b? He could do so legitimately by recalling the fact that he did receive Christ into his life and became a child of God (John 1:12; 1 John 5:11, 12); that the Spirit had often borne witness to his spirit that he is a child of God (Rom. 8:16, 17; 1 John 3:24); that he is even now miserable because he feels he has been thinking "out of character" and not as he knows is the Father's will for His child; and that he has produced fruit in the past. Thus Dick could say, "Father, I have sinned against You so absurdly. I know I belong to You, for I claim the promises You can never fail to keep. There has been fruit of Christ in my life before, and I do desire more fruit. I confess the sinfulness of my attitude and the things it has led me to do (he may specify here). Thank You for forgiving me and cleansing me according to Your word in 1 John 1:9."

Marty's case is quite different. He professed to become a Christian a long while ago, was received into church membership, participated in activities with other Christians, and even zealously witnessed to others. But after about a year, he withdrew from his regularity in meeting with others for any type of fellowship. Soon he dropped this altogether. Some of the Christians sincerely sought to look him up and help him, but they found that he tried to avoid them and learned that he had fallen in with a bad crowd. Through a casual conversation with one of Marty's new friends, the fact came out that he had been sleeping with a divorcée, had also had a string of immoral escapades with other women, and frequented stag parties to watch lewd films. When one of the Christians finally caught up with Marty himself, Marty was quite nonchalant. He said, "Oh, I'm a Christian, but I've read some other viewpoints too, and I think some of these other religions have a lot going for them. Since you know something about these women, well, I'm not denying it. As a matter of fact, frankly, it's really fun, and I like it. Maybe sometime I'll see things the way you do, when I'm ready, but right now I just don't feel the way I used to about it."

There is a vast difference in the attitude Dick and Marty take toward their sin. Also there is the difference that Dick, while defeated for several days, desires to walk with his Lord; Marty's sin follows a persistent pattern over a longer period of time and displays a callousness as shown by his illicit relationships with several women.

Does Marty fit into the description of 15:2b? In the final analysis, "the Lord knoweth them that are his" (2 Tim. 2:19), and the judgment of men, though based upon what appears to be ample evidence at the time, is by no means above error. However, Paul's encouragement to Timothy is immediately followed by an exhortation: "Wherefore, let every one that nameth the name of Christ depart from iniquity." Also, there is the perilous possibility that the seemingly fruitful works of a person like Marty at an earlier time were only apparently and outwardly so to men and not genuinely and inwardly so to God. Moreover, we are to take New Testament warnings seriously when they say that those who practice the works of the flesh shall not inherit the kingdom of God (Gal. 5:21).

Second, Christ says "every" branch, and this is comprehensive in an absolute sense. It admits of no exceptions. Here again is encouragement for the Christian as he meditates upon the mind of his Father and the implications in the word "every." He can exult, in worshipful awe: "It is a blessing to consider that my Father does not overlook one single branch. This 'every' encircles even *me*. He will not lose sight of me in the crowd, slight me, or fail to pursue His good intentions in me. I can be altogether confident that He will be about His business in me — this year, this month, even this very day! What strength of poise this gives me to cope with whatever may come. I can be sure, as I truly seek to do His will, that He will not withhold from *me* the things He chooses as best for me. Some things may be comfortable and pleasant, others painful and distasteful. But whatever my lot I can be of good cheer by recalling with understanding what I see here. An experience does not come to me because my Father stands around the next corner in my life and delights in springing some unexpected situation upon me to see me squirm. It comes because my Father is altogether wise and sees that it is the finest experience that could happen to me just at this time. There is some lack in me that it is intended to supply in some way that I will understand perhaps only later. And it comes because I am one of the many suggested by the Father's 'every branch' and by His 'every son' (Heb. 12:6)."

So we see that when Christ speaks here of the branches the Father prunes, He means those which bear *fruit* (that is, the genuinely saved), and He emphasizes that this is true of *every one*. So if the Christian grasps which individuals are given this attention and can say, "This care of the Husbandman includes even *me*," he also needs to be aware of what the pruning really is. If he knows the meaning of the word he can have a mental predisposition that prepares him to take it all in stride. He will not be caught by surprise when the Father begins to prune him in some difficult experience of life.

The idea of the pruning. Just what does Christ mean when He says of the Father, "He purgeth it"? The Christian may visualize the picture more fully if he reflects on the character of natural branches and then sees that things true for them are true for spiritual branches also. We will look first at the natural branches, and second at the spiritual branches (persons).

(1) The natural branches. Christ chooses the word *katharei*, which is from the verb *kathairo*. The word basically means "to make clean." The only other place we see it in the New Testament is in Hebrews 10:2, where it has the spiritual sense of worshipers being cleansed from the consciousness of sins. In a number of references in early non-biblical writings, the word referred to various types of

cleansings in the work of farming. It is used in reference to *cleansing* corn by removing waste matter during the winnowing process and *ridding* the ground of weeds before planting seed. But the type of usage in John 15:2 appears in the writings of Philo (20 B.C. to A.D. 53). He says:

> As superfluous shoots grow on plants, which are a great injury to the genuine shoots, and which the husbandmen cleanse (kathairousi) and prune (apotemnousi), knowing what is necessary; so likewise the false and arrogant life grows up beside the true and humble life, of which to this day no husbandman has been found to cut off by the roots the superfluous and injurious growth. [2]

It is clear that Philo was thinking about some phase of removing parts of a plant and using this to show a similar truth in regard to persons. As Bernard states, one can hardly distinguish Philo's word for "cleanse" from the word for "prune." [3] A similar statement occurs in the writings of Xenophon: ". . . for the purpose that the vines might become cleansed (katharai) of wood." [4] Here, the plural noun occurs rather than a verbal form, just as the noun form "cleansed ones" appears in John 15:3 after the verb in verse two.

Since the context is using the illustration of a vine and branches, the sense of the word here must be "prunes," for that would be true of the natural branches.

[2] Philo, *De Somm.*, II, 64, cited by J. H. Bernard, *A Critical and Exegetical Commentary on the Gospel According to St. John*. International Critical Commentary (Edinburgh: T. & T. Clark, 1928), p. 479. Also see C. H. Dodd, *The Fourth Gospel*, p. 136, for the opinion that while *kathairein* is used of pruning in Philo, it does not appear to have been common in the vocabulary of viticulture. Dodd points out that even Liddell and Scott and also Moulton and Milligan give no example of the word meaning "to prune" apart from John 15:2. "I have gone through a number of vineyard leases and the like among the Oxyrhynchus papyri, which enter into elaborate detail about the various operations, without coming upon $\kappa\alpha\theta\alpha\acute{\iota}\rho\epsilon\iota\nu$. I do not think it was a word which a vine-grower would naturally have used." He proposes that here Christ's metaphorical application, the spiritual meaning (speaking of men) He had in view in using the allegory, has influenced His choice of language.

[3] Bernard, *ibid.*

[4] *Ibid.*, citing Xenophon, Oeconomicus, 20:20.

What is involved in pruning vines, and what did Christ mean to illustrate in the spiritual realm?

Detailed statements in recent years by leading authorities on grape growing show us much about pruning which was probably true in some measure in first-century Palestine. One expert spells out various types of removals for a vine. [5] Outside of harvesting itself, the most important removal is the process of pruning which involves the removal of canes, shoots, leaves, and other vegetative parts. This takes place during the growing season itself, and includes several particular acts. There is *pinching* with the thumb and finger to remove the growing tip of a vigorous shoot so that it will not grow too rapidly and be broken or damaged by a gust of wind. *Topping*, or the removal of one or two feet off the end of a growing shoot to prevent a later loss of the entire shoot which might be snapped off by the wind is another helpful measure to insure growth. *Thinning* — the removal of flower-clusters, grape-clusters, or parts of a cluster — enables the rest of a branch to bear more and better quality fruit. There is also *pruning* or cutting away of suckers — the shoots that arise from below the ground or from the trunk and main branches.

The grape farmer not only removes parts during the growing period, but later "prunes the vine back" severely in the autumn or winter by cutting off everything except the main stock and perhaps two canes (matured shoots). He has carefully "trained" these canes to incline along some type of support or trellis. Now he leaves them until the next spring when they will be "positioned" for more advantageous growth and fruit, according to his desires. Engel depicts this scene when he says that each winter a vine grower "sees the vines cut back to the stock and every vineyard nothing but rows of dry butts, bereft of all branches." [6]

---

[5] H. E. Jacob, "Grape Growing in California," Circular #116 (California Agricultural Extension Service, The College of Agriculture, University of California at Berkeley, April, 1940).

[6] F. G. Engel, "The Ways of Vines," *The Expository Times,* 60:111. Of course the precise physical act of cutting off most or all branches in the fall is not transferable to the spiritual realm. It is not Christ's point in verse 2b. The Father does not prune off whole *branches* (believers) themselves, but only *parts* of their lives that hinder full fruitage.

(2) The spiritual branches. What, then, does Christ mean when He applies the word "purgeth" to spiritual branches or believers? He is evidently referring to the removal of whatever things hinder the believer from his full potential of expressing the essence of Christ in fruitfulness. The Father, as Vinedresser, guards him, like the branch, against sucker growths, diseases, and pests that drain away and waste his life.

Pink applies only a limited meaning to the word. He insists that the term "purgeth" does not here mean "prunes"; instead, he favors the translation "cleanses." From this he concludes that Christ specifically alluded to the cleansing away of insects, moss, and other parasites infesting a plant. [7] This, of course, would have its analogy in the sins which deter the Christian and must be cleansed during the life experience of sanctification.

It appears better, however, to recognize in the word an even wider reference. It should not be restricted to one aspect but is general enough in scope to include various particular ways in which the Father might remove the Christian's sin. Many translators see the appropriateness of reading here "he prunes it" (as RSV, Phillips, NASB, etc.). The idea is that he cleanses *whatever* does not serve the best interests which the vinedresser has in mind. For the grape farmer, this would involve removing parasites, diseased parts, or the undesired growths within the branch itself. For the Father, in the spiritual analogy, it would include every aspect of the removal of sin, regardless of what the particular means might be. The complexity of sin in the believer can involve various aspects of cleansing. Here are some examples: (1) cleansing away some sin which is a particular issue temporarily blocking one's experiencing the joy of fellowship with God; (2) cleansing away sin in which a believer has not been consciously and deliberately resisting God on a specific matter but which new light from the Word now pinpoints as an issue and which he obediently forsakes; and (3) cleansing by

[7] Arthur W. Pink, *Exposition of the Gospel of John* (Grand Rapids: Zondervan Publishing House, 1945), 2:480.

sufferings, which can do the Christian service by dislodging him from countless unwholesome aspects of the self-life. Let us consider these in more detail.

First, there is cleansing from sin that is a definite issue. A Christian may tolerate some particular sin, fully aware that it is contrary to the will of God who is Light. It is a point-blank issue which he cannot continue to sidestep, for God faithfully presses it upon his thoughts so that he may confess and forsake it (Prov. 28:13; 1 John 1:9). If this is not effective, it becomes necessary to confront him through some special discipline for his own good and the glory of God. When he confesses the sin, he "agrees" with God. This means that he sees "eye-to-eye" with God, so to speak, or "says the same thing" about that sin that God says. This is the actual idea in the Greek word for "confess" *(homologeo)*. [8] If a person does confess, God is faithful (to His promise) and just (on the basis of Christ's death) to cleanse or to remove that sin in a twofold way. He acts to *forgive;* that is, He pardons the sinner and so removes his guilt. But He also cleanses *(katharise,* a form of the word in John 15:2b). This means that He *purifies* the Christian's life from the defilement which he has allowed, giving His child a fresh experience in His righteousness.

/ Second, there is cleansing from sin that new light reveals. No Christian, either young or old in the faith, has at the present moment an absolutely perfect awareness of all that God's light can involve, all possible twists of sin he might commit, and a forsaking of them all. *Every* child of God is a participant in a lifelong experience of being progressively set apart to God and released from the dominion of sins. He is to be ever growing in grace (2 Peter 3:18), and he never gets beyond need of more light from God's Word. As he lives in the Word, he sees godliness in which he is to participate by faith. The Holy Spirit may also crystalize specific sins to his consciousness in such a way

[8] A helpful discussion of the Christian's confession is found in John R. W. Stott's book, *Confess Your Sins* (Philadelphia: The Westminster Press, 1964).

that he now recognizes them as an affront to God and a hindrance to his life. They will have to go! He responds to the new light he has seen, putting his finger on these sins, so to speak, and trusting God to cleanse his life of them.

While God cleanses, the believer himself very definitely is responsible to deal with the sin. He has will, intellect, and emotion, whereas a literal branch does not, yet there is even a sense in which a literal branch prunes itself. Haaf reminds us: "In experience every follower of Christ must apply the pruning-knife to his own life if fruit is to be produced. Yes, even plants prune themselves by forming an abcission layer between themselves and the offending member till that offender drops off by its own weight." [9] And Johnson says, concerning reckoning or putting sin to death in our lives: "So, in the believer's life, since he has now been grafted into the Last Adam and His new life, he must by the Spirit put to death any products of the old life that may appear (cf. Rom. 8:13)." [10] Cf. also Romans 6:11; 1 Corinthians 9:24-27; and Colossians 3:5.

The believer, seeing truth that is new to him and obeying it, will often say to himself: "How slow I have been to learn this! Oh, that I had seen it in the light of the Spirit a long time ago and had trusted God to take it away then and implement His own will in this area of my life! How much more fruitful I might have been if I had recognized and applied this truth earlier."

Third, there is cleansing from sin by sufferings. As the Father prunes the fruit-bearing branch, He frequently uses the painful method of suffering in some sense. He may or may not necessarily be doing this to remove some specific sin in which we know we are resisting Him. It may be that by affliction the Father intends to develop the sinews of our faith which are imperfect and so call us to a deeper, richer fruitfulness. He may be seeking to purge away pos-

[9] G. S. Haaf, "The Physiology of the Vine and the Branches: John 15: 1-9," *The Lutheran Church Quarterly* (1938), 11:404.

[10] S. Lewis Johnson, "Studies in the Epistle to the Colossians: Christian Apparel," *Bibliotheca Sacra* (January, 1964), 121:24.

sibly unsuspected areas of self-centeredness, self-sufficiency, self-applause, or any of a number of other twists in the subtle self-life which are still at work even in the sturdiest saints. His motive is to set us apart to a yet greater commitment to Him alone. Through the process of troubles, we learn valuable lessons about trusting Him more unwaveringly and having a more watchful distrust of ourselves (2 Cor. 1:9). In each case, His purpose is to cleanse and perfect us.

God has shown us in the Bible a great variety of kinds of suffering that He allows His own to experience. What are some of these? God's people may suffer from sickness (Job; Phil. 2:26-30; 1 Tim. 5:23); some physical problem like Paul's "thorn in the flesh," which may be either sickness or some other handicap (2 Cor. 12:7-10); hardships such as those of the fatherless and widows (James 1:27); loss of material goods (Job; Heb. 10:34); affliction through theft or maliciousness that causes difficulty and grief (Joseph); slander, which will inevitably be connected with a person's claim to be a Christian (Ps. 31:13; Rom. 3:8); a difficult work schedule imposed by others and beyond one's personal control (Jacob); loss of loved ones (John 11); agony through spiritual struggles prompted by concern for others (2 Cor. 1:6; Gal. 4:19); grief over a loved one whose waywardness or death God is allowing as part of an object lesson to speak to others (Hosea; Ezek. 24); persecution by those antagonistic to the Lord and to His message that His servant is faithfully proclaiming (Jer. 20; Matt. 5:10-12; John 15:18-27; 16:33); horrors of war, which fall upon the just as well as the wicked, though their ends are altogether different (Ezek. 20:47; 21:4); and oppression by the rich or powerful in the sense of perverted justice or even bodily harm (Amos 8; James 2; 5).

God-ordered troubles can do us a great service by stretching us beyond our present extremities and revealing those points where our dependence has been upon Him and where it has been misplaced. Even the Chirstian who has the sturdiest faith may be deeply rebuked as God uses His "messengers of mercy" (troubles!) to point out elements of self-trust still treacherously entrenched within. God faithfully crystalizes to him the yet immeasurable need for further perfecting and, though he may have wonderful faith, new rays of light focus upon dark areas that must also be cleansed.

Whatever the type of cleansing the believer encounters, he, like a branch in a vine, is receiving care by which the Father may realize some wonderful purpose in him. This naturally leads us to Christ's own explanation of what that purpose is.

The intent of the pruning. We may be sure, by faith, that the Father's intent with us when He performs this ministry of affliction is always good. But we do not always see it this way. In fact, our reaction to His pruning effort is often very bad. We may suddenly blank God out of our vision, look only to "second causes," and whine in self-pity that this bitter pill can never do us any good. We fret, complain, and indulge in a dark mood as though blind chance has imprisoned us as victims in some dark web of circumstances beyond God's control.

Or perhaps we acknowledge that God has allowed this predicament, but stoop to the fool's absurdity of charging, under fire, that He has blundered in His plan for us. We assault His wisdom, doubt His love, impugn His gracious intentions. We cry out to remind Him that *we* would have been too wise to think that anything worthwhile might be accomplished in a mess like this. We act as though we know better than He the ways in which He might best display the sincerity of His love. Or we wail, "Oh, God, why this — when we have been working so hard for You and trusting You completely? Why? Why? Why?"

But in contrast to that attitude, He wants us to understand His intent and have a sound outlook. In fact, if we keep in mind that we are like branches, our attitude of response to cleansing can be twofold. We are to *recognize* the Father's purpose, and then *rest* in that purpose.

(1) Recognize the Father's purpose. The intent or purpose in pruning the branch, Christ says, is "that it might

bear more fruit." In this purpose clause there is a special emphasis on the word "fruit" *(karpon)*, since it immediately follows the word "that." Literally it reads, ". . . for the purpose that fruit more it might bear." He is making the point clear that the Father cleanses the branch to prepare it to bear more fruit. The same point under a different figure, that of sonship, appears in Hebrews 12:4-11. The Father chastens every one of His sons for the purpose of their becoming partakers of His holiness (v. 10) and having the fruit of righteousness (v. 11; cf. Rom. 6:22; Phil. 1:11).

Our Father would have us recognize also in other realms of life the necessity of training which causes pain but works out for good. He has been faithful to prepare us by emphasizing this principle over and over again throughout His Word. There are many vivid examples.

The soldier sacrifices many ordinary privileges of life and suffers painful hardships in the process of pleasing the "brass" above him (2 Tim. 2:3, 4). The athlete endures agony in his body but strives within the rules to qualify for the eventual victor's crown (2 Tim. 2:5). After much painful toil, the diligent farmer finally harvests his crop (2 Tim. 2:6), while the slothful man, shirking the duties that hurt, courts failure (Prov. 24:30-34). The refiner of gold seeks by intense heat to remove dross and finally gain purified metal (Job 23:10; 1 Peter 1:7; 4:12).

But perhaps the most touching example of all in the Bible is the relationship in which a father chastens his son. It is expected that a human father should discipline his son to fit him for future responsibility. He does not indulge him with all that he might prefer to do, since to do so might make him incapable of carrying out his responsibility. All of this is true in the natural bond of father and son, where the father's discipline is, at best, to some extent arbitrary. However, in the spiritual analogy the heavenly Father's discipline of every son is with a wisdom and love completely free of arbitrary whim or caprice.

It is fitting to ask here if "chastening" in Hebrews 12: 3-15 is the same as "pruning" in John 15. Certain factors point to the conclusion that it is:

JOHN 15	HEBREWS 12
(1) The context turns the spotlight on persecution as the particular thing Christ's "friends" will face (15:18ff; 16:1ff).	(1) The context speaks of the Hebrews as facing the contradiction of sinners (v. 3).
(2) The Father as Vinedresser cares for His vine branches by pruning.	(2) The Father cares for His sons by chastening (vv. 5, 6). This is a different figure but the same point.
(3) *Every* branch is involved.	(3) *Every* son is involved (vv. 6-8).
(4) Love of the Father is emphasized.	(4) Love is emphasized (v. 6).
(5) The purpose in pruning is, specifically, that we might "bear more fruit."	(5) The purpose in chastening is "that we might be partakers of his holiness" (v. 10) and be given the "fruit of righteousness" (v. 11).

The believer, then, is a branch, a soldier, an athlete, precious metal, and a son. He is to recognize the purpose of the greater vinedresser, general, coach, refiner, and Father. He can discern that even in the times of pruning through sufferings, he is being better prepared to glorify God. Though the pruning knife may cut away at him with pain, the end can be more fruit. The training routine may involve maneuvers that seem unreasonable at the moment, but the end can be an ability to do by conditioned reflex the right thing at the right time and come off a winner from the field of life. Training for the Olympics may inflict agony to the body, but at last there can be the victor's medal. A refining process may call for fire of intense heat, but the result can be purified gold. Discipline for a son growing up in the faith may be difficult, yet his future can shine with bright glory and honor.

We are not only to *recognize* the Father's purpose in cleansing, but also to —

(2) Rest in the Father's purpose. A Christian may not understand the particular reason of the Father for some

difficulty or affliction which He has directly brought or allowed to come into his life. But he can be sure of one thing. Fruit can result from it. Has he not committed his life to the Father who is wise and loving? So it can be his joy to look by faith past all second causes and take everything ultimately as having come under the Father's watchful eye and past His faithful hand. He may settle it in his heart that nothing can occur in his life as a branch that is outside the orbit of the heavenly Vinedresser's care. His spirit may rest in confident poise, since he knows that the Father is there and that he may think of even this situation as included in the details of His good plan for him.

All of this prepares us to look now at how the Father prunes us.

The instrument of pruning. A husbandman uses a pruning knife (cf. Isa. 18:5), various kinds of knives, in fact, with his natural branches. But what is the heavenly Father's knife for pruning or cleansing believers? Some emphasize sufferings or trials as the means through which we are purified; others say that it is the Word which cleanses. Let us look at these.

It is proper to associate purification with sufferings if we understand their relationship properly, for certain passages connect cleansing with afflictions (Ps. 66:10-12; 1 Peter 1:6,7, et al.). John Owen, writing at length on this, pointed out four ways in which afflictions are related to cleansing: (1) They become tokens to the believer of God's displeasure against sin and cause him to see and hate sin and therefore seek a remedy. (2) When the believer is afflicted, he often is caused to take his affections off things around him to which he had been inordinately attached, for he sees that they have no beauty and allurement after all and are insufficient to give relief. (3) Afflictions curb affections within the Christian which would carry him into sin. (4) God uses afflictions to excite all the graces of the Spirit to diligent exercise so that the life may be cleansed from sin. The believer is led to put his trust rightly in God. [11]

[11] John Owen, *A Discourse Concerning the Holy Spirit* (Philadelphia: Presbyterian Board of Publication, n.d.), pp. 269, 270.

This is true in our afflictions, yet in the final analysis it is not the afflictions themselves that purify us. Rather, it is the Word of God doing its work in our hearts as they are vigorously exercised. This is evident for several reasons:

(1) Christ's specific word in the context is to this effect (v. 3). "You are already clean because of the word which I have spoken to you." Here we are to distinguish between an *initial,* past cleansing (v. 3) and the *perpetual* present cleansing that goes on throughout the Christian life this side of glory (v. 2b). In 13:10, 11, we see a differentiation in harmony with this. There was the washing or bath already effected for the eleven disciples, that is, cleansing at the point of initial salvation. Then, after this, there was required the washing of their feet, picturing daily spiritual cleansing of which they continued to have need. At the time of the initial cleansing one receives through grace the imputed righteousness of God, and God justifies him (declares him righteous). From that point forward, sanctification is at work in the believer's life. In this, also by grace, God progressively sets him apart from sin to Christlikeness in which he may find his proper usefulness in the will of God. The Spirit of God, using the Word of God (John 17:17), works with the Christian's own grace-directed thinking and conquering in the warfare of faith to develop him from one stage to the next in that sanctifying process (2 Cor. 3:18). This will be consummated in future glorification when he shall at last be wholly perfected in likeness to Christ (Rom. 8:29; Phil. 3:21; 1 John 3:2). Paul's argument in Romans 1 - 8 develops all of the three aspects — justification, sanctification, and glorification.

Here, then, is the logic of our point. If Christ plainly says in verse 3 that the disciples are initially clean *through* (stressing agency or instrument) the Word, then any cleansing which follows subsequent to this must be by that same instrument. And the rest of the context also emphasizes the Word (John 14:21, 23; 15:7, 10).

(2) Our Lord's prayer in John 17:17 bears out the fact that cleansing is basically by the Word: "Sanctify them in the truth; Thy word is truth."

(3) This agrees with what the psalmist experienced. A man is cleansed by the Word (Ps. 119:9-11).

(4) This harmonizes with the rest of the New Testament. We are born through the Word (1 Peter 1:23) and then grow by it (1 Thess. 4:1; 1 Peter 2:2, 3).

A practical question arises here. If trials themselves appear to be God's knife by which He cuts away the undesirable shoots of the self-life, in what sense is the *Word* His pruning knife?

At the outset it will help to remember that the picture of husbandman and branch, while generally analogous to the relationship between the Father and the believer, does not demand an exact correspondence at every point. Parts of a vine branch may be cut away by a knife simply as an external act. There is no internal, rational thinking process in that branch which corresponds to a believer's response to the Word of God in the capacity of his will, intellect, and emotions. When a Christian is pruned in the sense of sufferings, he, *unlike* the nonrational branch, may experience two things. There are the painful external circumstances which seem to cut like a sharp blade, by which the Father prunes him. But there is also the sharp knife of the Word which reaches into the deepest recesses of the life to expose things in their naked reality before God's searching light. For the man who is genuinely in Christ as a branch, the Father's pruning work involves a combination of circumstances in the outward experience and the Spirit's ministry of the Word in the inward life that responds to those circumstances. Both of these, in actuality, serve the Father's purpose in seeking to make that person more fruitful.

However, we may credit the Word alone as the final pruning instrument. A trial can bring pressure to bear upon spiritual muscles and be used to develop them. But the Word, not the trial itself, is the instrument working within the Christian to prune away attitudes, words, and deeds that please self and to replace these with others that honor God. In the difficult situation God simply arranges a setting, a fitting occasion, to extend a Christian beyond the extremity of his own puny resource and confront him with

a fresh opportunity to depend upon God as his whole sufficiency.

It is of rich benefit to meditate upon some of the great
statements that show the connection between adversity and
the Word.

First, F. B. Meyer, emphasizing the fire of difficulty itself, says the Father's chastisement is

> not that we expiate the wrongdoing by suffering, but that
> we may be compelled to regard it in its true light. Amid
> the pain we suffer we are compelled to review our past.
> The carelessness, the unwatchfulness, the prayerlessness
> which have been working within us pass slowly before our
> minds. We see where we had been going astray for long
> months or years. We discover how deeply and incessantly
> we had been grieving God's Holy Spirit. . . .
>
> Times of affliction lead to heart-searchings, and we be-
> come increasingly aware of sins of which we had hardly
> thought at all. . . . We cannot forget our sin so long as the
> stroke of the Almighty lies on our soul; and we are com-
> pelled to maintain a habit of holy watchfulness against its
> recurrence. [12]

Andrew Murray, turning our attention to the pruning
knife, writes:

> What is the pruning knife of this heavenly Husbandman?
> It is often said to be affliction. By no means in the first
> place. How would it then fare with many who have long
> seasons free from adversity; or with some on whom God
> appears to shower down kindness all their life long? No;
> it is the Word of God that is the knife, sharper than any
> two-edged sword, that pierces even to the dividing asunder
> of the soul and spirit, and is quick to discern the thoughts
> and intents of the heart. It is only when affliction leads to
> this discipline of the Word that it becomes a blessing; the
> lack of this heart-cleansing through the Word is the reason
> why affliction is so often unsanctified. Not even Paul's thorn
> in the flesh could become a blessing until Christ's Word —
> "My strength is made perfect in weakness" — had made

---

[12] F. B. Meyer, *The Way Into the Holiest. Expositions of the Epistle
to the Hebrews* (New York: Fleming H. Revell Company, 1893), p. 218.

him see the danger of self-exaltation, and made him willing to rejoice in infirmities. [13]

Charles H. Spurgeon has given us a fuller explanation:

How does the Lord prune his people, then? It is generally said by affliction; I question if that could be proved as it stands; it needs explanation. It is generally thought that our trials and troubles purge us: I am not sure of that, they certainly are lost upon some. Our Lord tells us what it is that prunes us. "Now," saith he, . . . "ye are clean (or pruned) through the word which I have spoken unto you." It is *the word* that prunes the Christian, it is the truth that purges him, the Scripture, made living and powerful by the Holy Spirit, effectually cleanses the Christian. "What then does affliction do?" say you. 'Well, if I may say so, affliction is the handle of the knife; affliction is the grindstone that sharpens up the word; affliction is the dresser which removes our soft garments, and lays bare the diseased flesh, so that the surgeon's lancet may get at it; affliction makes us ready to feel the word, but the true pruner is the word in the hand of the Great Husbandman. Sometimes when you lay stretched upon the bed of sickness, you think more upon the word than you did before, that is one great thing. In the next place, you see more the applicability of that word to yourself. In the third place, the Holy Spirit makes you feel more, while you are thus laid aside, the force of the word than you did before. 'Ask that affliction may be sanctified, beloved, but always remember there is no more tendency in affliction in itself to sanctify us than there is in prosperity; in fact, the natural tendency of affliction is to make us rebel against God, which is quite opposite to sanctification. . . . Alas! some people are of such a character, that if they were stricken till their whole head were sick, and their whole heart faint, they would not be benefitted; if they were beaten till they were all bruises and putrifying sores, they would still go on to rebel, for these things only provoke them to a greater hatred against the Most High. We must be pruned, but it must be by the word, through affliction. [14]

[13] Andrew Murray, *The True Vine* (Chicago: Moody Press, n.d.), pp. 31, 32.
[14] Charles H. Spurgeon, "A Sharp Knife for the Vine-Branches," *Metropolitan Tabernacle Pulpit* (London: Passmore and Alabaster, n.d.), 13: 562, Sermon 774, preached May 12, 1867.

This same identification of the pruning instrument was made about a century after the death of the apostle John by Clement of Alexandria (A.D. 155 - 215). He wrote on verse two:

> For the vine that is not pruned grows to wood. So also man. The Word — the knife — clears away the wanton shoots; compelling the impulses of the soul to fructify, not to indulge in lust. Now, reproof addressed to sinners has their salvation for its aim, the word being harmoniously adjusted to each one's conduct; now with tightened, now with relaxed cords. . . . [15]

All of this pruning, as we have seen, is to the end that we may bear even more *fruit*. This is what the divine Husbandman so greatly desires in us, as Christ emphasizes in verse eight: "Herein is my Father glorified, that ye bear much fruit." With this on our hearts, then, as it is on the Father's heart, we are prepared to see in the next chapter why fruit is so very important.

---

[15] Clement of Alexandria, "Paedagogus," Book I, ch. VIII, in *The Ante-Nicene Fathers*, ed. A. Roberts and J. Donaldson. American reprint of Edinburgh edition (New York: The Christian Literature Company, 1893), p. 226.

WHAT IS SO IMPORTANT ABOUT FRUIT?

Herein is my Father glorified, that
ye bear much fruit (John 15:8).

Christians are always using the word "fruit," but some apparently do not think carefully about what a Christian's fruit actually is. This is unfortunate since fruit is the very product of life itself. God says that fruit bearing is what life is all about. Any servant of Christ who longs for no less than a life of the highest fulfillment can discover momentous possibilities in the bearing of fruit. This is true whatever his particular role of service is in the body of Christ, in accordance with his gifts. He may be a fascinating evangelist who sways great crowds to action, a businessman faced with hard decisions of ethics in a dog-eat-dog world, a lawyer seeking to relate Christianity in a meaningful way to his profession, a housewife slaving over a sink of dirty dishes or teaching a little child, or a student confronted with the compromise and confusion of unsound philosophies about life. Whatever the Christian's present niche in life, what God says to him about fruit has up-to-date relevance for every moment of life.

It is our purpose here to see why fruit is important to us. Later we will ask what it actually is. Fruit is important for at least two basic reasons. First, God stresses it, and this makes it significant. Second, God Himself is the source of good fruit, and therefore it is important because it is of the very essence and outflow of His life.

God stressses it. The Bible brings up the concept of fruit with a frequency that should snap us to attention. The main Old Testament word for fruit, *periy,* appears no less than 106 times, and *Young's Concordance* lists eleven other Hebrew terms which denote various aspects of meaning relating to fruit. The most used New Testament word, *karpos,* occurs nearly seventy times, and there are also other Greek terms such as *gennema* (2 Cor. 9:10) and *opora* (Rev. 18:14). Other words that are variations of these exist also, such as *akarpos* ("unfruitful," Eph. 5:11; 2 Peter 1:8). The important place that fruit held in the thinking of New Testament writers becomes apparent when we discover that twenty-four of the twenty-seven books refer to the idea in some clear manner. The only exceptions are Philemon and the second and third epistles of John. But even these three books, though not referring to the specific word "fruit" or some related word like "seed" (1 John 3:9), still have something to say about fruit by other words which obviously indicate it. For example, they speak of love, joy, and peace. Some might question whether fruit is mentioned in 1 Timothy. There is a metaphorical suggestion of fruit in 6:10 which says, "The love of money is the root of all evil." Fruit is the natural result which issues ultimately from a "root" as that root has its effect through the plant it serves. The love of money is a root, and the evil is the fruit.

God has reminded men of fruit through references to plants that bear fruit, as well as by the phrase "the fruit of the womb" (Gen. 30:2; Ps. 127:3). After creation, His first mandate was the command to be fruitful (Gen. 1:28). The Bible not only begins, but also ends, with this emphasis upon fruit. The last chapter of the book of Revelation pictures the tree of life "bearing twelve *kinds* of fruit" (22:2). The predominant type of Israel's economy, the agricultural, furnished daily illustrations of fruit as the inevitable result where there is normal life. If you look at the listings for "plants" in a Bible dictionary, you will be impressed with how many there are. Bible writers, profoundly influenced by the object lessons contained in the natural world, capitalized upon them to draw vivid analogies between *natural* fruit and *spiritual* fruit. We see the great highlights in

Psalm 1, Isaiah 5, John 15, and Galatians 5. Besides these, there are many, many other Scripture references to plants and fruit bearing. [1]

It becomes clear from the message of the Bible that the thrust of every life in every moment is unavoidably toward fruit bearing. It may be either evil or good, but it is fruit (Matt. 3:7-12; 7:15-20; 12:33). In this sense, every person is somewhat like Walt Whitman's poetic creation "The Noiseless Patient Spider."

> "A noiseless patient spider
> I marked, where on a little promontory it stood
>   isolated,
> Marked how, to explore the vacant vast surrounding,
> It launched forth filament, filament, filament,
>   out of itself,
> Ever unreeling them, ever tirelessly speeding them.

> "And you, O my soul, where you stand
> Surrounded, detached, in measureless oceans of space,
> Ceaselessly musing, venturing, throwing, seeking
>   the spheres to connect them,
> Till the bridge you will need be formed, till the
>   ductile anchor hold,
> Till the gossamer thread you fling catch somewhere, O
>   my soul." [2]

The person, though possessing by the will and gifts of God a potential immeasurably greater than that of the spider, also sends forth from his life "filament, filament, filament." He, too, seeks by many fine, thin threads to form meaningful, bridgelike relationships in life. With certain thoughts, words, and acts he builds and fulfills his life. And if he is a Christian, a branch in Christ the Vine, the whole thrust of his life can be toward bearing the "much fruit" of John 15:5. His span of life is longer and his opportunities more

---

[1] See, for example: Jer. 11:19; 17:7, 8; Ezek. 15; Hosea 14:4-8; Matt. 3:7-10; 7:15-20; 12:33; 13:3-8, 18-23; 21:43; John 12:24; Rom. 6:21, 22; 7:4, 5; 15:28; 2 Cor. 9:10; Eph. 5:8-13; Phil. 1:11, 22; Col. 1:6, 10; Titus 3:14; Heb. 6:7-9; James 1:21; 3:17, 18; 2 Peter 1:3-11.

[2] Included in Charles D. Warner, *Library of the World's Best Literature Ancient and Modern* (New York: R. S. Peale and J. A. Hill, Publishers), 27: 15, 910.

varied than the spider's. A year has 8,760 hours. Should a person live 50 years after becoming a Christian, he fills more than 438,000 hours as a Christian. Allowing for eight hours of sleep per day (which is more than for many students I know!), his daily schedule of 16 hours for those 50 years would give him 292,000 hours or 17,520,000 minutes. He *must* fill these with thoughts, words, and/or deeds. This makes it imperative that he grasp the importance of fruit as God sees it and that he be very clear as to the true nature of fruit.

The second fact that clarifies the importance of fruit in the New Testament is its *source.*

God is the source of it. The Bible teaches unmistakably that men must have good works to live in prosperity with God, and those who live in prosperity with Him have good works. Wedded with this is the concept that God, the giver of all physical life, is also the source of all spiritual life and fruit. This means that if a person's works are to be a delight to God, they must originate in an inner reality of life appropriated from Him. This utter necessity in the spiritual realm is analogous to the physical realm in which the branch of a vine assimilates the very life essence within the vine (John 15).

Many passages thus paint the spiritual reality in the pictorial imagery of plant life receiving rain from heaven and bringing forth fruit (Isa. 45:8ff; Joel 2:22-24; Heb. 6:7-9, et al.). Isaiah, for instance, employs the heaven-to-earth picture as a background when he speaks of God raining down righteousness upon His people so that they might flourish in it (vv. 8, 17, 24). The Scriptural point is that God Himself is the source of all good fruit, and this makes fruit important.

The same essential fact is taught in various ways in the Bible.

(1) There are statements tracing fruit directly to God. The prophet Hosea, picturing Israel's future kingdom blessings, represents God as saying, "From me comes your fruit" (14:8 NASB). Later, in John 15, Christ emphasizes *positively* that only the person who abides in Him bears fruit (v. 4) and

negatively that without Him we "can do nothing" (v. 5). Paul repeats the concept in Philippians 1:11 when he speaks of "the fruit[3] of righteousness which is by Jesus Christ."

(2) There is also the example of Christ Himself. He frequently claimed that His works were completely in accord with the Father's will; He even said that they were the works of the Father done through Him (John 5:19, 30; 8:28; 14:10). When He said, in a metaphor, "I am the bread of life" (John 6:35), He applied this to believers by analogy: "As the living Father hath sent me, and I live by the Father; so he that eateth me, even he shall live by me" (v. 57). We may add to this the truth that Christ, living truly as a *man,* did His works by the enablement of the Holy Spirit (Matt. 12:28; Luke 4:1, 14, 18; Acts 10:38). So may we ever live!

(3) There is explicit teaching that spiritual power is of God. The psalmist knew that "power belongeth unto God" (Ps. 62:11). True ability for any conceivable situation is in Him. Paul places emphasis upon this: "It is God which worketh in you both to will and to do of His good pleasure" (Phil. 2:13), and "I can do all things through Christ which strengtheneth me" (4:13).

(4) Finally, there are specific commands to live in the power of God. He is the very spring and source for our lives. The divine imperative, communicated through Paul, is this: "But I say, live habitually by the rule of the Spirit" (Gal. 5:16 *author's translation*). [4] The apostle urges the absolute necessity of the Spirit's direction. Why? First, He can enable the Christian to triumph over the lusts and

---

[3] The singular form of fruit, in the accusative case *karpon,* is substantiated by the best manuscripts and preferred in more recent translations, such as the *New American Standard Bible.* Reference to fruit in the singular is found often, as in such a key passage as Galatians 5:22. However, the plural "fruits" does appear in Matthew 7:16, 20; James 3:17 etc., and 2 Corinthians 9:10 refers to the "fruits of righteousness" (though *gennemata,* not *karpous,* is used).

[4] Paul's sense is evidently that of a dative of direction or rule as in Romans 8:14 and Galatians 5:18 (cf. C. J. Ellicott, *A Critical and Grammatical Commentary on St. Paul's Epistle to the Galatians,* Vol. I in Ellicott's Commentaries, Critical and Grammatical, on the Epistles of Saint Paul (Boston: W. H. Halliday and Co., 1868), p. 129; J. B. Lightfoot, *Saint Paul's Epistle to the Galatians* (London: Macmillan and Co., 1900), p. 209.

works of the flesh. Second, He can produce, as the very source and origin, the qualities specified in verses twenty-two and twenty-three as "the fruit of the Spirit." Here the emphasis is on the *origin* of the fruit which, as Eadie reminds us, is "not man's spirit, or the new and better mode of thinking and feeling to which men are formed by the Holy Spirit . . ., but the Holy Spirit Himself, the Author of all spiritual good." [5]

It is very clear, then, that the Christian is the recipient and channel of life imparted from God, and fruit originates in this life. Evidently it is right to define the nature of fruit, at least partially, in terms of its *source.* "Fruit" denotes the gracious dispositions and characteristics which the Spirit produces as He makes good the very life-essence of Christ the Vine within and out of the believer. This concept probes deeply, like an X-ray, to inner reality and authenticity and is not satisfied merely with external and often arbitrary criteria. In any given episode, two Christians may act out the same set of motions and convey the outward impression that they are equally fruitful, yet one may be fruitful and the other unfruitful. The acts of the one are permeated by God's authentic vine-life which has been released freely through him, while the acts of the other are counterfeits with no quality higher than the performance of fleshly and earthly ability. God, who sees through the externals to the essence, unerringly distinguishes what is fruit from what is fake.

The Bible shows us the importance of fruit, then, by revealing God's own stress on it and God as the source of it. It is our privilege and responsibility to apply this, making it wholly important to ourselves also. (As we often say when playing checkers, "It's your move!" Let us emphasize that we are responsible for the *bearing* of fruit, and let us trust God to be the *source!*

---

[5] John Eadie, *Commentary on the Epistle of Paul to the Galatians* (Grand Rapids: Zondervan Publishing House. Reprint of 1894 edition), p. 422.

THINGS THAT SOMETIMES PASS FOR FRUIT

The Lord looketh on the heart (1 Sam. 16:7).

A discerning believer, in light of the definition of fruit given in the preceding chapter, is able to screen out popular but false ideas of what is fruit in practical situations. It should help to clarify these here, and then, in the next chapter, go on to look at positive examples of what the New Testament itself calls fruit. One sometimes hears fruit linked rather automatically with certain external matters per se. These now follow.

Success. When a Christian seems to be successful in his niche and is regarded favorably, it is popular to label him in some particular situation as "fruitful." Christians place others into neat little categories on the strength of impressions, and these may or may not spring from true discernment. It is still true, as the Lord told Samuel long ago, that "man looketh on the outward appearance, but the Lord looketh on the heart" (1 Sam. 16:7; cf. Luke 16:15). It is possible to confuse outward success of the moment with fruit, even though there is actually a big difference. Both fruit and true success (i.e., success as God sees it) are matters of reality and quality. [1] They go deeper than impressions. Things are not always what they appear to be, whether we are talking about Christians or non-Christians. Do you remember Edwin Arlington Robinson's poem entitled "Richard Cory," and how everybody was so sure he

[1] Eric Fife helpfully articulates this point in his article "Beyond Success," *His,* April, 1963, pp. 5-7, 16.

had everything and was a grand success? Robinson's point was simply that outward appearance alone does not always reveal what is going on inside a person.

Whenever Richard Cory went down town,
We people on the pavement looked at him:
He was a gentleman from soul to crown,
Clean favored, and imperially slim.

And he was always quietly arrayed,
And he was always human when he talked;
But still he fluttered pulses when he said,
"Good morning," and he glittered when he walked.

And he was rich — yes, richer than a king —
And admirably schooled in every grace:
In fine, we thought that he was everything
To make us wish that we were in his place.

So on we worked, and waited for the light,
And went without the meat, and cursed the bread;
And Richard Cory, one calm summer night,
Went home and put a bullet through his head.

We are so easily fooled, for things are not always what we think they are. We cannot look into the hearts of other persons, and we seldom really know them. As a high school boy, I walked into a small cafe one day and a pretty girl in my class came over to meet me. She was holding a beautiful flower as she sat down with me in one of the booths by a window. From across the table I thought the flower must have a very delightful fragrance. As she toyed with it quite nonchalantly, I was overcome.

"Let me sniff it," I coaxed. She held it across to me. At first I took a very light sniff without looking at it closely and could smell nothing.

"Sniff really hard," she urged, "so you can get the full effect."

Gullibly, I did. With concentrated effort, I drew in my breath. At the same time, she squeezed a tube below! I got a nose full of fine pepper. The joke was on me. And the lesson was one I have never forgotten. Behind the candy-sweet faces and smiles of people there may be hidden desires to hurt us and take advantage. And, like that flower, a person who outwardly seems to be so lovely may be dominated at the moment by the pepper of sin.

Apply this to the Christian. He may appear to be very fruitful in a given situation but may, in fact, be in quite a sad state with regard to genuine fruit or success within. The real secret behind what others interpret as "success" is an indomitable drive or the shining dramatics of a fleshly performance. A missionary, for example, may appear to be a failure in some aspects of life, such as winning converts immediately on a difficult field. Some people of the home church constituency, looking for quick, visible "results" and appraising the missionary without access to all of the "inside" facts as God unerringly knows them, would question his fruitfulness. Take, as an example, William Carey (1761 - 1834). [2] During his first seven years as an English missionary in India (1793 - 1800), he worked hard and gained not a single convert. During his later years of service, many became Christians. Any careful and perceptive study of what is known about Carey's attitude and service during those seven seemingly blank years will reveal that his life was quite fruitful. There are many areas of life other than direct witness in which a Christian may bear true spiritual fruit. It is true, however, that for a time Carey was not visibly successful in terms of the *one* specific aspect of the conversion of others to Christ. Yet every Christian should honestly search his own heart here, for it can become a tempting convenience to rationalize his ineffectiveness in touching other lives and thus to excuse himself from his responsibility.

Sensationalism. Sometimes people virtually equate fruit with something sensational. The flashy missionary is more likely to rally a large number of people to his support than is a rather common person. Some who are attracted to the sparkling personality with the entertaining line of talk may be so with very God-centered attitudes. Others, however, lacking wise value judgments, choose whom they pre-

[2] Frank D. Walker, *William Carey: Missionary Pioneer and Statesman* (Chicago: Moody Press, 1951), pp. 180ff.

fer to be drawn to on the shallow basis of fleshly values. Christian service, for some people, has to be rather earth-shaking or go off like a blast of dynamite to be worth anything. It must have an explosive sound before they will be likely to label it as effective — and fruitful.

Thus, because of what others seem to expect, a Christian may be misguided by the idea that he has to become emotionally charged and worked up to a high pitch to be really spiritual and fruitful. Often this is because those in his church or group, whom he desires to please, make this virtually a status symbol, "the only way to fly," and so he must do the sensational thing.

It appears to be an assumption among some Christians, expressed often in little unguarded comments they make, that the more outwardly spectacular a person is the more godly he must be. In their minds, the great Christian is the speaker who sways the crowds or the youth leader with all the scintillating "answers" and color and flash. In reality, these *may* be very godly and fruitful, or they may not be. Certainly, if they are, it is not the outward bombastics that make them so. It is the inner life contact with Jesus Christ, the Vine. Remember that many ministries for Christ are comparatively quite undramatic. Take, for example, working in a nursery program in the church, teaching a class of small children, or doing office tasks like typing and stuffing envelopes to be mailed. An interesting incident that illustrates this occurred in the lives of John and Betty Stam, missionaries to China who were martyred later. When John was serving in Suancheng, he once put up sixty quarts of preserves and jams for the absent housemother. He made the comment, "Didn't think *that* had anything to do with missionary work, but it seems to!" [3]

One Christian, exercising the gift of the Spirit he has been given, may be cast in the limelight on the stage of life and appear more sensational than another believer who has a less dramatic gift. The one is on the "big news" end of things, and makes the big splash. The other is in a

[3] Mrs. Howard Taylor, *The Triumph of John and Betty Stam* (Philadelphia: The China Inland Mission, 1935), p. 77.

comparatively obscure phase of service behind the scenes, where the results are not so readily noticeable and are less likely to register with others. Yet the two Christians, with different gifts and types of service, may be equally fruitful before God as they are good stewards of what has been committed to their trust.

It is possible that sensationalism and fruitfulness *may* be combined, but let us be sure they are not identical.

Sectarianism. A Christian serving in a denomination that honors the Lord and maintains true doctrine can be abundantly fruitful in the sphere in which God directs him. But we have always with us those who rabidly equate "fruit" with dedicated zeal for outward group protocol or "the program." Actually one may work "the program" and be wonderfully fruitful before God, or, tragically, he may be merely going through the motions. It is not the service per se, or the outward facade of chalking up denominational work, that constitutes true fruitfulness. It is the sap of the Vine, Jesus Christ, imparting within the person engaged in the service God's authentic essence of life. Someone has appropriately said, "The secret of effectual service [and fruitfulness, we may add] is not overwork but overflow." Men may highly praise us for what God would emphatically disown (Luke 16:15).

Sacredness as opposed to the secular. The Christian should wholly avoid any spirit of heart that is secularistic (i.e., worldly or empty of genuine spiritual attitudes). He should rather nourish within himself a sacred spirit. But one can stagger under the self-imposed burden of a false sacred-secular antithesis. He can artificially compartmentalize his life by the criteria of external tasks and places in themselves. For example, he might feel at ease in a church atmosphere surrounded by stained glass windows and he might be soothed by reassuring organ music. But when he ventures into the "world" at the office on Monday morning, he is disturbed by a gnawing doubt that Christ as the Vine can really *relate* Himself as closely to "secular" acts as to acts done in "sacred" service or surroundings. Yet the truth is that fruit is basically a product of Christ's life from within the Christian. God dwells in his body, making it His spiritual temple (1 Cor. 6:19, 20). This means that *wherever* the believer goes and *whatever* his daily work, providing it is not inconsistent with biblical principles and values, he may devote God-centered and God-glorifying attitudes in that place and in that task, doing all for God's high honor (1 Cor. 10:31; Col. 3:17, 23). In a chapter entitled "The Sacrament of Living," as well as in many of his other writings, A. W. Tozer has shown that spirituality toward God cannot be relegated into a cramped mold of "sacred" suroundings only. [4] Sacredness and fruit-fulness reach into events and places of as infinite a variety as all the aspects of life itself. The Christian can say confidently of the total myriad of activities in which life involves him just what Christ his Vine says in John 8:29: "I do always those things that please Him."

Pleasing God involves the motive of the heart. Right here is the crux of the matter. In my life as a branch, what is my motive, incentive, or purpose for any specific thing I do? Is it to please and glorify my Father who is the Husbandman? Is it to live to carry out the will of Christ, the Vine with whom I am related? I may do the right things for the wrong motives. Is it merely to fulfill someone else's ambitions or for some personal advantage? Is it to gain recognition or prestige for myself, or to receive some business or social promotion because my action projects a good image and will look good on the record? Do I teach the Sunday school class simply because it gives fulfillment to me or exalts *me* over a little kingdom? The inventory of motives could go on and on.

When I stand before Christ some day, He will uncover the thoughts of my heart (1 Cor. 4:4, 5), the way I treated others (Rom. 14), and my work (1 Cor. 3:11-15). [5] He

[4] A. W. Tozer, *The Pursuit of God* (Harrisburg, Pa.: Christian Publications, n.d.), pp. 117-128; see also his *Man: The Dwelling Place of God* (Christian Publications, 1966), pp. 53-56.

[5] It is recognized that 1 Corinthians 3:11-15, in context, is immediately emphasizing more specifically the judgment of leaders in the church. However, as Alexander Maclaren has so capably shown, it is proper to apply the *principle* to all Christians (see his *Expositions of Holy Scripture* on the passage).

will be concerned about the *quality* of my works, of what
"sort" they are. Of course He, the Vine with whom I am
in union, is concerned right now. I need to appear often
before God, not only with my mouth open to speak to
Him but also with my Bible open and my heart receptive.
There, alone with Him, I will discover that something else
lies open also — heaven itself. And I can enter into the
motives that are on the heart of God, and He will enter
them on my heart and make me to be like Him. Then, in
my life at least, His will can be done "in earth as it is in
heaven." This will transform the ordinary things of life out
of a merely secular status and make them sacred matters
touched with the glory of God. Every day can be, to me,
a great day. And in the things I do that are permeated
with His glory my heart is truly bearing fruit.

Simulation.   There is also this subtle danger of reducing
the Christian life to an external simulation of the life of
Christ. Many slavishly try to imitate what they believe the
ideal model to be, or mimic some exemplary Christian with
whom they are enamored. Now, admittedly, there is every
reason to be guided by good principles that please God,
and to imitate Him *in power appropriated from Him* (Eph.
5:1, 14, 18 et al.). What I am speaking about is the tragedy
of letting one's Christian life dwindle to a human project
of self-improvement. One may look at the life of Christ
or that of some fruitful saint which is the authentic product
of the Vine. But when one merely simulates this pattern,
he is guilty of a double counterfeit. First, he is straining
to duplicate *on his own* the life that *Christ Himself* is living
through the person he seeks to copy. Whereas the fruit is
spontaneous in that other person, it is artificial in the one
who copies him. Second, he is laboring to be *the other
branch.* The German philosopher Arthur Schopenhauer has
reminded us, "We forfeit three-fourths of ourselves in order
to be like other people." He was not writing of Christians.
But when a Christian seeks to be a carbon copy of another,
he is saying, in effect, "I do not believe that Christ is
adequate to be in me, as my own unique self, what He is
in this other person as his unique self."

These, then, are concepts of fruit that are popular in certain circles. It is indeed refreshing for the Christian to meditate on what the New Testament itself says about fruit. This we will see in the next chapter.

WHAT GOD LABELS AS FRUIT

Herein is my Father glorified, that
ye bear much fruit (John 15:8).

Fruit in the Christian life is "a many-splendored thing."
It grows in as many aspects and forms as there are expressions in life itself. Let us consider five broad categories
of such fruit, chiefly as found in the New Testament.

It is character that is Christlike.   This is clear in key passages such as John 15 and Galatians 5:22, 23 and other vital
references, like Ephesians 5:8-13, James 3:17, 18, and 2 Peter
1:3-11. Christ's focus in John 15 is upon love (v. 9), joy
(v. 11), and obedience (v. 14). In John 14, just before
His illustration of the vine and fruit bearing, He refers to
peace (v. 27). Each of these is, in essence, an attitude
characterized by the very nature of Christ's life, just as the
fruit of a vine is permeated by and is the very life-essence
within the vine itself. We live by Christ's life, enabled by
the Holy Spirit, "the Spirit of life in Christ Jesus" (Rom.
8:2; cf. Eph. 3:16, 17). Pusey, among others, felt that the
Holy Spirit in the Christian corresponds with the sap flowing in a vine. [1]
Galatians 5:22, 23 lists the ninefold but unified "fruit of
the Spirit" in direct contrast to the discordant and chaotic
"lusts (plural) of the flesh." Meditate on the analogy here.
As the *invisible* or hidden lusts of the flesh result in *visible*
works, so the *invisible* power of Christ's life imparted by

[1] E. B. Pusey, *The Minor Prophets, A Commentary* (Grand Rapids:
Baker Book House, 1961), 1:99 (on Hosea 10:1).

the Spirit of life produces *visible* fruit. [2] The first three aspects of fruit which Paul mentions (love, joy, peace) correspond with three examples Christ gives in John 14 and 15. Paul simply expands the list in more detail, though even his enumeration is only representative. He clarifies this by a Greek word, *toiouton:* "Against *such classes of things* there is no law" (Gal. 5:23).

Later, in Ephesians 5, Paul refers to the "fruit of light" (v. 8), but his context indicates that this is the same as the "fruit of the Spirit," for the Christian must be "filled with the Spirit" (v. 18). "Fruit of light" evidently concentrates upon the *essence* or *character* of the manifestation (as light, opposed to darkness, vv. 8a, 11). "Fruit of the Spirit," however, emphasizes the source of origin, the Spirit who is God and perfect Light. Paul clarifies that the "fruit of light" is in the sphere of all goodness, righteousness, and truth (v. 9). He says "Be imitators of God" (v. 1) and stresses walking in Christlikeness (v. 2). Specific examples of such "fruit" follow in the passage. First, there is love which sacrifices for the good of the other person rather than exploiting him for selfish pleasure as in promiscuous sex relations (vv. 2, 3). Second, there is wholesome language (v. 4). These ways of being like Christ, executed in the grace of God are part of what Berkouwer defines as a true imitation of Christ, whose mind we are to have (Phil. 2:5-8) and in whose steps we are to follow (1 Peter 2:21). [3]

This New Testament picture of fruitfulness is in harmony with the Old Testament concept. In Isaiah 5, where the Lord found *corrupt* fruit in His vineyard, the immediate context sets forth exhibits A, B, and C of such fruit (vv. 8ff). Good fruit, the opposite of these un-Christlike characteristics, would be such virtues as giving rather than taking advantage (v. 8), disciplined self-control by the Spirit rather

[2] W. E. Vine, *Expository Dictionary of New Testament Words.* 4 vols. in 1 (London: Oliphants, Ltd., 1959), 2:133. See also William Barclay, *Flesh and Spirit, An Examination of Galatians 5:19-23* (Nashville, Tenn.: Abingdon Press, 1962). The latter is a 127-page study of the words for the "works of the flesh" and the "fruit of the Spirit."

[3] G. C. Berkouwer, *Faith and Sanctification* (Grand Rapids: Wm. B. Eerdmans Publishing Co., 1952), ch. on sanctification and the imitation of Christ.

than being controlled by wine (v. 11; cf. Eph. 5:18), and truthfulness rather than dishonesty (vv. 20, 23; cf. Eph. 5:9).

It is plain that fruit is Christlikeness before God and others. It is shown by a Christian who says a kind word on another's behalf when others are "throwing him to the snakes." Or when he himself is rebuffed for a mistake, he acknowledges it and answers in softness and kindness instead of resentfully lashing back. On the highway, another driver darts in front of him, then stops to turn left and holds him up for a long line of oncoming traffic; but instead of leaning on his horn or being peeved for long, he wishes blessing on the unthoughtful driver. Or, as a mechanic, he practices honesty in appraising the car he is working on, whereas many would pad the bill with the rationalization that "it's just good business if you can take advantage of someone and get away with it." Or suppose he comes home tired and his wife has ideas about rearranging the furniture. He can respond in good cheer, love, and helpfulness. In another case, he is delayed a few minutes unexpectedly, and this throws him off schedule at a crucial time. He can spend that time doing something very worthwhile in loving, joyful prayer instead of fussing. God can show him how to use his time profitably as he waits. Do you remember the miller's daughter in the childhood story spinning straw into gold with the help of Rumplestiltskin to satisfy the whims of a king? Contrast that fanciful tale with what can be wonderfully true for a Christian. God's sons and daughters may turn their situations into golden opportunities for fruit with the help of Christ who lives in them! The story has been told of the painter, John Sargent, being told many years ago in Italy that his train would be quite late. Others in his traveling party paced back and forth at the station, suffering from the heat and agitating about the delay. But Sargent sat down, took out his painting equipment, set us his easel, and began to capture a scene of a yoke of oxen nearby on the street. He literally turned the delay into a masterpiece! And in spiritual matters that are far more important than painting, we also may turn our irritating circumstances into occasions of creativity.

Fruit of Christlikeness is what our Father desires from us in situations like these. But we must go on to look at other aspects of fruit.

It is confession of Christ's name in praise (Heb. 13:15). The writer to the Hebrews shows that believers may offer up a sacrifice of praise to God through Christ. This sacrifice is the fruit of a Christian's lips. The "fruit of the lips" refers to utterances of thanksgiving in a spirit of true worship. In the Old Testament, this phrase seems to have been a Hebrew idiom (Isa. 57:19; Hosea 14:2). Hebrews is citing Hosea from the Greek translation of the Old Testament, which renders "fruit *(karpos)* of our lips" as a paraphrase of the Hebrew wording "calves of our lips." Hosea's literal words place "of our lips" in opposition to "calves," meaning that the people of Israel will one day offer a genuine type of sacrifice, namely their lips, in pure worship. [4] These utterances, which are "fruit," will be like the calves offered on Israel's altars long ago, and will be more acceptable to God than the past animal sacrifices, which were often presented in a hollow, ritualistic sham worship. The idea of Hebrews 13:15, then, comes more into focus. Jewish Christians, having embraced Christ Himself as the perfect sacrifice, are not to go on offering animals which pointed to Him. Yet they still do have a sacrifice to offer, the sacrifice of praise-words from their lips. Such sacrifice is fruit to God. In uttering such praise, they are "giving thanks to his name" (KJV), or, more literally, "confessing" or "agreeing" or "saying the same thing." The word is the very term used in 1 John 1:9, where John says that men may "confess" sins. This is the basic sense of agreeing with God (that is, evidently, in regard to the true nature of their sins as opposed to His character as light in verse five). The writer to the Hebrews means, then, that as the believer offers the fruit of his lips as a sacrifice to God, he is agreeing with regard to the name of Christ, agreeing that He is wonderful and altogether adequate.

Fruit here can be, as in John 15 and Galatians 5, the life-

---

[4] Theodore Laetsch, *The Minor Prophets* (Saint Louis, Missouri: Concordia Publishing House, 1956), p. 107.

essence of Christ within the believer, including such aspects as love, joy, and peace — which are at the heart of praise. But there is still more to fruit.

It is a contribution to those in need.   A loving gift from the Christians in Philippi to Paul in his Roman chains (cf. Acts 28:20) called forth his words of Philippians 4:15-17. Though he was grateful, he was not primarily concerned for a gift to *himself.* Above all, he desired fruit that might be credited to *their* account. He used commercial language to draw a mental picture. His use of "fruit" *(karpos)* is in accord with the Hebrew word *periy* for "fruit," which Judaism applied at times to the business realm. It meant financial interest. [5] Paul's context itself shows that the image in his mind was that of banking, for his word "account" is definitely a business word. As Hendriksen writes, the gift prompted by the Holy Spirit in the hearts of the Philippians was fruit because it *"was really an investment* entered *as a credit* on the *account* of the Philippians, an investment which is increasingly paying them rich dividends . . ." (italics his). [6] Evidently the contribution to Paul had originated in an attitude or essence of love (thus fruit) in the believers' hearts. The gift itself, inasmuch as it is intimately intertwined with that life-flow of love, is also fruit in a sense.

In Romans 15:28, Paul wrote of the financial gift for needy Jewish Christians in the area of Judea. He called it "fruit," evidently because it was the product (harvest) of God-imparted love shed abroad in hearts, a concern for others. Paul was to visit those in Rome while on his way to Spain, but only after he had "sealed" this fruit. His act of sealing refers to finishing the task of delivering the "fruit," just as "sealing" a sack of grain was a sign of the *completion* of the transaction in Greek literature. [7] In Paul's thinking, fruit as love and fruit as the gift issuing from that love formed one unified idea.

    [5] Friedrich Hauck, "Karpos," in *Theological Dictionary of the New Testament,* ed. Gerhard Kittel, trans. Geoffrey Bromiley (Grand Rapids: Wm. B. Eerdmans Publishing Co., 1965), 3: 614, 615.

    [6] William Hendriksen, *Exposition of Philippians* (Grand Rapids: Baker Book House, 1962), p. 205.

    [7] Hauck, "Karpos," 3: 615, footnote 7.

Do some immediate applications occur for your own life? If contributing to the lives of others in need is fruit bearing, how can this be put in "shoe leather" today? Is there any connection with such situations as the following: mowing the yard for a man who is down with back trouble and embarrassed about the long grass growing up, preparing supper for a family burdened with illness, sending a check to a person who has been in an accident and has some extra bills to pay, and giving to a student who is struggling to meet his expenses and stay in school? "Herein is my father glorified, that ye bear much fruit."

However, the concept of fruit bearing is broader than that of helpfulness to those in need.

It also includes conduct in general. Fruit, according to the New Testament, can appear in all acts of the life. Paul conceives of the Colossian believers as "being fruitful in every good work" (Col. 1:10), a concept expanded in our next chapter. A realization of this can add zest and spark to any life. Paul often names specific good works (e.g., 1 Tim. 5:9, 10; Titus 2:7-10; 3:1, 2). A revealing example is his list of what a widow can do (1 Tim. 5)! She is to be "well reported of for good works." One good work is that of bringing up children, evidently with the countless spiritual attitudes, words, and acts that a woman abiding in Christ may devote to a task having such far-reaching influences. She may also bear fruit in showing hospitality to strangers, washing the saints' feet and offering a helping hand to those in distress. Her washing of the saints' feet refers to the custom of washing the dusty feet of those who came into one's home — a custom that was a sign of cordial hospitality. Christ used it as an example to believers that they should humbly serve one another in love (John 13: 2-15). We may paraphrase Paul's conclusion in this way: "To sum it all up, the widow is acceptable if she has devoted herself to every good work (i.e., such as these I have just mentioned as prime examples)."

A true concept of fruitfulness sees, then, that eternity's values may be invested in even the seemingly routine acts of the home. And this concept can put sparkle in the Christian's life. This means at all times, in every way, and in all places. Life need never be monotonous but can ever be momentous. Still, however, there is more to the concept of fruit.

Fruit also consists of those who are converted through one's witness. Our Lord, after conversing with the woman of Samaria at the well, talked with His disciples (John 4). He discerned that their primary interest was in satisfying their own personal, physical needs rather than satisfying the spiritual needs of others. He seized the golden opportunity to share with them His own sense of priority which elevated the Father's interests above all else (vv. 31-34). Then He applied this to them by His analogy between those who reap a physical harvest of grain and those who reap a spiritual harvest of persons (v. 35). The comparison rises to its climax in verse thirty-six with the reaper gathering "fruit" in the sense of *converts* possessing eternal life in Christ.

Paul was thinking of fruit in a similar sense when he spoke of converts as the "firstfruits of Achaia" (1 Cor. 16: 15). Though he used the word *aparche* for "fruits," not *karpos* for "fruit," his figure was drawn from the farmer's "firstfruits" (Lev. 23:10). These were the first, token fruits representative of the full harvest he was yet to reap. His point must be that some were the earliest converts (fruit) in the region of Achaia; others there were introduced to Christ later.

Another passage often used for teaching that "fruit" means "converts" is Romans 1:13. Paul stated the purpose of his desired visit to the people in Rome in these words: ". . . that I might obtain some fruit among you also, even as among the rest of the Gentiles." It is possible that Paul thought of converts when he spoke of fruit, but, quite frankly, the case for such an interpretation is not clear-cut. He could have meant the fruit of Christian character — love, joy, peace, and the like — in his own life or the lives of those under his ministry which would be for the greater glory of God. Either meaning is possible but, of course, the two concepts are intimately related to each other.

This leads to an important question. Exactly what does Christ mean by "fruit" in John 15? We have already looked briefly at this, but we need to become aware, if we do not already know it, that there have been emphatic disagreements over this. A. B. Bruce, for example, insists that it must mean souls led to Christ, whereas R. C. H. Lenski as strongly claims that it is basically such traits of Christian character as love, joy, and peace. Bruce writes:

> While urgent in His demand for fruit, Jesus does not, we observe, in any part of this discourse on the vine, indicate wherein the expected fruit consists. When we consider to whom He is speaking, however, we can have no doubt as to what He principally intends. The fruit He looks for is the spread of the gospel and the ingathering of souls into the kingdom of God by the disciples, in the discharge of their apostolic vocation. Personal holiness is not overlooked; but it is required rather as a means toward fruitfulness than as itself the fruit. [8]

Later, he defines the fruit as being "in the shape of a church of saved men believing in His name."

But Lenski counters this idea in these words:

> Strange things have been said about the term "fruit," *karpos,* making the branches themselves the fruit of the vine, and then reasoning that the fruit of the branches must be similar, namely other branches, souls joined to Christ by us. Such thoughts only confuse and spoil the allegory. No branch ever grafts another branch into the vine. The production of branches is wholly the business of Christ, the vine. The fruit of the branches consists in grapes. What this fruit in reality is, is plainly told in Scripture: "The fruit of the Spirit is love, joy, peace, long-suffering, gentleness, goodness, faith, meekness, temperance," Gal. 5:22, 23; "in all goodness and righteousness and truth," Eph. 5: 9; "the peaceable fruit of righteousness," Heb. 12:11. . . .[9]

[8] A. B. Bruce, *The Training of the Twelve* (New York: George H. Doran Co., fifth edition, revised, n.d.), pp. 412-414. Cf. George Johnston, "The Allegory of the Vine: An Exposition of John 15:1-17," *Canadian Journal of Theology,* Vol. III, No. 3, July, 1957, p. 152; John Marsh, *The Gospel of St. John* (Baltimore: Penguin Books, 1968), p. 520.

[9] R. C. H. Lenski, *The Interpretation of St. John's Gospel* (Minneapolis: Augsburg Publishing House, 1943), pp. 1029, 1030.

Later, he adds that "the fruit consists in all manner of Christian virtues and in the thoughts, words, and deeds in which they manifest themselves. . . ." A. C. Gaebelein and John R. W. Stott agree, but use the term "Christlikeness." [10]

What is the solution? The nature of the question is complex and therefore we will best arrive at a sensible answer by looking at the matter carefully. To do so, we will follow two steps.

(1) There is fruit in the image of the vine. If we are to be true to the precise image in view in John 15, we can find much to agree with in Lenski's words. This is because of four factors. First, fruit is from *within* the vine and branches, the very life-essence of Christ expressed. In the physical branches it is grapes, as Lenski insists, and not other branches. Second, Lenski argues that a branch does not add other branches in the physical vine, so it does not appear that this would be the meaning of fruit here. Third, although some are sure that verse sixteen which says, "Go and bear fruit," definitely refers to converts as fruit, it can just as well be understood as calling us to go and bear the fruit which is love, joy, and peace. We *go* to do that, too. Fourth, the context itself appears to make this explanation more likely, since both before (vv. 8-12) and after (v. 17), its particular emphasis is on love. Examples of what is evidently fruit in the passage itself also include joy and peace. And these are part of the fruit in Galatians 5:22, 23. Christlike character is in view there, and so it seems to be here also. The emphasis on witness, which leads to converts, appears later, in 15:26, 27.

Now, having said this, must we exclude converts from being called "fruit"? No. We must recognize that the total biblical teaching of what can come under the term "fruit" is wider than what is consistent with the strict facts of one image, the vine. This leads to our second step.

(2) There is fruit in the image of the harvest. In other passages, as we have shown earlier, converts can be fruit. First, there is John 4:35, 36 (cf. also Matt. 9:36-38), where

---

[10] A. C. Gaebelein, *The Gospel of John* (New York: Publication Office, *Our Hope*, 1936), p. 296; John R. W. Stott, *Christ the Liberator* (Downers Grove, Illinois: Inter-Varsity Press, 1971), p. 52.

the image is that of a harvest, not the same as that of a vine. Second, and much like the first picture, is the figure of firstfruits (1 Cor. 16:15). Third, persons introduced to Christ and born again can evidently be referred to as fruit in view of other statements of Paul. For example, he speaks of begetting others (1 Cor. 4:15; Philemon 10). A Christian can say that he has begotten another person in the faith as he is God's instrument in this, though in the greater sense God has begotten that person unto life and sonship (1 Peter 1:3; 1 John 5:1). Paul also refers to certain men as his sons in the faith (*Timothy:* 1 Cor. 4:17; Phil. 2:22; 1 Tim. 1:2, 18; 2 Tim. 1:2; *Titus:* Titus 1:4; *Onesimus:* Philemon 10). If this is true in a spiritual sense, then it is reasonable to say that such "sons" who are "begotten" are fruit just as sons begotten physically are "fruit of the womb" (Ps. 127:3; Acts 2:30). Fourth, we may give a word of caution about the second argument under the first step above. In one sense a physical branch in a vine *does* add other branches, for it puts out yet other branches from itself. Lenski fails to recognize this physical fact as well as its spiritual analogy when he says, "The production of branches is wholly the business of Christ, the vine." It is more sensitive to the overall aspect of the picture to say that Christ also *uses persons* to bring other persons into union with Himself. The vine image, seen in the limited light in which Lenski views it, would not permit the thought, but Lenski's statement about branches not adding other branches is susceptible to challenge.

It appears to be the wisest conclusion, then, to say that fruit in the New Testament has more aspects than one image alone is capable of conveying. Fruit appears in different senses and can refer *both* to Christlikeness and to converts. Yet Christ's *emphasis* in the context of John 15, as Paul's in Galatians 5, seems to be on the first meaning, in line with the illustration of the vine. In the context of a harvest, fruit can mean converts, but the fruit of a vine branch is more naturally grapes, not other branches.

This provokes an important question. What, then, is the relationship between fruit as Christlikeness and fruit as converts?

First, when some limit fruit to refer only to people led to Christ, they convey an unfortunate emphasis. The writer has heard some stress "soul winning" as fruit to the virtual exclusion of any consideration of fruit as love, joy, and peace. The importance of Christian character is lost sight of. There are churches where evangelism is emphasized, but the people are hungry and impoverished for teaching on the Christian life. The Christian who sees the different elements in the concept of fruit in his Bible will rightly desire a life of all-around symmetry in fruit-bearing, not simply an all-out drive on one aspect while the other suffers. Second, however, we must ever be sensitive to the fact that our Lord did place great emphasis upon taking the message to others (cf. Matt. 28:19, 20; Luke 19:10; Acts 1:8). The Book of Acts goes on to record the acts of the risen Christ by the Holy Spirit through men captivated by the passion of introducing other men to their great Lord. The epistles fit in primarily as "follow-up" material. The Christian must realize that fruit as character and fruit as converts need not exist in a mutually exclusive either/or relationship but may relate in a both/and unity. After all, doesn't it make sense to ask what Christian *character* could there be without Christian *characters?* One sins against his Lord if he rationalizes, "I am relieved to learn that fruit can be many things besides just leading others to Christ. I will live my life and bear my fruit in these respects, and leave the witnessing part to others." How can the Christian exclude himself from responsibility in the light of the inseparable connection that must exist between his love and obedience to the concerns that are on Christ's heart (John 14:21; 15: 9-14)? The person who truly lives in the love of the Spirit, as an abiding branch, will want to be sensitive to the heartbeat of Christ who came "to seek and to save that which was lost" (Luke 19:10).

Now the question is pertinent, how does the fruit of character actually relate to the fruit of winning people to Christ? It is in this way. Our love, joy, and peace have at their very core the Word of God with its message of the Gospel (good news). In the New Testament type of Christian life, these fit closely together. The Christian who truly bears the fruit of love, joy, and peace will also in some measure be properly related to the Word (John 15:2, 3, 7; cf. 14:21). By his character he arrests and impresses others, and by his word (shaped by the Word of God) he communicates his secret and reveals how they also may receive life in Christ. This word falls into the soil of another life as seed (Matt. 13:3-9, 18-23) and begets the person unto eternal life (1 Peter 1:23). It is an implanted word (James 1:21). There is, then, an analogy between what is true in the realm of *plants* and what is true of *persons* as shown in the following diagram:

PLANTS	PERSONS
(1) A branch produces grapes (fruit).	(1) A believer produces spiritual fruit such as love, joy, peace.
(2) A grape gives forth the seed that is within it.	(2) Such fruit has seed, the Word of God, or Gospel, as its essence (1 Pet. 1: 23).
(3) The seed goes into the soil and new life (a new plant) springs up.	(3) The seed (the Word) enters into the heart-soil of a person and new life springs up (Matt. 13:23).

Here it is evident that already we have gone beyond the vine-branch image. Now we have a new, separate plant, not another branch on the same one plant, the vine. The total New Testament imagery in relation to the spiritual life is broader than the aspects that the vine illustration alone can depict.

Conclusion about fruit. The five areas of fruit we have discussed in this chapter indicate a variety of things fruit can be and situations to which it is related. Truly it is, for one thing, a character that is Christlike, and we ought to sing with deep sincerity, "My desire, to be like Jesus; my desire, to be like Him!" But it is also confession of Christ's name in adoring praise, giving to those who are in need, every act of life in general, and, among all these things, it is the converts who have come to believe through our witness by life and word. Indeed, fruit is as varied as life itself and so it is "a many-splendored thing." Shakespeare has reminded us: "One man in his life plays many parts"; [11] and the person who loves Christ loves the things Christ loves, and desires fruit in the many roles in which he is cast. Just as his heavenly Father looks for the precious fruit, so he longs to see that which is, in its essential quality, the inlived and outlived product of the authentic life, the life of Christ who is "the vine, the true one."

[11] William Shakespeare, *As You Like It*, Act 2, Scene 7.

ARE GOOD WORKS FRUIT?

. . . being fruitful in every good work (Col. 1:10).

Are we right according to the New Testament if we call good works fruit? The question is simple, but certain aspects of biblical teaching have been turned to the advantage of different views. Most scholars equate good works (also thoughts, words, and converts) with fruit. But some expositors dogmatically distinguish good works (in true faith) from fruit, insisting that fruit is in inner character only.

The position taken here is that fruit may appear in a variety of forms including even good works. John Owen was perceptive when he said:

> Unless believers have uninterrupted influences of grace, and spiritually vital nourishment from Christ, "they can do nothing"; that is, nothing which appertains to fruit-bearing. Now every act of faith and love, every motion of our minds or affections towards God, is a part of our "fruit-bearing"; and so are all external duties of obedience. Wherefore, our Lord being judge, believers themselves cannot, without new actual supplies of grace, do anything spiritually good.[1]

The conviction here is that the fruit of the Spirit consists first in those dispositions such as love, joy, and peace dominating the life. Emphasis should first be upon what a person *is* in character before considering what he *does* in conduct. Yet there is a vital relationship between these. When the qualities of his disposition are the fruit of the Spirit, he manifests these virtues in works. The gracious, God-given attitudes inspire, permeate, flavor, and give tone and value to the works themselves. So the Christian may

[1] John Owen, *A Discourse Concerning the Holy Spirit* (Philadelphia: Presbyterian Board of Education, n.d.), p. 302.

be "fruitful in every good work" (Col. 1:10), meaning that a quality of Christlikeness is invested in, and imparts true worth to, every outward good work. He can "abound to every good work" (2 Cor. 9:8), be "abounding in the work of the Lord" (1 Cor. 15:58), and be "full of good works" (Acts 9:36). Good works, then, may themselves be the believer's produce or fruit as well as the context or occasion in which he bears the fruit of inner Christlikeness.

This appears to be the proper view to which the Scripture leads us when we carefully weigh the evidence as a whole. We now turn to this evidence.

(1) If works of the flesh are contrasted with fruit of the Spirit (Gal. 5:19-23) and can even be designated as "unfruitful works" (Eph. 5:11), then fruit of the Spirit would seem to be works of the Spirit. This includes both inner attitudes and outer acts. Several of the works of the flesh can be in either the attitude or the act. An obvious example is murder (the act) and hate (the attitude, 1 John 3:15). Another example is adultery, for when a man lusts after a woman in attitude, he has in a sense already committed the act of adultery with her (Matt. 5:28). A very close relationship exists, then, between inner attitude and outer act. If this is true of fleshly attitudes and works, is it not also true of good fruit? Could we not say that fruit may be either an attitude of love or a *work* of love expressing that attitude?

Some have sought to maintain a distinction between the fruit of the *Spirit* (disposition) and the fruit of the *Christian* himself in service (works). But this has not been thought through carefully. Actually, there is a beautiful coordination in which the fruit of the Spirit is the fruit of the believer himself in the power of the Spirit.

(2) The New Testament gives an analogy by stating that good works are a product of the Christian just as fruit is the product of a tree. Hauck argues from the fact that John the Baptist and Christ refer to the works of men as their fruit and as evidence that repentance is genuine (Matt. 3: 8, 10; 7:16-23; 21:43). [2] This is reasonable, since the Old

---

[2] Friedrich Hauck, "Karpos," *Theological Dictionary of the New Testament,* ed. Gerhard Kittel, trans. Geoffrey W. Bromiley (Grand Rapids: Wm. B. Eerdmans Publishing Co., 1965), 3:614-616.

Testament preparation for the New speaks of fruit as coming from thoughts (Jer. 6:19), words (Prov. 12:14; 13:2; 18:20; Isa. 57:19), and works of the hands (Prov. 31:16). All of these were empirical fruit, not just inner dispositions.

The context of Matthew 7:16-24 supports this. It links "good fruit" (v. 19) with "by their fruits ye shall know them" (v. 20) and then with "he that doeth the will of my Father which is in heaven" (v. 21) and hearing and doing Christ's sayings (v. 24). In the parallel account in Luke 6:43-45 (especially v. 45) and also in Matthew 12:33-37, Christ very closely identifies fruit with *words* in His analogy. Hebrews 13:15 also refers to our words, "the fruit of our lips." When the particular emphases of all the passages are put together, the more complete picture crystalizes. Fruit equals works and words (or teachings) as well as inner dispositions.

(3) Later Judaism considered the works of men their fruits, as Hauck shows. [3] This fits with the linking of works with fruit in Scripture: "Bring forth therefore fruit meet for repentance" (Matt. 3:8) and "Do works meet for repentance" (Acts 26:20).

(4) If converts are fruit in the analogy of a harvest (John 4:35, 36; 1 Cor. 16:15), the New Testament thus going beyond the limit of allowing only character as fruit, then surely works and words may also be called fruit. They are products of a life.

(5) Fruit would seem to include works and words, since judgment is in some passages said to be according to *works* (Matt. 25:31-46; Rom. 2:6, 13; 2 Cor. 11:15; Rev. 20:12, 13 et al.) and in others according to *words* (Matt. 12:33-37). It is those who lack good fruit who are cast into the fire of judgment (Matt. 3:10; 7:19). The lack of good fruit appears to be the lack of good works and words, as well as evil dispositions.

(6) Revelation 2:19 equates works with qualities that are

---

[3] *Ibid.* The Jewish midrash says, on Psalm 36:6, that as the mountains which are sown bring forth fruits, so the righteous bring forth fruits or good works. See H. L. Strack and P. Billerbeck, *Kommentar zum NT aus Talmud und Midrasch* (Munchen, 1956), 1:466.

among the fruit of the Spirit. Christ commends the Church of Thyatira. "I know your works," He says, "your love and faith and service and patient endurance, and that your recent works are more numerous and greater than your first ones." Many interpreters understand "works" as the main consideration and say that the four qualities that follow — love, faith (or faithfulness), service, and patient endurance — are simply those characteristics from which the works have come. [4] However, A. T. Robertson refers to Revelation 2:2 where a similar series of virtues occurs, and the word "and" (Gr. *kai*) between words can mean "even" or "namely." [5] If this is true in 2:19, then "works" is the equivalent of love or love-works (fruit of the Spirit brought out in the form of acts), faith, and so on.

(7) John 15:1-6 in its emphasis upon the inner-life essence of the vine imparted to the branches is not really opposed to the concept that good works are fruit. It is true that the life is *within* the branches, but the fruit comes out *on* the branches eventually and is permeated by that inner life. Similarly, the Christian has the imparted life quality of Christ within, yet bears fruit that also shows up on the outside of his life, whatever may be invisibly true within. Fruit that appears on the outside may be in attitudes, words, and works, for all are closely related.

(8) Galatians 5:22, 23 specifically defines the "fruit of the Spirit" in terms of the inner life — Christlike character, attitudes, or dispositions. From this, some wrongly insist that good works are not fruit but rather that fruit is the pervading spirit, quality, or virtue underlying, inspiring, and giving value to the works. But one part of a definition of fruit such as in Galatians 5 should not be allowed to shape one's entire New Testament concept. Rather, it ought to be correlated as one aspect along with other aspects in the total picture which is broader than the one passage emphasizes. Fruit as inner disposition is beautifully harmo-

---

[4] For example, Leon Morris, *Revelation of St. John* (London: The Tyndale Press, 1969), p. 70; A. T. Robertson, *Word Pictures in the New Testament* (Nashville, Tenn.: Broadman Press, 1933), 4:308.

[5] Robertson, *ibid.*

nious with fruit as words and works extending the inner life into Christlike action.

(9) Some resist with the logic that God's love, joy, and peace are in a sense distinct from His bountiful works themselves and so must it be with a Christian's fruit and good works. In response to this, we acknowledge a distinction between attitude and act, certainly, yet they are often inextricably bound together as one, since the qualities of love fill the acts. Also, fruit is basically a product and, as in the Old Testament, words and works are just as really products as inner thoughts.

(10) This is consistent with situations which seem to require a distinction between the fruit of the Spirit as inner character and good works in outer behavior. Some do not see how our view could be true in such cases. But let us look at the matter. Suppose that a Christian woman is bed-ridden, scarcely able to move even a hand, and thus incapacitated for outer good works. She may still be trusting in the grace of God and radiating the fruit of the Spirit. Or take a believer in prison, even in the rare situation of having suffered the loss of tongue and hands. His spirit is Christlike. Does this not prove a distinction between fruit and good works? Not really. The fruit of these Christians may be all concentrated within their dispositions only, for they have no opportunity for outer works as most of us do. They are bearing fruit in one of its forms within their range of possibilities. This, however, does not affect others who have wider possibilities, for they may bear fruit also in many works. And we must also call to remembrance the truth that what a believer does inwardly is still in essence a work, and a good one if the Spirit controls. Should the bed-ridden Christian be able to translate that inner fruit also into outer works, he would do so. But the life he lives in disposition may bear as much fruit or more to please his Lord as the life a healthy believer lives in attitude, word, and act.

(11) Some have contended that 1 Thessalonians 1:3 proves a distinction between inner characteristics and outer activity. From this they will argue that a good work is not

fruit itself (as love is). Paul commends the believers of
Thessalonica for their "work of faith, labor of love, and
stedfastness of hope." There are, admittedly, various views
on how the Greek construction may be understood, and
W. Hendriksen has conveniently listed the main ones. [6] The
most plausible is that which Hendriksen himself expresses
in his translation, a view also favored by A. T. Robertson. [7]
In this position, Paul is speaking of "your work resulting
from [i.e., springing from, accomplished by, and revealing]
faith, and (your) exertion prompted by [and revealing] love
and (your) endurance inspired by hope. . . ." This recognizes a clear-cut distinction between labor and the love (a
fruit of the Spirit) which has prompted it.

In response, it should be said that although it is true
that we may recognize the distinction between love which
can be an inner quality only, apart from any form of outward expression such as a labor which love inspires, yet
when love as inner fruit is expressed in a love-work as outer
activity, the love-work is simply a visible form of the same
essence. The work is fruit; that is, fruit in an outlived and
extended manifestation. This is consistent with points 1-3
and 6.

(12) Passages inconclusive in themselves may best be
interpreted in harmony with the explanation we have taken.
There are a number of such verses.

Philippians 1:11 refers to "the fruits of righteousness,"
where much good textual evidence argues for the singular
"fruit of righteousness," just as "fruit" is singular in Galatians 5:22. This is most likely the same fruit as in the
Galatians passage — basically Christian character, and then
also other forms in which it may appear, as in words and
works. The meaning of the phrase is "fruit characterized
by righteousness," just as the expression "fruit of light"
(Eph. 5:9 RSV) is "fruit characterized by (or of the essence
of) light." Another translation, which would still be in harmony with our basic view, is "fruit of (from the source of)

---

[6] Wm. Hendriksen, *Exposition of I and II Thessalonians* (Grand Rapids:
Baker Book House, 1955), p. 47.

[7] Hendriksen, *ibid.*; A. T. Robertson, *Word Pictures*, 4:8.

light." This would point to God the Holy Spirit who is the source of fruit as in Galatians 5:22. Fruit may be in disposition, word, or work, since each may be characterized by righteousness or be from the source of righteousness.

Paul's words in Philippians 1:22 are more difficult. He is torn between two possibilities, to live on in the flesh or to depart to be with Christ. If he lives in the flesh, he says, "this is fruit of my work." What is the fruit he has in mind? The Greek wording "of my work" is in the genitive case and is open to different meanings. For example, "of my work" may be a genitive of apposition in relation to "fruit," calling for the meaning "fruit which is my work." Bengel, favoring this, says Paul thinks of his *work itself* as fruit. [8] But we may also regard the words "of my work" as a genitive of source or origin. The meaning would then be "fruit of (from the source of) my work," or "fruit secured by or resulting from my work." Many are inclined to this, such as Hendriksen and Jamieson-Fausset-Brown. [9] We have, then, five main possibilities as follows:

(a) Fruit as work itself (above). This is possible, in view of the broad spectrum of meaning for fruit in Scripture.

(b) Fruit as love, joy, peace, etc. These would come as a result of Paul's work in sowing the Word. Men would receive it into their hearts, be saved, and then yield fruit as in Galatians 5:22, 23. In one sense, it would be "fruit of the Spirit"; in another, "fruit of the believers themselves"; and still another, "fruit of Paul's labor," emphasizing the human instrument through whom it became possible.

(c) Fruit as Christ. According to the *Beacon Bible Commentary*, "Christ is the fruit of Paul's labor. . . ." [10] This also is a possible interpretation in view of Paul's words in

[8] Bengel in *Gnomon of the New Testament,* cited by B. C. Caffin, "Philippians," *The Pulpit Commentary* (New York: Funk and Wagnalls Co., n.d.), 47:6.

[9] Hendriksen, *Exposition of Philippians* (Grand Rapids: Baker Book House, 1962), pp. 76, 77; A. R. Fausset, "I Corinthians — Revelation," in *A Commentary Critical, Experimental and Practical on the Old and New Testaments* (Grand Rapids: Wm. B. Eerdmans Publishing Co., 1961), 6:427.

[10] John A. Knight, "Philippians," *Beacon Bible Commentary* (Kansas City, Missouri: Beacon Hill Press, 1965), 9:307.

verse twenty-one: "To me to live is Christ." He might have meant that Christ would be the fruit of his labor; that is, the very life of Christ or Christlikeness in love, joy, and peace within himself and others because of his work as he lived as a branch in the vine. If to live is Christ, then the fruit of his labor will in some sense also be Christ.

(d) Fruit as converts, the salvation of souls as a good result of his work. Hendriksen [11] and Braune [12] are disposed to this. The fruit is a harvest of souls as in John 4:35, 36 and 1 Corinthians 16:15. Some, as Charles Hodge, also teach this from Romans 1:13.

(e) Fruit in the general sense of that which is "worth-while." Grotius sees "fruit of my labor" as an idiom. [13] If Paul should continue in the flesh, it would turn out to be worth his while, since he would carry out Christ's cause. But although this point is true, it seems better to be more specific in explaining the fruit, as in one or more of the preceding points.

It is difficult to decide among these choices what Paul really intended. All are consistent with our concept of fruit in the New Testament. If he meant the first, it would harmonize with the idea that fruit may be work as well as word or disposition. This possibility is different from all the others in that they all speak of fruit as in some sense the *result* of work. It does not appear likely that he meant the first since it is usually works (plural) that are equated with fruit. But when we look at the other explanations, we wonder if Paul's total concept of fruit might have been broad enough to carry all four aspects — (b), (c), (d), and (e). The fruit resulting from his labor could very well be all, though this writer is not inclined to include (e) in the final analysis because it is found nowhere else in the New Testament and is not specific as the others. Paul realized, then, that should he live on in the flesh, his work would

[11] Hendriksen, *Philippians*, pp. 76, 77.

[12] Karl Braune, "The Epistle of Paul to the Philippians," trans. and ed., Horatio B. Hackett, in *Lange's Commentary on the Holy Scriptures* (Grand Rapids: Zondervan Publishing House, 1960 reprint), Vol. 11 (on Phil. 1:22).

[13] Grotius as cited by Fausset, *Commentary*, 6:427.

result in fruit including Christlikeness in those his ministry brought to Christ, Christlikeness in his own life, and the very converts themselves.

The next verse to consider is Colossians 1:10. Paul conceives of Christians as "being fruitful in every good work." What does he mean? There are two main possibilities.

(a) The believer may bear fruit, namely Christlike character, which imparts and manifests its wholesome influence (including a quality of goodness) in every type of work in which he engages. This could be his point, since in the very next verse Paul immediately places emphasis upon the power of God that strengthens within, evidently that of the Holy Spirit (cf. Eph. 3:16), and qualities of fruitfulness which this enables one to produce, such as stedfastness, longsuffering, and joy.

(b) The believer may be fruitful in every fruit. Fruit is the same as good work in some cases, though it is a broader concept in that it may also be in other forms. Hauck says this verse teaches that "works are the fruit of the righteous." [14] In the process of growth the Christian may become involved in all of the possible areas of fruitfulness, all that are possible in the will of God for him in particular. This is the more likely meaning in line with the evidence we have already seen that fruit may be the same as good works.

Two passages which are somewhat alike are Hebrews 12:11 and James 3:18. Both link the "fruit of righteousness" with peace. In both, the phrase "of righteousness" (in the genitive case) is most plausibly to be understood as explaining or defining "fruit." This means that it is a genitive of definition or apposition and we could translate it literally, "the fruit which consists of righteousness" or "the fruit, namely righteousness." Even if we looked at the words "of righteousness" as a genitive of origin, it would still be in accord with the overall view of this chapter. It would then simply mean "the fruit which grows as a product of righteousness." Both verses are speaking of fruit as Christlikeness, and this could be in different forms — attitude,

---

[14] Hauck, *Theological Dictionary*, 3:616.

word, work — all relating to righteousness. The idea of the genitive of definition may be preferable in James 3: 18 because, as Mitton reasons, it

> falls into line with the thought also expressed in Jas. 1:20. There we read that "the anger of man does not work the righteousness of God", the corollary of which might be that when man has a quiet mind and composed spirit he may be able to achieve righteousness. In that case peacemakers and the peace they produce may be regarded as the needed condition in which righteousness may flourish. [15]

We should add here that this is not out of man's composed spirit alone, but is in the power of the Holy Spirit whose fruit it is.

Two other verses in which some would undoubtedly make a distinction between works (the acts) and fruit are Hebrews 6:10 and 10:24. In the first, we read that "God is not so unjust as to overlook your work and the love which you showed for his sake in serving the saints, as you still do" (RSV). The second passage speaks of stimulating one another "to love and good works." In both cases, love is evidently a motivation for and a permeating quality in the work. Although we recognize a distinction between love as attitude and the act itself, we should still maintain that love is so expressed in the good work that the good work itself is of love's essence and is the particular form that fruit takes in that given instance. Why, then, does the writer to the Hebrews list love (a fruit) and good works separately? It is conceivable that he wanted to focus special emphasis upon one quality (love), the greatest of the virtues (1 Cor. 13), which was present in a marked way in those who had good works. He singled it out for special recognition, realizing that good works (as fruit) may reflect a number of virtues all at the same time. The separate listing of love would serve to highlight it especially.

In the foregoing discussion, then, we have seen evidence that seems sufficient to verify calling good works fruit.

---

[15] C. L. Mitton, *The Epistle of James* (Grand Rapids: Wm. B. Eerdmans Publishing Co., 1966), p. 143.

WHAT MAKES A GOOD WORK?

Be careful to maintain good works (Titus 3:8).

When a Christian is really serious about doing the will of God, he finds among other emphases in the Bible the recurring theme of good works. Christ Himself said, for example, "Let your light shine before men in such a way that they may see your good works, and glorify your Father who is in heaven" (Matt. 5:16 NASB). Paul often repeated the stress on good works. We have been "created in Christ Jesus for good works, which God prepared beforehand that we should walk in them" (Eph. 2:10 RSV). The wealthy believers in this world are to be "rich in good works" (1 Tim. 6:18). Scripture can equip a Christian for every good work (2 Tim. 3:17). Paul wanted Titus to speak the truth confidently so that Christians might "be careful to maintain good works" (Titus 3:8).

But wait a minute! What is a "good work"? On what basis is one work "good" and another not "good"? And is the "good" in a "good work" related to the fruit of the Spirit, which includes "goodness"? We will look at these questions.

What is a good work? Gerstner defines a good work in the biblical sense as having three aspects. It is "any activity of a moral agent which proceeds from a right motive (love), is in accord with a proper moral standard (law), and aims at the glory of a worthy object (God)." [1] This is a helpful definition. Kuyper, in his famous work on the

---

[1] John H. Gerstner, "Good Works," *Baker's Dictionary of Theology* (Grand Rapids: Baker Book House, 1960), p. 253.

Holy Spirit, says a work is good when (1) it is conform-
able to God's law, for He alone possesses the right to determine what is good or evil; and (2) it is done in faith. [2]
By this last point he means it must be in *our* faith and *we*
must actively do the work, realizing that, although the
Spirit works *in* us, He does not work *in our place*. Yet
without Him we can do nothing that is truly good. So it
is we ourselves who do it, making the work our own, but
all the while it is He that has wrought in us so that He
deserves all the glory. Gerstner and Kuyper have spoken
well.

Two different Greek words are used mainly for the word
"good" in our English translations. They are *agathos* and
kalos. In seeking the particular meaning of each, one soon
becomes aware that at times they seem to be interchange-
able in the same verse (Luke 8:15; Rom. 7:18; 1 Tim. 5:10),
in the same context (Matt. 12:33, 35; 1 Thess. 5:15, 21),
and in parallel passages (Matt. 13:8; Luke 8:8). But some
writers today attempt to make a basic distinction in meaning between the two. Vine, for example, proposes that
agathos concentrates upon the potential within a thing to
be of practical usefulness or benefit in its effect. *Kalos*,
he says, focuses more upon the intrinsic beauty, pleasing
quality, nature, or value in itself. [3] Barclay's differentiation
is very similar. *Agathos*, he holds, is that which is practically and morally good in the result of its activity; *kalos*
is that which is not only practically and morally good but
also lovely, gracious, winsome, and pleasing to the eye so
as to make a direct impression on those who come in contact with it. It is agreeable, desirable, and worthy of praise
in itself. [4] In view of the words being used interchangeably
on occasion, it is difficult to defend exact distinctions consistently. We run the risk of being arbitrary at times.
Walker, for instance, shows that even *kalos* can have the

[2] Abraham Kuyper, *The Work of the Holy Spirit* (Grand Rapids: Wm.
B. Eerdmans Publishing Co., 1941), pp. 497-501.

[3] W. E. Vine, *Expository Dictionary of New Testament Words* (London:
Oliphants Ltd., 1959), 2:163, 164.

[4] William Barclay, *More New Testament Words* (New York: Harper &
Brothers, 1958), pp. 92, 93.

sense of "useful" (for practical purposes) in such expressions as "good fruit" (Matt. 3:10), "good ground" (13:23), and "good seed" (13:24). [5]

Whatever is our uncertainty about the particular distinctions we have just seen, we can be certain about some things relating to the word "good." Only God is good *(agathos)* in the ultimate sense (Matt. 19:17), and there is no good thing in man, that is, in his flesh (Rom. 7:18). So it is only when a man is participating in genuine goodness, the Source of goodness Himself, that he can relatively be called "good" and distinguished from the "bad" (Matt. 5:45; 12:34). By God's impartation that is actually transforming him as a person, a Christian is good in the sense of having intrinsic goodness, and he is good in the sense that both he and what he is doing are of outreaching benefit or usefulness. He is useful to God (Acts 11:24; 23:1) and to others (Rom. 12:9; Gal. 6:10; Eph. 4:28).

In the light of this, we can now look at the next question.

Is the good related to fruit? Yes. In a good work, the "work" is the act itself, involving the motions or what is done. The quality of "goodness" which constitutes it a "good" work is the goodness *(agathosune,* noun form of *agathos)* which is a fruit of the Spirit. Paul tells us in Ephesians 5:9 that "the fruit of the light consists in all goodness and righteousness and truth" (NASB). A Christian's invisible attitude of goodness and the translation of it into a visible work or audible word are both specific examples of fruit. Fruit is the inlived and outlived product of God's character and so may be reflected even in the form of some act or word in particular that is permeated by that nature. The fact that it is a "good" work places descriptive emphasis upon one basic aspect characterizing it. It is good. Apart from that quality it would be bad. But it is also possible in a particular case to describe it in line with other emphases as a "righteous" work or a "truthful" work. For the fruit of the Spirit is in the sphere of goodness, righteousness, and truth — all of these.

---

[5] W. L. Walker, "Good," *International Standard Bible Encyclopaedia* (Grand Rapids: Wm. B. Eerdmans Publishing Co., 1960), 2:1277.

What about the good works of the unsaved? Whatever these appear to be outwardly among men, whose judgments are relative and fallible, they are not truly "good" in the appraisal of God. The unsaved are likened to trees that are corrupt and therefore can bring forth only corrupt fruit (Matt. 7:16-23). In the first epistle of John (3:1-12) the apostle draws a sharp contrast between children of God and children of the devil and their corresponding works.

Certainly an unsaved person can do an act prompted by what he judges to be sincere concern. He may show kindness, generosity, thoughtfulness, or hospitality. The non-Christian person is often alert toward helping those in need. He sometimes seeks to raise his children with clean habits as far as he understands them. The rich young ruler who spoke with Christ had kept the commandments from his youth up, outwardly at least (Luke 18:18-27). Yet our Lord confronted him with a deeper issue, true commitment, and he was sorrowful, clinging to his possessions, which in the final analysis were of a more ultimate value to him than God was. The Bible does not specifically call the deeds of this man "good works." They were not truly good by God's standard of judgment. Olshausen says:

> The natural man, destitute of the knowledge of God, of himself, and of sin, dreams that by his own strength and efforts he can produce a form of virtue which can stand before the bar of God. He does not know that of necessity, and by a law of his nature, he can only produce evil fruit, just as a wild tree can produce only bitter fruit. Even should he succeed in calling into exercise all the good he has in the most perfect form, it is so destitute of love, and so corrupted by conceit, that it merits condemnation, as fully as though life were openly immoral. The beginning of truth, of which holiness (which is true liberty), by a like organic necessity and law of nature, is the fruit, is for man the acknowledgment that death reigns in him, and that he must be imbued with life. [6]

Even the Christian, who does the will of God and maintains "good works" by God's grace, is still far from meeting

[6] Cited by Charles Hodge, *Commentary on the Epistle to the Romans* (Grand Rapids: Wm. B. Eerdmans Publishing Co., 1964 reprint of 1886 revised edition), p. 210.

the perfect standard. Gerstner, writing on good works, reminds us:

> Nothing that he ever does, even after justification, merits anything; because nothing which he does is ever perfectly good. That is, nothing which he does proceeds from a perfectly good motive, is directed perfectly according to the good standard, and is aimed perfectly at the glory of God. Nothing short of this is truly good. Since no justified person, in this life, ever does anything which meets such standards he does no meritorious good work. Therefore, he never has any merit to claim which in any way supplements the merit of Christ. . . .[7]

What will be the end of good works? We are talking about good works in *this* life, for certainly good works will continue eternally as we reflect Jesus Christ's glory in all of our activities after this life. First, there is to be reward for the believer. Although no person can merit salvation by his works, the Christian will receive reward on the basis of the life he has lived since trusting Christ. His fruit will come up for evaluation. Christ is to appraise good and bad aspects (1 Cor. 4:5; 2 Cor. 5:10). Every attitude, word, and work, having been brought under the unerring judgment of Christ and shown in its proper light, will be recognized in accordance with what it is truly worth. The believer is to be assigned the reward appropriate for the sum total of quality the Lord finds in his life and ministry.

Second, there must be glory to God. While the reward is very directly in recognition of the honor that comes to the Christian himself, and he will receive deep, satisfying personal fulfillment in it, he will also give all the glory to God through whose rich grace it was made possible (1 Cor. 1:31; 4:7).

Since this exciting prospect is true, and his fruit is a result of abiding in Christ, it is very important for him to know what abiding really means. This is the subject we are to consider in the next chapter.

---

[7] Gerstner, "Good Works," p. 254.

THINGS INVOLVED IN ABIDING

Abide in me, and I in you (John 15:4).

Ordinarily, a Christian lives for some years on earth after his conversion. Sometimes we grow homesick for heaven, but still God would have us wait. A friend of mine once led a young man to Christ. A few days later, after the new convert had begun to study the Scriptures, he sat down and wrote my friend a letter. He wrote, in essence: "I've just read through Romans 8. Man, am I excited. I feel as though I could sprout wings right here and fly away into heaven!" The Bible sometimes give us a longing for heaven, as we consider the pleasures that are "at God's right hand forevermore" and eagerly await the joy of being with Christ, which is far better than any joy we have yet experienced. But God leaves us here as branches of Christ. Our exciting privilege is to *abide* in Christ *now*, to have our dwelling place in Him until that day when He calls us up into the intimacy of fellowship in those dwelling places He is preparing for us (John 14:1-3).

This abiding in Christ involves two basic concepts: the period of *time* during which a person abides and also the *quality* of the relationship involved. Let us consider these two concepts.

The Concept of Time

We can better grasp the meaning of "abide" if we learn how it is used in its references and gain a perspective of how it relates to other words about the spiritual life.

The relation of "abide" to time. The word "abide" (Gr. *meno*) appears more than a hundred times in the New Testament and often in the Greek Old Testament, or Septuagint. It means, basically, "to remain" or "to continue," and it also usually conveys a concept involving some period of time. [1] Early papyri writings used it in a wide variety of settings. One typical use of it is in the following clause: "In order that the hay of Theoxenis may not *remain* too long uncut." [2] The idea of time is always inherent in some way, but the time element may fit into one of four specific categories.

(1) It may be a stated period that is only temporary. In such a case, "abide" has some specific phrase limiting

[1] "Abide" in the English translation also occurs many times in the Old Testament and covers a broad range of ideas in Hebrew words. Some of these suggest a life of spiritual intimacy approaching the warmth and richness our Lord invests in the word "abide" of John 15. In the Greek translation of the Old Testament, the Septuagint, *meno* (our Lord's word) often emphasizes endurance or continuing. It is used in translating various Hebrew terms: (1) *yashav*, to stay, remain, as in Rebekah's abiding with her family a few more days (and we can imagine how golden those days were before she parted with them to become the bride of Isaac!) (Gen. 24:55), or as the Lord abides forever (Ps. 9:7; 102:12); (2) *amad*, to stand, endure, abide, as the counsel of the Lord abides forever (Ps. 33:11), and His righteousness and that of a man fearing Him abide forever (Ps. 111:3; 112:3, 9), and a man is blessed who does not abide in the way of sinners (Ps. 1:1; here *amad* occurs, but the Septuagint does not use *meno*); (3) *chakah*, to wait, abide, as in Isaiah 8:17, where Isaiah says, "I will wait for the Lord . . . I will even look eagerly for Him" (NASB); (4) *hayah*, to exist, last, abide, as in Psalm 89:36, where it is said that David's descendants shall abide forever.

The English word "abide" has also appeared in many Old Testament passages where *meno* is not the Greek translation. For example: (5) *leen*, as in Psalm 91:1, where it is said that the person who dwells in the secret place of the Lord shall "abide under the shadow of the Almighty" just as one would continue or lodge as a guest overnight, for some longer period, or permanently; (6) *sha'an*, to support oneself, lean, rely, abide, stay, as in Isaiah 50:10, where a man is to "stay upon his God," i.e., support himself by leaning on the Lord for stability; (7) *gur*, to tarry, sojourn, abide, remain, as the Patriarchs sojourning in Palestine (Gen. 26:3), or as one lodging in a home with others (Exod. 3:22), or as evil abiding, as in Psalm 5:4, "Evil cannot be a guest of thine" (translation of Francis Brown, S. R. Driver, and C. A. Briggs, *A Hebrew and English Lexicon of the Old Testament* [Oxford: The Clarendon Press, 1957], p. 157), or as abiding in the Lord's tent, in which case an intimacy of relationship as well as duration of time is suggested (Ps. 15:1; 61:4, 7; cf. Ps. 27:5 for a similar thought).

[2] James H. Moulton and George Milligan, *The Vocabulary of the Greek Testament Illustrated From the Papyri and Other Non-Literary Sources* (Grand Rapids: Wm. B. Eerdmans Publishing Co., 1963), p. 397.

the time. Mary, destined to be the mother of Jesus Christ, visited Elizabeth and "abode with her about three months" (Luke 1:56). Jesus, invited to extend His visit among the Samaritans, "abode there two days" (John 4:40; cf. also Matt. 10:11; John 11:6; 19:31).

(2) It may be an obviously temporary period, even with no mention of exact length of time. Christ, enveloped with sorrow in Gethsemane, said to Peter, James, and John: "Abide ye here, and watch with me" (Matt. 26:38; cf. also Luke 8:27; 10:7; Rev. 17:10). Abiding in such a case is evidently brief.

(3) It may be an uncertain length of time. In Rome "Paul was allowed to stay (abide) by himself, with the soldier that guarded him" (Acts 28:16 RSV). Nothing in the immediate statement itself even intimates the length of time involved. But the context later clarifies that two years elapsed (v. 30).

(4) It may be a lifetime or even eternity. Paul says of the believer who gives to help others: "his righteousness abides forever" (2 Cor. 9:9). He exhorted Timothy to "continue in the things" which he had learned (2 Tim. 3:14), obviously all through his life. Peter says that the word of God "liveth and abideth forever" (1 Peter 1:23; cf. v. 25). Christ "abides as a priest continually" (Heb. 7:3; cf. v. 24). The Jewish Christians who had suffered through the plundering of their goods were buoyed up on joy because they knew that they had in heaven a better and an abiding possession (Heb. 10:34). The "things which cannot be shaken" (Heb. 12:27) and the city called the New Jerusalem, which the saved will inhabit (Heb. 13:14), are to abide forever.

Christ's words in John 12:24-26 illustrate that the word "abide" can describe the entire, overall thrust of a person's life. Jesus used a physical illustration concerning a grain of wheat to convey what is true in the principal realm. He saw before Him His impending death (v. 23), in which His selflessness was to be the culmination of a whole life of service to others. But He was also teaching, by principle, that any man who would serve Him must follow Him (v. 26), and more particularly, that he must be one who

"hates his life in this world" (v. 25). A man in whose experience this self-denial is a fact shall not lose his life but
"shall keep it unto life eternal," and, Jesus said, "him will
my Father honor." It is clear here that the contrast is between a saved man and an unsaved man, with the whole
life sweep or characteristic life style of each in view. The
word "abide" (v. 24) is involved in this contrast. Just as
a seed "abides alone" if it does not fall into the ground
and die, a person "abides alone" if he does not "serve" and
"follow" Christ by faith. That must mean, in the light of
verse 25, that he is unsaved. On the other hand, by implication, the opposite would also be true. The man who,
like a grain, does fall into the ground and die, abides with
"much fruit," and that is a picture of a Christian as described in John 15:5. It is plain, then, that Christ's description of each of the two types of men is general or comprehensive. He does not, for example, break down the saved
man's experience into small segments of time like a week,
a day, or an hour. He does not even mention for consideration that there might be *certain* times and situations in
which such a man's life is embarrassingly inconsistent with
his *usual* life style. But in Luke 9:23, where He says a man
is to follow Him, He also says, "Let him take up his cross
daily" (cf. also Matt. 10:37-39; 16:24-26; Mark 8:34-38).
Christ does not pinpoint some failure and raise the question
we like to ask: "What is the status of a person when he
fails?" Evidently the inconsistent week, day, or hour does
not change or nullify the general life pattern. This man is
still a "much fruit" man, a man who "hates his life in this
world," a man who serves and follows Christ, even though
there are those times when he must confess he is out of
character.

How, then, does this relate to John 15? The big point
is that Christ selected a figure in the physical realm to illustrate a spiritual contrast in the characters of two kinds
of people. He had in mind *the rest of their lives.* They
abide one way or the other. In John 15:5, 6, also, He employed a physical figure to depict two kinds of men. One
type of man abides in Christ and brings forth "much fruit"
(v. 5; cf. 12:24). The other type (v. 6) does not abide in

Christ and evidently brings forth "nothing" (v. 5; cf. 12:24, [the grain abides "alone"]) and faces judgment (v. 6; cf. 12: 25, 26, [the man loses]). Just as in chapter twelve, our Lord's reference to abiding here appears to characterize the life of each man as a whole, according to his true character. The one who abides as a general life orientation is the genuinely saved person, as the one who does not abide is the unsaved person.

The relationship of "abide" to other words. What we have just said about "abide" is in harmony with other words in the New Testament which describe a man by his life-characteristic. They size him up in one glimpse, and categorize him, without delving into qualifying statements, in view of isolated, partial segments of his life. These, like the word "abide" in John 12 and 15, also have the long-range view.

The word "keep" is an example. It frequently has in view a person's attitude toward Christ's word — an attitude which is an acid test of his profession. He who obeys Christ's commandments, by the energy of God-given faith, of course, is the one authentically saved (John 14:21, 23, 24; 15:10; 1 John 2:3, 4, 5; 3:22, 24; 5:3). "Follow" is also like this. Christ says, "My sheep . . . follow me" (John 10:27; cf. vv. 4, 5; 12:26). Evidently, the fact that a spiritual sheep is sometimes foolish, wanders, and must be disciplined temporarily (Ps. 119:67, 176) does not off-set the overall trend of perseverance in his life. He is still a sheep that basically hears and follows Christ, his Shepherd, and not some other shepherd. Still a further word is "look," as in Hebrews 9:28: "and unto them that look for him shall he appear the second time without sin unto salvation." The term expresses the basic, life-shaping spiritual occupation of the believer with the Person of Christ. It does not demand an absolutely flawless consistency in maintaining such a proper gaze of faith at every moment, for no believer lives without committing acts of sin for which he is ashamed. The terms "love," "loveth not," "abideth," and "hateth" in 1 John 3: 14, 15 are also used in a general sense to describe a pattern of life as a whole. The unsaved man who "hates" can never at any time express the essence of genuine love, for he is not related to the source of authentic love, God Himself. But the true believer is not shut up to such limitations. Christ does express His love through him as fruit, but there may be heart-breaking times when this is interrupted and not true of him at all, when he acts as if he does not even know Christ.

It is evident, then, that a number of New Testament words designate a man by his broad pattern even though there are some deviations from that. So a person is a Christian and "abides," "keeps" Christ's words, "follows" Christ, "looks" for Christ's appearing, and "loves"; or he is not a Christian and does not do these, though he may cleverly counterfeit them. With the word "abide" in John 15:4, 5, Christ looks at the believers' lives in one sweep, and expects them to obey the exhortation by faith. He is saying, in effect: "Let it become your principle for the rest of your lives that you continue in Me, and I in you. The abide-in-me type of man is the man who bears much fruit."

THE CONCEPT OF QUALITY

But "abide" has meaning far richer than simply a relation to time or eternity. In most places, it suggests at least some degree of quality. It speaks of intimacy in a relationship. It is true that all who are authentically saved abide in Christ as a characteristic orientation of life. But there is great variation in the quality content that constitutes each different Christian's abiding. That is, there is flexibility or elasticity as different believers are at varying stages of growth with regard to involvement with Christ. There may also be great deepening and enriching in the quality of a given Christian's abiding during the process of his maturing through the years.

We may see that "abide" is a word of quality-involvement by considering first the proof of it, then certain particulars of it as shown in John 15.

The proof of it. Think of abiding as the guest of a dear friend. Obviously, "abide" has rich connotations. Much greater things will be involved than simply putting in time there. Time, like space, is often only a framework for some type of relationship or content. Mary abode in the home of Elizabeth (Luke 1:56); the disciples, with their hosts during a speaking tour (Luke 10:7); Jesus, at the house of Zacchaeus (Luke 19:5); Andrew and Peter, with Jesus (John 1:39). In each of these instances, one does not do full justice to the abiding if he does not get the "feel" of the implications in personal interactions. Abiding, in any normal Palestinian guest-host situation, was a warm and wonderful arrangement. The guest received many courtesies from the host, such as a kiss of greeting, a washing of the feet, and an anointing of the head with oil (Luke 7: 44-46), as well as drink and food, the honor of being temporarily lord of the house in a sense, and even protection if necessary. [3] The oriental host was graciously concerned to put his guest at ease and lavish upon him every possible benefit. Naturally, the relationship was reciprocal. The visitor displayed his delight and gratitude in receiving such attention. It would be a dark deed if he knowingly damaged any object belonging to the host, showed disrespect, or was unappreciative. His abiding, then, involved a relationship with whatever people, events, issues, or objects made up the atmosphere and circumstances during that time.

Consider the two disciples who walked with Jesus on the road to Emmaus after His resurrection (Luke 24:13-35). Seeing that the shadows of evening were rapidly lengthening, they urged Jesus, "Abide with us," and "He went in to stay with them" (v. 29). In our Lord's brief abiding with these disciples, He received food from them and entered into the occasion by blessing the food, breaking it, and giving it to them. The hosts, having felt their hearts strangely warmed in His presence along the way, were now deeply stirred as they listened to His prayer to the Father, detected His mannerisms, and felt the radiating warmth of His personality. Abiding involved not only continuing for a certain length of time but also an unusual intimacy of relationship. It reached its high point of quality when "their eyes were opened, and they knew him" (v. 31).

John 15 also conveys a quality involvement in the vine-

[3] Fred Wight, *Manners and Customs of Bible Lands* (Chicago: Moody Press, 1953), pp. 72-78.

branch illustration. A branch, of course, has no will, intellect, or emotion to feel as a person, nevertheless its abiding in a vine has more implications than just the passing of time. It silently receives all the good of the living essence in the flow of the sap and responds by fulfilling its purpose to bear fruit. The very fact of abiding, for a branch, inevitably implicates it to some degree at least in a quality relationship with the vine.

Spiritually, this is true for those related to Christ. To abide in Him certainly includes quality content as well as a length of time. There are definite reasons why it is necessary to see this elasticity in the term "abide" in John 15.

First, it allows for a growth in fruit. It is plain that a genuinely saved person may, to some extent, be already bearing fruit as he abides. Yet he can bear even *more* fruit (v. 2b). Since fruit is the product of Christ's living in the Christian as he abides (v. 5), and one may become more fruitful, there is in some sense a change in the quality of his abiding relationship. There has been a deepening, an enriching, a broadening, a stretching in capacity. From this it follows that two believers may be at widely different points of progress in the Christian life; one may be a novice and the other very mature, and yet both abiding. For one the depth of abiding can be greater, with Christ making His difference in many more areas of his life.

This concept is in harmony with many descriptions in the epistles that show a believer's expanding capacity for fruitfulness. Paul wrote to the Thessalonian Christians that he and his associates were "praying . . . that we might see your face, and might perfect that which is *lacking* in your faith" (1 Thess. 3:10). He added, "And the Lord make you to increase and abound in love . . . " (v. 12). In 4:1, he wrote of abounding more and more, in 4:10 of increasing more and more. Finally, in 5:23, he wrote, "The very God of peace sanctify you wholly. . . ." Then there are other passages on growth that follow a similar pattern (2 Cor. 3:18; Phil. 1:9, 25; 3:12; 2 Thess. 1:3, 11; 2 Peter 3:18). It is clear, then, that one may be abiding in Christ but experience change involving growth in fruitfulness. His quality of abiding becomes richer.

Second, this elastic nature of abiding allows for expanding knowledge of the Word and progressive awareness of, and response to, God's will in new areas. Consider Peter, for example. It is clear in John 13 that he was chosen (v. 18) and clean in the sense of being saved (vv. 10, 11; cf. also 15:3). He was a branch abiding and bearing some fruit (15:2b). On the Day of Pentecost, as a Spirit-filled man, he proclaimed the first great message of this age. Three thousand said yes to his appeal for a verdict, changing their attitudes toward Christ (Acts 2). Here and in later episodes, it is obvious that Peter is bearing fruit. Yet this fruitful branch had much yet to learn about the Word of his God and new areas in which he might respond obediently and fruitfully. While he waited for lunch on the seaside housetop of Simon the tanner at high noon in Joppa, God spoke to him in a dramatic, three-phase vision (Acts 10). By receiving new understanding about God's plan to save Gentiles as Gentiles on a grace basis equal with His program for Jews, Peter was conditioned for a ministry among the Gentile throng in the house of Cornelius. Though his old Jewish prejudices flared up at first, the Word of God, emphasized three times, so persuaded him that his former ideas began to be pruned away. He became a more usable branch, more fruitful in the work of Christ.

God, through His written Word, is still insistently speaking to His branches today. His way is just as real as in His direct confrontation of Peter. Through new light from His Word, speaking to an abiding and fruit-bearing believer, He perfects the quality of that abiding (cf. Ps. 138: 8). He does this so that He may yet realize fruit in new aspects of life and more fruit in the old.

We can see, then, that abiding involves not just time, but quality.

The particulars of it. It is evident that "abide" embraces far more than simply continuing (persevering) with Christ in a time sense. If we say, as some do, that it means "to continue," but then do not go on to explain what that involves, we have only a generality.

Andrew Murray, the famous devotional writer, authored

several books in an attempt to plumb some of the relationships possible in the quality involvement of abiding. In one definitive chapter, he clarified the "branch-life" as a life of absolute dependence, deep restfulness, much fruitfulness, close communion, and absolute surrender. [4] The definition of the French scholar Godet, written about a hundred years ago, has often been quoted: "*To abide in me,* expresses the continual act by which the Christian sets aside everything which he might derive from his own wisdom, strength, merit, to draw all from Christ, in these different relations, through the deep longings of faith." [5] Another popular definition is that of the much-used Scofield Reference Bible:

> To abide in Christ is, on the one hand, to have no known sin unjudged and unconfessed, no interest into which He is not brought, no life which He cannot share. On the other hand, the abiding one takes all burdens to Him, and draws all wisdom, life and strength from Him. It is not unceasing *consciousness* of these things, and of Him, but that nothing is allowed in the life which separates from Him. [6]

More concisely, Ryrie defines "abiding" in terms of obedience as in 1 John 3:24: "To abide is to keep His commandments." [7] Gaebelein states it more at length:

> To abide in Him means the continued exercise of faith in Him, that faith which is the very breath of the new nature, which realizes constantly that Christ is all, that depends on Him for everything and knows its utter helplessness apart from Him. As a result of such dependence the believer clings to Him and lives the life of close and intimate communion with Him. [8]

[4] Andrew Murray, *Absolute Surrender* (Chicago: Moody Press, n.d.), pp. 111-127.

[5] F. L. Godet, *Commentary on the Gospel of John* (Grand Rapids: Zondervan Publishing House. Reprint of 3rd ed., 1893), 2:295.

[6] C. I. Scofield, ed., *The Scofield Reference Bible* (New York: Oxford University Press, 1945), on John 15.

[7] C. C. Ryrie, "The First Epistle of John," *The Wycliffe Bible Commentary,* ed. Charles Pfeiffer and Everett Harrison (Chicago: Moody Press, 1962), p. 1474, on 1 John 3:24.

[8] A. C. Gaebelein, *The Gospel of John* (New York: Publication Office, *Our Hope,* 1936), p. 295.

Kelly agrees that abiding in Christ involves both negative and positive elements, "not merely distrust of ourselves, but cleaving to Him and counting on Him." [9]

These writers see beyond the time concept in "abide" a whole world of meaning for life in all its complex ramifications. They discern a quality relationship that invests a life with fullness of significance, whatever might make up each individual believer's set of experiences. Some of the statements (such as those of Godet and the Scofield Reference Bible) make abiding sound too absolute, however, with words like "all" giving the impression that only those abide who are totally perfect and without inconsistency.

Can we crystalize some specific features, then, that are a distinctive part of any abiding life? Yes. There are certain characteristics inevitably true *to some degree* in the personal matter of abiding with another person. These are also true in the relationship of a branch abiding in a vine, and are suggested in the very atmosphere of John 15. Abiding involves a person's *relating* himself, though imperfectly, to Christ the Vine, to His Person and His purpose; *rejecting* attitudes, words, actions, or interests which Christ's Word reveals He cannot share; and *receiving* the quality-essence of Christ's imparted life for authentic fulfillment. These involvements may be very pronounced in one Christian, who has learned to open his life up in many aspects to Christ, but they may be weaker in another Christian because of his short experience in this life or his wilful toleration of much of his self-life. We are ready now to consider in detail these elements of the quality aspect in abiding.

(1) Relating of the life to Christ. A man truly born of God has passed over into a new orientation. Now he can learn more and more to relate himself always to Christ, his Vine. Christ is the nourishing source of his life and spirituality. He is his very food and inner life content. Truly, the believer is like a branch which, if it could think and speak, would say: "I am identified irrevocably and completely with this vine, with what it *is* in its very essence

[9] William Kelly, *An Exposition of the Gospel of John* (London: F. E. Race, 1923), p. 306.

and what it *does* in its effect. My sphere, my orientation, my relationship, my potential for fulfillment are here, by God's plan in putting me here (cf. John 15:16). And so, under His good arrangement, it is my privilege to relate myself always to this vine." In this same way, the Christian's abiding involves relating himself both to Christ's Person (what He is in attribute) and to His purpose (what He does in activity).

First, he relates himself to Christ's Person. Since he is now united with Him, he will never again be alone in that awful sense of a man who does not possess the Son who is life (1 John 5:11, 12; cf. John 12:24). A Person-to-person relationship has begun, with all the intriguing interchange that can be invested in that relationship. Each is to be freely accessible to share and be shared in an inner flow of heart with heart. The Christian is no longer to do anything in terms of himself alone. Before this new life began for him he asked, and now he asks even more, "What is God like? How may I visualize Christ?" And he discovers the answer in an ever-growing way in the Word of God, where his heart may be caught away in utter fascination daily as he gazes upon the images of the Person with whom he is related. He meditates upon such statements as "God is light" (1 John 1:5), "God is love" (1 John 4:16), God is "the God of peace" (Phil. 4:9), and God seeks continual fellowship with His own (John 4:24). As he grows, life's doors are flung open to show him new and unimagined aspects of the relationship he may have with this Person, and this Person with him. All of this is in accord with what the Person is like and what he himself is like as the unique individual God made and understands him to be. The indelible imprint of the very *Person* of Christ, what He is in essence and as reflected by scriptural episodes where one may see Him in action, is in harmony with the *purpose* of Christ.

Second, the abiding believer therefore relates himself in some measure to Christ's purpose. He is compelled to ask, if he reads the Word of Christ with a responding heart: "Am I investing my life in purposes dear to Him?" And he is impressed, for example, that Christ came to minister,

and to give His life a ransom for many (Mark 10:45); that
He came to seek and to save the lost (Luke 19:10); that
He expended Himself for others (Matt. 27:42); that He
came to do the Father's will (John 5:19; 6:38; Heb. 10:7);
that He was always in sensitive touch with the Father
(John 11:42); that He sought out a place alone to com-
mune with the Father (Mark 1:35); that He lived for the
Father to live through Him (John 14:10). The Christian
learns, as he grows, that the new life is not a life of coaxing
Christ to involve Himself in *his* plans devised without reference to Christ's will. How dare he seek to "use" Christ
as a "tool" to further his own ends! He sees, by contrast to
this, the truth that he may involve himself in *Christ's* plans,
with Christ using him as an instrument for His ends, which
are really worthwhile ends. Through victories and failures,
God teaches him never to be so wretchedly careless as to
lose sight of the reality that he is in Christ, the Vine. And,
in practical blood-and-flesh terms, that has implications for
him whatever happens, wherever he goes, and all the time.
Even a Christian wife, ironing her husband's shirts, can relate this to Christ and His purpose. "Lord, how wonderful
that I can iron this shirt, and the man who wears it this
week will have your love, your joy, and your peace, and
will be sharing you with others!" Abiding, then, involves
relating, but let us go on to the second element in abiding.

(2) Rejecting attitudes, interests, and concepts which
Christ does not share. In the person's life as a "branch,"
abiding also calls for continual discernment and rejection.
A natural branch does nothing "of itself" (v. 4), and, should
it be severed from the vine, it withers and becomes useless
(v. 6). The Christian, too, can do nothing of himself,
though he differs from the branch in the sense that he possesses will, intellect, and emotion. He must be merciless
toward the attitude of living without Christ (v. 5). He
must learn to repudiate relentlessly the fool's deception of
expecting good out of what he is apart from Christ. All
through the New Testament, he sees that he is to "deny
himself" (Luke 9:23), "love not the world" (1 John 2:15),
"resist the devil" (James 4:7), "abstain from fleshly lusts"
(1 Peter 2:11; cf. Titus 2:12), "mortify" the deeds of his

body (Rom. 8:13), "reckon" himself dead to sin (Rom. 6: 11), "have no anxiety about anything" (Phil. 4:6 RSV), keep himself from idols (1 John 5:21), and put away filthiness and receive the Word (James 1:21). These prohibitions and negative commands make sense because of the very nature of antitheses in the universe. The Christian is on a new side now. There are God and Satan, Spirit and flesh, righteousness and sin, light and darkness, love and hate, good fruit and bad fruit, truth and error, heaven and hell.

A Christian's life with Christ began with both negative and positive elements of true separation, turning, "to God *from* idols *to* serve the living and true God" (1 Thess. 1:9). With any spiritual discernment at all, he can never put his whole heart into the sometimes popular cliché "Let's forget the negative and emphasize the positive!" It is not either/or but both/and. Yet it is a spiritually healthy perspective for him to avoid the negatives of sin by a positive appropriation of Christ to be his life.

The necessity of rejecting bears relevance in all of life. The parent who really cares and is responsible withholds from little Johnny the things which would be disastrous to him: the box of matches, the bottle of poison, the razor blade. The farmer practices rejection when he sprays his fields to rid them of pests. A housewife dusts the house, washes the dishes, and peels the potatoes. A manufacturing company "irons out the bugs" in its new product or rejects it. This principle of rejecting is not only a fact of life but an utter imperative spiritually if a man is to abide in Christ. We will look at some examples in our next chapter. But now let us give our attention to the third element of the quality aspect in abiding.

(3) Receiving the quality-essence of Christ's life. One word summarizes the attitude of the abiding, fruit-bearing man. It is faith. All other proper responses to a giving God are included within the broad outreach of this word. Our reaction to all of God's truth ultimately boils down to faith. Someone has said, "Great saints are only great receivers." Another has thoughtfully stated that the totality of John Calvin's famous theology, *The Institutes of the*

Christian Religion, comes down to this one basic essence: depending upon the faithfulness of God. [10]

Visualize again the branch abiding in the vine. Certainly if it is healthy, it is relating itself in a life-union with the vine and at the same time rejecting all opposed to this union. But it is also *receiving* that which the vine supplies and would be utterly helpless apart from it. Assume that it could talk and we had some way of listening to its words. What would the branch say? "I will live today without reference to the vine. After all, I am a very strong branch now, and I am doing remarkably well. It will not hurt me if I am without vital contact." Of course, you say that would be sheer nonsense for a branch. Christ iterated an unalterable maxim of physical law when He said that "the branch is not able to bear fruit of itself . . ." (v. 4). Obviously the branch is able to bear fruit only when it is in contact with the vine so as to share its life-flow. Christ added this fact in His positive emphasis: ". . . except it abide in the vine." In other words, the branch must not vest dependence in itself but in the vine alone. It lives by relying. It must forever be receiving its entire sufficiency from the vine.

But our Lord's primary intent was to convey the analogous fact in the experience of a Christian. He added His crucial point: ". . . no more can ye, except ye abide in me." Then, to strengthen the point, He stated the entire relationship again in verse five in both its positive and negative aspects: "He that abideth . . . the same bringeth forth much fruit: for without me ye can do nothing." It is unequivocal, direct, and utterly true. The Savior was decisive as to His estimate of all that men might do apart from being receptively in touch with Him. Such doing would all add up to "nothing." This was true of us entirely when we were unsaved and "without" Him. Now, in principle, it is still true of us to the degree that we live in self-sufficiency as we did in our unsaved state. In what sense do we do "nothing" without Him? Surely Christ did not mean that a person is inflicted with total paralysis, that he is incap-

[10] Murray, *Absolute Surrender,* pp. 112, 113.

able of making the slightest movement. In fact, the Lord once showed that a man might be a dynamo in doing, impressively involved in so-called "spiritual" activities. Yet at the end of everything in this life, he might have all of his effort appraised as "nothing," for while it elicited applause and was highly credited here below, it was put down in the only register that ultimately matters as a mere zero, an empty thing. Christ said that He will say to some: "I never knew you" (Matt. 7:23). Our Lord does not esteem a person's doing as "nothing" by the criterion of quantity, but rather of quality. If He does not find in it the quality-essence of His own imparted life which is available to spiritual branches for whom abiding involves receiving, the doing is nothing, in the sense that it is barren of Christ and the Holy Spirit, and so is opposite to fruit which is the living expression of God's nature. The believer whose eyes of understanding have been enlightened to perceive this, and who takes it seriously, is driven to an awesome sense of dependence upon Christ. He excitedly wants to open up to the spiritual reality of living in Christ in all things. To him, this can become as habitual, and is as necessary, as breathing.

One day when I was a boy, two of us were arguing over who could hold his head under water longer before coming up for air. We were at his father's house several miles from a pool or tank of water where we might put the issue to the test. But the argument went on until we finally hit upon a way to settle it once and for all. We filled a large bucket with water and timed one another with a watch. He dipped his head first and stayed under for forty-five seconds. Then it was my turn. I put my head down into the bucket and waited and waited and waited. At first I thought I would estimate and count off the seconds the best I could in my mind, but soon I lost track and had no idea of how many seconds had gone by. Finally, I felt that I had to come up for air, yet I held on, determined to take no chances of losing. After a while longer, the desperation for air became almost intolerable. "No," I told myself, "I can still last a little longer." When at last it seemed that my lungs would explode, I came up. For a moment, I did not even think of winning. It was gratifying to learn later that I had won by holding my breath for one minute and forty-five seconds. But the only sensation that gripped me just then was a most fantastic desperation to breathe. All I wanted in all of this whole wide world was an enormous gulp of air and then more air. What a change would come into our lives if we would have something of this sense of desperation to receive what we need spiritually from Christ. We would receive Him to be all things to us.

Now, in what specific ways can this receptivity toward Christ display itself in us? There are endless ramifications, but we may point out three specific areas.

First, there is receptivity toward Christ's Word (v. 7; cf. James 1:21). "If ye abide in me, and my words abide in you, . . ." our Lord said. The abiding branch is the receiving branch, that is, the person who receives the word of his Lord. This, in effect, is being receptive to Christ Himself, whose "I in you" (vv. 4, 5) is experientially tantamount to "my words . . . in you" (v. 7). Christ assures the abiding man in whom His words abide that he will receive that for which he prays. This is because the Holy Spirit puts the very will of heaven into his heart by the Word of Christ, and that will issue in his offering prayers back to heaven. "And this is the confidence that we have in him, that, if we ask anything according to his will, he heareth us: And if we know that he hear us, whatsoever we ask, we know that we have the petitions that we desired of him" (1 John 5:14, 15). Christ taught an inseparable relationship between discipleship and abiding in His Word (John 8:31). John links a responsive obedience to Christ's commandments with abiding in Him (1 John 2:14, 24; 3:24).

The young believer ought to meditate searchingly and believingly in passages that speak directly about the Word in his life. Especially rich in this among Old Testament portions are certain psalms (1; 19:8-14; 119). Psalm 1, for example, depicts a godly man: his focus (vv. 1, 2), his fruit (vv. 3, 4), and his future (vv. 5, 6). This is supremely true of Jesus Christ as a man on earth, but it may also be true to some degree in any man who is genuinely His. The believer is characterized by a "delight" in the law of his God which the Spirit of God is faithful to nurture within him as he exposes himself to that word (1 Peter 2:2, 3; 2 Cor. 3:18). The Christian can go on to trace in Psalm 19 the glory of God in the sky (vv. 1-6), in the Scriptures (vv. 7-10), and in the saint (vv. 11-14).

The Word will, for the receptive believer, be "profitable for doctrine, for reproof, for correction, for instruction in righteousness" (2 Tim. 3:16). God is real and life-transforming to him when he seeks to draw near to God through the Word, saying, "Father, I feel stale, flat, dead — anything but primed to be really receptive to You as I come right now. Yet I know that You are real, Christ is real, and I am a branch in Him. I feel as if I am dragging my feet, but I am confident that You know me perfectly, through and through. As I begin to read now, Father, I do desire that my inner life will be fully exposed to the light of Your Word. I am willing to be made willing. I am waiting before You, knowing that this is what You delight to do in those who come in weakness to be made strong in Your strength. Remove from the eyes of my understanding any obstruction that I am unable of myself to define, that I may see Your will, and work in me that I may will and do what is Your good pleasure. Thank you, Father." Then he can read with the helplessness of a branch in utter need of the Vine, receptive to Him even for the enablement to be receptively obedient to His Word.

From such a "refresher" in the Word, the believer can step into the activity in which he is involved. Through power which Christ is prepared to supply, he is receptive to obey the aspects of the Word which his Spirit-quickened thoughts crystalize as relevant to his situation. In the next chapter we will look in on him in some actual situations where he lives out this receptivity toward the Word. Let it be enough now to say this: the abiding believer, receptive to the Word, exposes the details of his life in a positive response that says yes to God even as His promises in Christ say yes to him (2 Cor. 1:20).

Second, think of receptivity toward God's pruning (John

15:2b). Here is one of the basic truths that even a young Christian should be taught. It is inevitable that his faithful Father will cleanse him at various times and in various ways. He does this with the good purpose that the Christian may bear more fruit. Whatever the aspect of cleansing, he must learn in each case to be receptive. If he has temporarily harbored known sin that spoils his sense of fellowship, and God presses some relevant truth of the Word upon his thoughts with a convicting power, his "yes" of response is in confessing that sin (1 John 1:9). "Confess" (*homologeō*) is a yes-word, a word of receptivity. Basically, it means "to say the same thing." It is the believer's response of agreement or harmony with God. And immediately he may have the sense of God's forgiveness and cleansing. Or, perhaps a truth of the Word is new to the believer or fastens upon his attention in some fresh, captivating way. It "smokes out" some element in his life with which the Father is displeased but which he has never before faced in just this clear light, even though he has been abiding in Christ. The overall attitude of his life has been to walk in the light (1 John 1:7), and now he can extend the same attitude also to this matter. Rather than sidestepping the issue or postponing a showdown when God's voice is speaking within, he can react with receptivity toward the Word. "Yes, Lord, You have made me aware of this matter which You want to prune from my experience. I know that I can be more fruitful without it. I do want Your will as my will, even in this, though it hurts to let go. I do not have power to turn loose and make my decision really last. But You, the Husbandman, have all the power I need. Take it, cleanse it away, and thank You that You have my good in view so totally that You could not stand by and tolerate what I am so prone to overlook." This is receptivity, another cleansing, and a step toward bearing more fruit.

Think also of another situation. Some matter, possibly beyond the believer's control, poses a problem. It is a type of trouble which the Father is using to chasten and to prune him. By a positive, receptive response, he can become a more useful branch. Now it is possible that he can

allow this incident to upset him so that he fusses, frets,
and complains. He lapses into an irritable disposition, an
ugly mood. He feels that these things are working against
him as impassable roadblocks thrown up in the way of his
pursuit of godliness. Or he simply resents them because
they cut against the grain of his own self-chosen way at the
moment. And so he may be negative toward the good that
might come even in such things. On the other hand, suppose he is receptive. It makes sense that if he has committed his way to an all-wise Father, he can live in un-
ruffled poise, confident that whatever circumstances enter
his life have first come past the Father's hand which en-
closes him (John 10:29), been noted by His eyes that take
note even when a sparrow falls (Matt. 10:29), and given
consent by His infinite love. His response may be a re-
sounding yes of receptivity, though the human viewpoint
would call life at the moment rough, tough, and even lousy.
His attitude may be what Lina Sandell Berg has expressed:

> Day by day, and with each passing moment,
> Strength I find to meet my trials here;
> Trusting in my Father's wise bestowment,
> I've no cause for worry or for fear.
> He, whose heart is kind beyond all measure,
> Gives unto each day what He deems best,
> Lovingly its part of pain and pleasure,
> Mingling toil with peace and rest.

When he is receptive in suffering, God will cleanse, take
away the dross, and make of him a better person fit to
bear more fruit.

Third, there is receptivity toward God's adequacy. Suppose that God really is in control of all things relating to
the life entrusted to His keeping. He must have a tremendous desire that the believer learn to be restfully trustful
in whatever He does or allows, wherever He sends, and
whenever He chooses for him. Why not think it through
this way?

"Do I believe that there is 'nothing' — no value — in
what I might do apart from Christ? Yes, I believe that.
Then where is my only source of 'something'? In Christ.

He wants me to face life and say with regard to anything, 'Thy grace is sufficient,' and actually count on it. I refuse to tolerate the absurdity of facing this present situation with any smug reliance on my own equipment — my wisdom, ability, personality — and thus elbowing in on Christ's prerogatives. Neither will I indulge in the subtle deceit of meeting the situation as though I must be strictly on my own, shut up to my own resources. I repudiate both the idea that I *can* do it without You, Lord, and still have it reckoned as fruit, and the idea that I *have to* do it without You. Instead, I am looking receptively to You, ready to meet this demand in terms of Your adequacy. This gives me a sense of confidence in the results that it will be Your good pleasure to work out. Thank you again."

It is possible for Christ's man to invest the work of his mind or his hands with dimensions that are Christ-sized. His work can be permeated with Christ's touch, His thrust, His glory, His sufficiency. Peter exhorts believers to serve out of the strength which God supplies (1 Peter 4:11). The sense of this supply goes beyond physical strength, which He also gives, to spiritual power, as is evident from the emphasis on spiritual gifts with which we are to serve (1 Peter 4:10). We can exult with ever-increasing enthusiasm that the Christian life was never conceived by God as a challenge for us to "measure up." How that would glorify us! Rather, God's message to us is that we may be continually receiving Jesus Christ as the adequate One who does measure up. To a degree that becomes greater and greater as we grow in Him, He can be His full measure in us. So He does not propose to look for a perfect person and use him. None would qualify. He proposes to take a person who, though he is very imperfect and sinful, is receptive toward Him, fill him with a perfect Savior's adequacy, and then use him. We can be "perfect" in the sense that we have come to live in the norm or pattern of His life as spiritually mature people, but even this is *His* work in us as we work, trusting Him.

LIVING WHERE GOD'S ACTION IS

"He that abideth in me, and I in him,
the same bringeth forth much fruit: for
without me ye can do nothing" (John 15:5).

A popular question of our generation has been, "Are you living where the action is?" But another question is more intriguing: "Are you living where *God's* action is, as a branch in Christ the Vine?" Are you relating your activity to life with this Person who said, "I came that they may have life, and have it abundantly" (John 10:10 RSV)? Are you caught up in the exciting challenge of rejecting many things for infinitely better things? You are, if God has gotten through to you with this message: "Christ is the Vine, the true One in whom is ultimate reality. Relentlessly reject all cheap imitations, all self-hypnotizing substitutes that flash with temporary glitter but would later mock you." And are you receiving continually from the fullness of His life (John 7:37), being refreshed by receiving Him as your whole sufficiency daily? If, to some degree, you are abiding, living out of Christ's overflow, then you are truly living where *God's* action is!

It will help now to look at some life examples of Christians living where God's action is.

RELATING YOUR LIFE TO CHRIST

Barney, a young Christian, looks like a Mr. America physically, but is dragging his feet in defeat spiritually. "I can't live the Christian life," he despairs. "I'm too weak, I guess, and I just feel like throwing in the towel." How does his situation touch the principle of relating? One thing is clear. He is a branch but, frankly, like so many, he is casting himself in the role of being the Vine, responsible for his own sufficiency. He is unskilled in the matter of being simply a branch. He has heard his pastor emphasize his identification with Christ who is all-sufficient while he is insufficient. But, by improperly relating himself to his Lord, he is still thinking that he must make it on his own. But now he thoughtfully meditates upon himself as a branch related to Christ the Vine, the Person who lives life out to the full, with all supplies for fruit bearing. As he considers the life of abiding, the Spirit of God speaks deeply within him. "Christ is the Vine. Do you see, the Vine! He is related to you as the One who lives *what He is* in you. In Him is love, joy, peace, longsuffering, gentleness, goodness, faithfulness, meekness, and self-control." Then he is impressed with the liberating thought: "Since He, as the Vine, is related to me as all in all for me, my response is that of receiving. And, in the measure that I am relating myself to Him and Himself to me, receiving all from Him, I will be living as a branch lives."

•   •   •

Bill, a middle-aged layman only recently saved, is asked to teach a boys' Sunday school class. This catches him somewhat by surprise. He will think it over for a few days. "Me?" he says to his wife in an incredulous tone. "There are a lot of things I *can* do, but I can't teach. I'd run out of anything to say after about the first sixty seconds." His wife, who has been a Christian somewhat longer, smiles knowingly. "Oh, it would be new to you at first, Bill, and you would have a lot to learn. All of us do. But I think you might be surprised with what you could do if you would just give yourself a chance." He laughs as though she is joking. After some time on the same subject, she says: "You know, it was interesting to me to see that the eleven disciples whom the Lord so wonderfully used were really just simple men. He took them, raw as they were, worked with them, and showed them that, being united to Him, they could do things they had never before imagined. Their secret was Christ's own power in them." That was a convicting blow to Bill. He had read something like that in his Bible, too, but he had not related it to this situation. Later, as he arrived at a decision about teaching, he said something like this to his Lord: "How foolish I've been, Lord, to consider that class only in terms of the limited abilities I now see in myself. I am related to You, and so I can think of it in terms of what You are and what your purpose is. Ultimately it is not a challenge to me, but to You, and I know that You have all power to get to the hearts of those boys through me. Thank You, at the same time, for opening my eyes to see that this truth of relating affects everything else in my life too."

• • •

Mary, a college student, is a Christian in need of a job. An opportunity to make phone calls for a magazine sales outfit opens up, and without carefully checking into it, she jumps at the offer. But after phoning a few people, she becomes painfully disturbed by the realization that there are subtle misrepresentations in the baited wording of the "pitch." What the people don't know *can* hurt them. Several thoughts now tumble upon one another in her mind. "God is light, and in Him is no darkness at all. This is what Christ is, and I am related to Him. I have been saved to walk in the light. I cannot go on giving this pitch, which I now realize is deceptive. Lord, as I look to You, I acknowledge that in my need for a job I was too quick to snatch at this opportunity, not waiting for what You must have had for me. I could rationalize because I am in a pinch where that pay check would really look good. But I will relate my life rightly to You and trust You for the right job." Shortly after this, Mary lands a job in a department store that satisfies her and meets her college needs.

• • •

Charlie is a hard-working layman in a fine evangelical church. But one matter gives him an uneasy sense of guilt. As he reads his New Testament, passages on witnessing prick at him with the thought, "All of this service can have a relationship, Charlie, but just what are you doing to relate yourself directly to my purpose of reaching men who need salvation? I came to seek and to save the lost. *You shall be my witness."*

"Lord," he responds, finally, "I want to do Your will. Though I am busy doing these things, many of which I feel I should continue to do, I long to get involved right at the heart of Your purpose. I want to touch lives and see them united to You. I have a lot to learn about witnessing, but I am willing to learn." In earnest about it, he writes down a list of people, begins to pray regularly for their salvation, then to share Christ with them. As he does so, in a spirit of loving concern, he finds that some are seemingly indifferent but others are really interested. He goes over to talk to his neighbors now, sometimes simply chatting about yard work, carpentry, cars, and the sports world. He does things for them, laughs with them, invites them over when he is able. And he is winning people to Christ! Abiding in Christ involves relating himself to Christ's purpose which, though having many other aspects also, includes sharing Him with others.

REJECTING WHAT IS OPPOSED TO CHRIST

As we saw earlier, various Bible passages make clear many things the Christian must avoid or lay aside. But some very harmful attitudes are so subtle that one may not at first recognize them. Many believers, staggering under self-imposed burdens, could simply drop them and enjoy blessed relief. Some labor under the strain of false concepts about fruit, equating it with such things as success, sensationalism, and the sacred-secular compartmentalization of life (see chapter 7). But there are still other false commitments to which Christians slavishly consign themselves so that they are imprisoned in self-made shackles of bondage. What are a few of these burdens?

Anxiety for results. Joe is a young pastor ambitious to push forward the cause of Christ in his church and community. Since coming here a year ago, he has been driving himself to the utmost to get his members into action. Many of them appear smugly complacent and at ease in the *status quo.* He has preached his heart out, carried on a whirlwind program of trying to visit every family in the church, challenged his people to do door-to-door evangelism, and worked to improve many other things. But after a fair-sized Sunday morning crowd, the Sunday evening service dwindles to less than half, a very small remnant shows up at the midweek prayer meeting, and it seems impossible to get even a half dozen out for visitation night.

Possibly one of Joe's problems is that he is anxious for big things to happen and so busy in activity to produce this that he is not disciplining himself in his own study of the Word. He has allowed himself to be pulled so many directions through the week that he gives out shallow messages from the pulpit. Frankly, it is not worth the people's time to hear them. The people come in hungry and go out empty. Joe is so frantic to get results that he has spent little quality time alone in counsel with God — and few long seasons in the praise, thanksgiving, and petition of prayer. Also, quite candidly, the fact that he tolerates a thin relationship with his Lord, while he maintains a zealous emphasis upon the program, betrays that his spiritual values are out of balance. In practical reality, he is dependent upon what *he can do* in terms of his own brains, plans, sermons, and fireball activity. The painful truth is that he has not lived with God in any sense of desperate need. He has treated Christ like some glorified elevator man who could be counted on for a little lift once in a while, and not as the divine Lord who wants to be counted on always as being life itself. He needs to think seriously on priorities and to insist that first things come first. This is not to forget that his problem may also be partially met by different emphases, a long-range strategy for imparting to laymen the concept of the Spirit-filled life, worshipful personal involvement in the Word, and workable methods for evangelism and follow-up.

It is also relevant to say a word about the impatient feeling that, at any cost, we *must* have certain results *right now.* Sometimes we may display a spirit of urgency about matters that we might better commit trustfully to God, confident in His attentiveness and His timing, whether it is His pleasure for us to wait briefly or perseveringly for the answer. It is true that some situations are of such a nature that we must have the answer to prayer immediately. But in many matters we should learn to wait as God's submissive servants lest we insinuate, in effect, that we are sovereigns who can set the ways and times He *must* work to answer our requests. God is not operating His affairs to fall in line with our neat little schedules. Paul expected to meet Titus at Troas (2 Cor. 2:12, 13); however, to his disappointment, but by God's appointment, Titus was not there. Paul learned more patience, prospered in the Lord's arrangement, and later met Titus (7:6).

Among the pastoral burdens of Joe's own making was the inwardly fretful insistence upon results to suit the plans he was engineering mostly in his own energy. What he needs is to reject the attitude "Lord, use me and this program" and to say instead, "Lord, *make me usable* and grant wisdom to me as I lead in planning a program so that it may be Your program and usable for Your purposes. And Lord, I reject this spirit that presumes to dictate when and how it will be best for You to work. Instead, even while I am faithfully serving You, lead me to wait in the quietness and confidence that give strength, and to know that You are endlessly dependable to work out Your sovereign pleasure. Things are going to be different with me, by Your grace. I will be spending much time alone with You, and learning more to discern and reject attitudes conceived out of accord with You — and to live and pray and work and play oriented always in You."

Absolute perfection.   It is possible to become obsessed with the idea that God requires us to be altogether sinless or even the idea that we *can* be sinless in this life. Of course, certain Bible passages may be so misinterpreted as to lend seeming support to this notion. There is a story of a man who was "sinlessly perfect." A preacher said to his audience, "Is there anybody here who is perfect or has ever known a perfect man?" He asked the question a second and a third time and finally a very timid man near the back rose to his feet. Everyone waited breathlessly. "Well," he said, "I know of a man who was perfect. I never met him personally, but I have heard a lot about him. He was my wife's first husband!" That man was not actually sinless, and neither is any other person anywhere on earth. Only the Lord Jesus Christ "knew no sin." But some live in the deception that they are or can be sinless. Such self-deception can lead a man to rationalize, believing that the sin he does commit is simply an "error" or "mistake," or it can impose a crushing burden that, when he commits a sin, draws from him the agonized cry: "All is lost!"

It is a false and wretched weight to bear, and no child of God need assume it. He can reject it, simply drop it. When one abides in Christ, he experiences a perfecting or growth as Christ lives within. But the sense in which he is perfect, at any time, is only relative and not absolute. He is to be perfect even as his Father is perfect (Matt. 5: 48) in the sense that his love does not limit itself just to certain people but can reach out to embrace all. Paul wrote of certain ones as being "perfect" (Phil. 3:15), but that is a relative perfectness, since he stated in the immediate context that there was a sense in which even he was not yet "perfect" (v. 12). The Christian can grow to *sin less,* but will not be *sinless* until Christ changes the body of his humiliation into a body of glory (v. 21).

Suppose that a believer says to himself, "I can be sinlessly perfect and I will trust Christ to make me so." He is saying, in effect, "I believe that *I* can be so flawless that *I* can maintain absolute unbroken trust in Christ so that *I* will not sin, and there will be no need for higher advance."

Binding oneself to a certain formula of devotions. One can fall into the scheme of setting up an inflexible routine of devotions as his prescription for blessing. He chooses his time, place, and formula for Bible meditation, and begins to expect unvarying results. This becomes a subtle habit in which it is possible for him to take his eyes off the Lord and lean on his "quiet time" itself as a crutch. He is thrilled with a certain fragrance of blessing as he nourishes his life by approaching his Bible in a particular way. He looks forward to it as an end in itself. Without realizing

it, he either gets the idea that Christ always blesses in the
same way or that the blessing is in the formula. He loses
focus on the reality that as a Christian he is a branch in
the Vine (Christ, a Person), and should not put his trust
in some *approach* to that Person.

Then a "dry" period sets in. It is the same time, the same
place, and the same formula, but the old blessing is not
there. Nothing in particular really lifts his spirit as before.
Finally, it is time for him to be off, and he did not get his
"blessing"! He feels spiritually dull and insipid the rest of
the day. This may go on for a week, perhaps longer, before he has some wonderfully refreshing "quiet time" again.

What is his problem? It may involve the harboring of
known but unconfessed sin, some bodily disorder, the lack
of proper rest or exercise, or even some combination of
these. In this case, let us suppose that a sin is involved
from which God desires to wean him. His sin may be a
subtle manifestation of the self-life, a motive that says, in
essence, "Lord, give me some blessing for myself," along
with a blithe ignoring of the fact that *God* should receive
something out of the "devotions." God seeks the adoration
of a believer's heart for *Himself* (John 4:24). Coupled
with the Christian's selfishness is the fact that he has misplaced his dependence by relying on a prescription when
he must rely on a Person. If such is the case, the believer,
seeing the lack of reality in his relationship with Christ
Himself, should reject his sin through confession. Then he
should seek to meditate always upon Christ, and not lose
Him in what he calls "*my* devotions."

However, it is also possible that a Christian may be very
much in fellowship with his Lord and still experience a
dry period. Why so? It may be a trial — in God's plan
for him — giving him opportunity to develop the muscles
of his faith to believe that Christ is still present even when
He has removed the normal manifestations of His presence.
As he searches his heart and honestly is not aware of any
estrangement in the fellowship, he can say, "Lord, I do
desire Your will, and I know You are in control. Even
while I pass through this darkness, I will walk by faith,
though not by sight" (2 Cor. 5:7).

Depending on some specific verse for every day.   The
Christian may have to learn to reject a false idea about
having to locate some particular verse for every day. Admittedly, one may possibly have his eyes very much on
the Lord and yet find help in this principle as a habit of
life. But for some this may become a spiritual fetish. A
believer can place himself under the burden of locating his
"strategy for the day." Sometimes this means that he feels
God is bound to speak to him so unmistakably each time
that he knows "this is my verse." This can be carried to the
extreme that a friend of mine shared from his Army days.
One of the men in his outfit suddenly went A.W.O.L. Upon
his return he was asked, "Why did you do it?" He said,
quite seriously, "I was reading my Bible in the place where
it says 'Arise, get thee out from this land' (Gen. 31:13);
so I took it that God was giving me a signal to rise up and
go!" Sometimes in testimony meetings believers will almost
as naively share similar incidents from their own lives. Let
us thank God that He worked things out all right for them,
despite their misuse of a verse in its context. Christ can
wonderfully bless the heart that is serious about obeying
Him, though we may yet be happily relieved of certain
misconceptions as we grow in Him.

Fixing blessings of the past.   A Christian may expect God
to bless him tomorrow in exactly the same form or in the
same type of situation that He did today. For example,
suppose that he leads three people to Christ today in thrill-
ing situations. He goes home rejoicing, "That's it! That's it!
That's the way God works." And so he fixes in his mind
the pattern of these specific experiences of God's working,
assuming that God must reenact such episodes every day.
Subtly, again, his commitment has been displaced to some
particular experiences rather than to Christ. He ought to
say, "Thank You Lord, that You led me in just the way
You did in these experiences today. My heart is filled with
exultation. Tomorrow, it will again be my privilege to see
Your good pleasure through me in whatever way You desire." This, of course, does not preclude preparing in advance a school assignment, office work, or any other item

that will help him to be ready. And one caught up in the heart passion of Christ for the lives of men will find himself on many nights thinking through ideas for sharing the "good news" with some individual or for meeting some group situation. All of this, however, is to have the attitude, "Lord, here are my ideas, but when the situation finally comes, You work it out the way that You know is best."

Maintaining a strict schedule. People today are on the run in a hectic age of intercontinental jets, busy freeways, crowded supermarkets, and pressing deadlines. The man who abides in Christ faces many challenges, like that of rejecting the attitudes of the flesh when a delay threatens some aspect of his preconceived schedule. His timing is thrown off. He can feel irked by a slow-up in the traffic when he has been trying to slice moments off to get somewhere in a hurry. He can fret when the supermarket line hits a snag because some person writes out a check that the manager, nowhere in sight, must "okay." He can make some caustic remark because his wife is still powdering her nose when he thinks they ought to be in the car ten miles up the road. Or, he can be secretly frustrated when some unexpected visitor or situation throws out of whack the schedule of things he was intent upon getting done. Rejecting attitudes like these in a busy life has right-now relevance.

Several facets of a total concept can be helpful to the man who is caught in the squeeze of pressures but desires to abide in Christ. One is that a man can commit the events of the day to his Lord and then follow up with a mental readiness for so-called interruptions or delays. "Lord," he may say, "my chief function as a branch today is actually not just to fill this position efficiently, like a robot, but to be in communicative contact with You and to bear fruit. Here is the schedule I foresee, but I am pliable as I realize that You will undoubtedly see the need for implementing certain changes where Your schedule differs from this. That is what I want. Thank You." I need to be prepared to say at every juncture of the day, I am here by God's direction and appointment. Then, when that interruption comes, learn to say, "Well, 1 never anticipated this, Lord, but obviously You are not surprised by it at all. I will not tolerate the frustration of looking at this as a threat to the schedule, but will assume that it is a part of it, from Your viewpoint. After all, I am not to live for myself, but for others. Of course, this may pose some knotty problems for the rest of the day, but there must be a way to work these out. I am not casting myself upon my own ingenuity alone, but am depending on You. Show me the way, Lord. Now, let me enter with gusto into this new development." All of this can be expressed in the essence of even a flash thought as a new situation arises. After a while, it can become a habit that is both physically and mentally relaxing, a spiritual reflex for the man on the job to whom Christ is present and real. Later, he returns to the schedule he knows and continues through the day. He may have to work a little late to meet some deadline. If his wife is expecting him at a certain time, he will surely feel it is the part of loving thoughtfulness to alert her about the delay. And, as he finishes the day, he can say: "Thank you, Lord, for the situations of today. Tomorrow, perhaps, I can do what I was not able to do today — and more."

Trying to be somebody else. For various reasons, a Christian may strive to be some other person. In so doing, he is making it difficult to discover his own unique self as the type of branch God designed him to be.

Perhaps the believer is afflicted with inner distaste for the abilities or lack of abilities that he sees in himself. So he wants to be somebody else. However, it may very well be that he has not yet gone far enough in Christian experience to give himself a hundredth of a chance in bringing out hidden and hitherto unrealized potentialities which God has invested in him to produce big dividends. Having scarcely begun in life with Christ, he impatiently jumps to the conclusion that he now sees at this early point all the possible uses that his life will ever have. And yet, when God wants to make a life a monument of His grace,

it is not His usual method to throw it up shantylike, overnight, or in a week, or even in a year. God is not in a
hurry.

We might as well face it realistically. We are not all of
the same vintage. Each has had a different heritage and a
different background, and each has a different psychological
make-up.

This desire to be someone else is in various ways inconsistent with simply taking one's place as a branch, and the
Christian should resolutely reject it. First, it issues from
grievous unbelief that is a slam at the wisdom and love
and power of God. To be quite pointed, the Christian is
saying, in effect: "Lord, I guess I am just going to have to
live with the fact that when You made me, You gave me
no good abilities. It was just my lot to draw a blank. It's
too bad for me." Or, "You gave me this ability, but it is
obvious that it is not worth much. If I don't do very much,
it will be easily explainable because I don't have very much
to work with, You know." In other words, even a child
of God, through a fleshly viewpoint, can "take a crack" at
God. He can say that God has made a blunder in slighting
him and that he is now in the rather embarrassing predicament of making the most out of a mess. He betrays a spirit
of doubt that God has been fair to him, rather than a
confidence that says, "Lord, I can now see only very little
in my abilities that appears to be of much value. However,
You are altogether wise and intelligent in Your good purposes, and I can be sure that You have credited even me
with potential to be worthwhile and to bear 'much fruit.'
Though I do not now have everything in view, I am trust-
ingly confident that You have arranged matters with regard
to me in just this way to qualify me more adequately for
what You have in mind for me. I need Your grace in bringing all of the potential out into action. Thank You."

Second, the desire to be somebody else may involve
covetousness, jealousy, and an unloving spirit. The Christian fixes his eyes of envy upon another believer and says
secretly, or even vocally: "Sure, people praise him. But
look at his money, his abilities, and the privileges he has
had. If I had these, I could do even better." And one of

two envious thoughts festers within the believer. He thinks either, *Sure, it's all right for him to have these abilities, but I want them, too,* or, *I wish that I could be in his shoes, and he in mine.* But he ought to remember Paul's thorn in the flesh. With Paul's abilities and privileges there was an attached thorn. Actually, the Christian should repudiate within himself any thought that is at variance with being precisely *the branch God has chosen him to be.* He should carefully avoid laboring under the false assumption that his fulfillment, or fruit, can be only in terms of what he is *in himself* as a branch. He reckons the useful good of his life as though he is a man alone, cast strictly upon what he has at his disposal. Even this he has received from the Vine, he admits, but it does not satisfy him. That other branch has more (enough!) and so the other person's life is one of great significance. As for himself, he is held back by a handicap, and so his life cannot be of real significance. He assumes that because there is a difference in Christ's gifts to men, there must necessarily be a difference in the adequacy of Christ to develop fruitfulness in each one. He fears that he will be on the short end, and so it ultimately comes down to self again — selfishness. The truth is that each person with his own God-given but differing abilities and experiences may live with abundant fruit and significance. No man in Christ the Vine should ever pity himself with the idea that he must face life only with what he now has from Christ but apart from Christ Himself. There need be no separation between Christ's gifts to us and His working in us with power. However small a Christian's gift might seem to be, he can find his daily experiences invested with God's eternal significance as he is receptive toward Christ. At the same time, he should reject (by harshly judging within himself) any attitude of envy toward another person. His brother's abilities are different and, perhaps, attract far more attention. But with those gifts come responsibilities and ultimately an appraisal at Christ's judgment seat. Would he care to answer for the use of those gifts as his brother will? And further, he might consider that God is Lord, far above all, with the right to do what He wills with each of His own. Along with this,

the Christian should serve his Lord with the gifts he does
have, seeking no splendor for self but gladly ascribing to
Christ every part of the glory — all of it.

Third, the desire to be somebody else intrudes the danger
of being unfaithful with present abilities. The believer is
a steward before God for all that is committed to his trust.
He may squander precious challenges of life where he might
have developed some gift. He discerns little in an ability
where his Lord sees vast potentialities, simply because he
does not look receptively, with Spirit-opened eyes, to discern values and opportunities held out within his reach.
Though he brings forth some fruit, there are many situations in which he does not share, but rather wastes his life.

It is evident, then, that the man who tries to be somebody else engages in the tragedy of unbelief, covetousness,
and unfaithfulness. He involves himself as a pretender in
a role in which he cannot be his own unique and natural
self that God has given him the opportunity to be. He is
a man who will never quite fit — except as a misfit — until
he drops his mask and walks out on the stage of life simply
as his undisguised and unique self. Perhaps he has fancied
himself as pretty hot stuff, just what certain people think
legitimately of the person he is trying to copy. It is a heavy
load to bear, because it is not his native role and he always
has to keep up the front. If he will be himself, though still
sinful, he will be in a better position to live life to the hilt,
growing up unto Christ. It is easier to live as *one* sinner
facing life than as a sinner also carrying a borrowed personality along with him!

The real you is what you do in nonstructured situations,
how you react to unexpected crises. This is when you are
caught with your guard down and simply react like yourself doing what comes naturally. At such a time, that which
has become a true and settled habit of life asserts itself
quite spontaneously and definitely. Why not be honest and
realistic about yourself before God, trust Him to help you
give up the airs you tend to assume before others, and expect from Him an imparted sincerity of life? He is in the
business of releasing us from phoniness and setting us free.

Assuming all knowledge.   Another burden a believer can carry is that of assuming, as a Christian worker, that he has to answer every question or problem about spiritual matters. He dares not admit ignorance on any point or all will be lost. That is, he will lose rapport with a non-Christian or with another Christian who looks up to him for answers. But being a branch has direct relevance even here. After all, if he will really admit that he is a branch, and not the Vine, he puts himself in the place of dependence and weakness where God has placed him. Even Christ, being a man on earth as the Father intended Him to be, did not know some things, such as the time of His future coming (Mark 13:32). That is one of the inscrutable facts involved in His being truly *man*. And Paul, polished in the finest scholarship of his day and filled with the Spirit of knowledge, admitted that he did not remember certain things (1 Cor. 1:16). It is an absurdity for the believer to feel compelled to flash back some answer, to spin it off his tongue and avert embarrassment, as though it all hinges on him! Certainly he should study very diligently to know the Word and how to relate it to practical matters. But if he feels that an occasional "I do not know" is likely to destroy the respect of others for him, then he is depending too much on his answers. He is simply not prepared, in this area of life, to live like a branch — dependently. What if he does not know an answer? Should not this in itself drive him even more to the sufficiency of Christ, who can save his "rapport" in many ways other than by having solutions to all questions?

Suppose a non-Christian asks him a question he cannot answer. "That's a terrific question," he might say. "I really can't say that I know just how to answer it. But I would like to see what I can find out about it. I'm glad to see you have questions just as I have had. But do you know, now that I have been a Christian for a while, I have even more questions than I had before. The more I study, the more I am exposed to areas I had never even thought about. It's like going on a sight-seeing tour. As you go along, you see details that never would have occurred to you before you started. But as I have learned more about God,

I have become more and more impressed that He is the
only Person in the universe who, without fear of embarrassment, could stand complete investigation. And He welcomes our questions, if we come in the attitude that we
really want to know. But also, as I have lived this life,
I have become more convinced of Christ's ability actually
to change our lives. The Bible shows us that all issues come
down ultimately to our personal relationship with Christ."
And he is back to the point of the non-Christian's greatest
need and positioned to share with him the "good news" in
the Person of Christ.

Abiding not only involves the elements of relating your
life to Christ and rejecting certain attitudes, interests, and
involvements in which He cannot share, but also receiving
from Christ.

RECEIVING FROM CHRIST

Let us now look at some examples.

Suddenly Harry is in a situation in which he can witness.
It just opens up beautifully. He is having lunch with a top
sales representative from a firm with which his own company is interested in doing business. His new acquaintance
is talking about his family life. Squeezing lemon juice into
his tea, he mentions that his wife has been going to some
church services recently and coming back talking about
their emphasis on "getting salvation." He looks up, grins,
and shrugs nonchalantly.

"The way I look at it," he says rather confidently, but
with obvious lack of real thought in the matter, "religion
is okay, but don't become a fanatic. If the notion strikes
you, fine. Otherwise, let it go. It'll come to you sooner
or later. You've got plenty of time."

Here is Harry's opportunity. But a voice within seems to
be saying that Handley will not really be interested in
spiritual things at the moment. Surely he will find some
excuse or divert the conversation in some nice way, or else,
if Harry does try to present the claims of Christ, he will
just not know how to say it the right way. Yet another
thought flashes into his mind. Just two nights ago at the
Bible study meeting the teacher emphasized the importance

of trusting Christ to be sufficient and to lead in all situations.

Handley is stirring sugar in the tea. "Isn't that about the way you see it?" he asks. Harry decides to trust the Lord to do what He can do. He smiles, praying as he does so, and begins to tell Handley how he himself had once felt this way but God had changed his thinking completely around. It is a splendid opening into Handley's life, and he listens with real interest. As they eat they continue to talk, and Harry brings the matter right down to the issue of a definite decision to receive Christ. Handley's eyes are glued to his own, in deep seriousness.

"Yes," he responds. "Yes, I would like to do that. How—?" He fumbles.

Harry explains how he may receive Christ right where he sits. He does this as they bow their heads together. Later, he follows out the steps Harry has shown him for beginning to walk with Christ, and even becomes a weekly participant in the Bible study with his wife. She, too, becomes a Christian, and both begin to serve the Lord in various ways in fellowship with others in a Bible-honoring church.

What Harry finally did in that lunch situation was what every believer can do in situations every day. He simply *received* by faith the adequacy of Christ to be all that was needed in that opportunity. But even if Handley had not trusted the Lord in the moments that followed, Harry could have gone on living like a branch, believing Christ his Vine to be sufficient in using the witness for His own purposes.

•   •   •

Bob arrives home from a hard day at the machine shop and drags his weary body through the door, looking for a chance to collapse and relax. But little Denny, Bob and Shirley's three-year-old, has been waiting all afternoon to hear that door open and see Bob come walking through.

"Daddy!" he shouts, springing up from his toys as though catapulted toward the door, "Pway wid me!" He rushes into the massive arms as though he is a halfback plunging in for a touchdown. Shirley joins them. The energetic fellow excitedly keeps up the clamor: "Pway wid me! Pway wid me!"

So Bob applies the principle of asking for grace to do what he does not really feel like doing. Rather than collapsing into an easy chair and becoming lost for a few minutes in the evening sports section, he gets down on his hands and knees in Denny's world. So, he is pushing little cars and trucks and tractors around the floor, with Denny's fertile imagination deciding the way they "pway da game."

In this, Bob looks to Christ for the grace to do what pleases somebody else in a practical situation of life.

•   •   •

Roscoe, an auto parts manager, spends his lunch break with a teenage boy in a little cubbyhole room at the back of the shop. They belong to the brown bag clan. While he munches, he weaves a faithful witness into the conversation and trusts his Lord to open the heart of his young friend, George. But George remains non-receptive for several weeks. It is all right for Roscoe, and he is willing to listen, but for him it is not "the way to fly."

One weekend after George has left to take another job, Roscoe is at home and there is a knock on the front door. George is standing there with a big smile.

"Roscoe," he exuberates, "I've been saved! It was last Sunday." And he goes on to tell Roscoe that what he had said during those lunch times had set his mind to thinking far more than was apparent on the surface. It had led him to read a Bible secretly himself and then receive Christ.

"Thank you, Lord," Roscoe prays later, "that You really were doing Your work when I was trusting You and it seemed at the time that I was not getting anywhere."

•   •   •

Elmer Lappen is an arthritic who had the privilege of running as a track ace in the Penn Relays but later was injured by a shell blast during Word War II. With his dedicated, Spirit-filled wife, Lee Etta, he has for sixteen years directed the Campus Crusade for Christ ministry on

Arizona campuses. Several hundred college men and women have committed their lives to Christ. Though Elmer is bed-ridden or in his wheelchair most of the time, those who know of his faith and activities are continually amazed. He has memorized many portions of Scripture and the Word of Christ dwells richly in him (cf. Col. 3:16), leading him to do exploits and to challenge others to step out boldly, trusting God for great things.

"Lord," he will say with confidence when a hard problem looms before the campus workers, "how You can work! We will do all we can do and receive from You what great things *You* can do." Then he will dwell lovingly on some Bible promise and thank God that this Word can come to pass if the Lord wills it in this situation. People often marvel, "How does he keep going? He is in such pain much of the time." In addition to a faithful wife with her encouragement and some staff members with a go-getting attitude, the basic answer is simply "receiving from Christ." He is abiding, and he lives as a branch can live. He lives where *God's* action is.

And so can you!

ABIDING — WITH OR WITHOUT EFFORT?

. . . without me ye can do nothing (John 15:5).

What did our Lord mean by His point-blank words "without me ye can do nothing"? This is a crucial question, because any follower of Christ wants his life to amount to something (certainly not *nothing!*), and there have been many misconceptions of the verse that he must avoid. Let us consider what Christ means. After this, we will look at how the words have been abused so as to result in misunderstanding and confusion about the relation of abiding and fruit bearing to personal effort.

WHAT CHRIST MEANS

First, notice that He did not mean, "Without Me you can do nothing of any type of activity whatever." Even an unsaved man, who is certainly without Him, may be a human tornado in doing things. He does do something! So does a carnal Christian (see 1 Cor. 3:1-4). A person may run about at full gallop like a race horse coming into the home stretch at Santa Anita. Our Lord is not talking about just going through the motions.

What, then, must He mean? He means that without Him a person can do nothing — nothing in the qualified sense of *that which is in the category of good fruit.* Fruit is the specific subject He is emphasizing in these verses as a whole. It is also His immediate point in the first part of verse five itself: "He that abides in me . . . brings forth much fruit. . . ." Christ surely means, then, that a person may have much activity, either outward or inward, but it is *on his own.* Such a person is not allowing Him who is

146

the Vine to live through him the only life that is fruitful. This is true of all the activities of an unsaved person, and may be true in varying degrees in the activities of a saved person. "Without me" may apply to either. [1]

Martin Luther caught something of this emphasis in his song "A Mighty Fortress Is Our God":

> Did we in our own strength confide,
> Our striving would be losing;
> Were not the right Man on our side,
> The Man of God's own choosing:
> Dost ask who that may be?
> Christ Jesus, it is He;
> Lord Sabaoth His Name,
> From age to age the same,
> And He must win the battle.

[1] The Greek expression "without me" (*choris emou*) is adaptable to either the saved or the unsaved. *Choris* as it is used in the New Testament does not favor one over the other conclusively. *Choris* is, admittedly, used in a number of instances in definite connection with one who is unsaved and so it could apply to an unsaved person in John 15:5. Take, for example, these instances: A man who has heard Christ's word and has not acted accordingly is like a man who built a house on the sand *without* any foundation (Luke 6:49). "At that time you were *without* Christ" (Eph. 2:12). "And *without* faith it is impossible to please Him" (Heb. 11:6 NASB). "But if you are *without* discipline, of which all have become partakers, then you are illegitimate children and not sons" (Heb. 12:8 NASB). "Pursue . . . after the sanctification *without* which no one will see the Lord" (Heb. 12:14 NASB). "And he must have a good reputation with those *outside* the church" (1 Tim. 3:7 NASB). In such a sense, our Lord in John 15:5 could be using "without me" in the strong meaning opposite to a valid "in me" in the same context. This would fit the thought of His contrast between one who abides and one who does not, taken as the genuinely saved person and the unsaved person. But *choris* in the New Testament sometimes has another meaning, *without some activity or assistance that is specified* in its context (cf. Wm. Arndt and F. Wilbur Gingrich, *A Greek-English Lexicon of the New Testament and Other Early Christian Literature* [Chicago: The University of Chicago Press, 1957], pp. 898, 899). There are examples such as these: "*without* him (that is, His power, His activity, etc.) was not anything made" (John 1:3). "For we maintain that a man is justified by faith *apart from* works of the Law" (Rom. 3:28 NASB). "And how shall they hear *without* a preacher?" (Rom. 10:14). In view of the various possible ways of understanding *choris*, either believer or unbeliever may be understood in John 15:5. This reference to both is somewhat analogous to Romans 8:4, 5, where walking according to the flesh is true of the unsaved but may also apply to the saved, although it is not the norm or characteristic that should describe one who has come to live as a Christian ought to live, walking according to the Spirit as the basic pattern of his life.

Christ's words "without me ye can do nothing" give the *negative* side of the picture and are directly in contrast to the *positive* side immediately before: "He that abideth in me, and I in him, the same brings forth much fruit." His negative words, then, strongly imply that there is an opposite: "*With Me* you can do *something* — bear good fruit, fruit that I accredit." The comment of Snell is apropos: "We who cannot so much as make a blade of grass grow without His cooperation, are not expected to accomplish the impossible and bring forth fruit of ourselves."[2] In all the activity we do put forth as Christians, we would have "nothing" qualifying for Christ's accreditation from our own natural power or wisdom but only by His spiritual life infusing it with the heavenly quality and value of true spiritual fruit. The branch has no essence of fruit *in itself alone, apart from the vine* (v. 4). How total is our need of Christ!

We realize that a person is unlike a natural branch in that he does have activity, but he is fruitful only in the measure that the quality-essence of Christ the Vine is flowing into and through his life. Opposition arises between one's *personal* effort and *Christ's* working through him only if he is struggling to do it in self-sufficient power and wisdom, that of the flesh, without truly relying upon Christ. But if he is Christ-dependent for sufficiency in power, wisdom, and everything else, then he must and will be active — possibly very much so — and his efforts will be fruitful in God's evaluation. Then his life would be a reversal of the words in verse four. We could read the idea this way: "As the branch can bear fruit out of the sufficiency of the vine, as it abides in the vine, so can you as you abide in me."

J. Oswald Chambers emphasized the principle "My strength is made perfect in weakness" (2 Cor. 12:9), when he wrote:

> God can achieve His purpose either through the absence of human power and resources, or the abandonment of reliance on them. All through history God has chosen and

[2] H. Herbert Snell, "Fruit," *A Dictionary of Christ and the Gospels,* ed. James Hastings (Edinburgh: T. & T. Clark, 1933), 1:625.

used the nobodies, because their unusual dependence on Him made possible the unique display of His power and grace. He chose and used the somebodies only when they renounced dependence on their natural abilities and resources. [3]

How well Paul illustrated this truth when he came to Corinth (1 Cor. 2:1-5). He did put forth effort in that he was *speaking*, but he was not relying upon some personal genius or persuasiveness of words to bear fruit among the Corinthians. He was simply living as a branch in Christ, abiding in Him. His dependence was on the demonstration of the Holy Spirit and power.

The relationship between the Christian's effort and God's power is shown more particularly in the writing of the words of Scripture: human instruments actively wrote in harmony with God's inspiration. The fact that *God* gave the words was not opposed to human effort and did not rule it out. God did not blank out men's thoughts, desires, and will (including word choices that would be natural to their individual vocabularies because of the particular backgrounds with which He had Himself prepared them). He did not render them robots who went through a mechanical process. He superintended and directed their own effort so that His word was the product. And so it is with Christ and those who abide in Him. As they trust Him to be their adequacy, they work, yet He is behind and in their work, inspiring it, enabling it, and investing it with true spiritual quality that is fruitful. What is *their* work, is, at the same time, *His* work through them. This does not demand that every point relating to the two realms be consistent absolutely, of course. For example, the result in the case of Scripture writers is infallible, whereas the result in fruit bearers is variable and subject to the imperfections of humanity not yet completely redeemed from sin. The one point of analogy between the two intended here stands. Abiding and fruit bearing, as Christ teaches in John 15, are perfectly compatible with human effort rightly understood.

[3] J. Oswald Chambers, "Man's Weakness — God's Weapon," *Missionary Crusader,* Dec., 1964, p. 7.

THE MISUNDERSTANDING IN QUIETISM

It is not true to the Bible, then, to use words conveying the impression that there is no effort in abiding and bearing fruit. Yet this very type of emphasis has often appeared in devotional literature, stamping upon the thinking of men a misconception of the truth Christ teaches in John 15:4, 5.

For example, a widespread trend known as "quietism" in seventeenth century France placed heavy emphasis on withdrawing from activity in the spiritual life. Champions of this mood were de Molinos, Madame Guyon, Fenelon, and others. There was, in this passivism, such an attempt to blot out one's own will and ban his own works that the emphasis swung mostly to God Himself filling and performing all things through him. This sounds attractive at first, but it was fraught with many errors and dangers. Fostered mainly by Roman Catholics, it grew out of the Reformation and counter-Reformation focus upon human depravity and the "miserableness of the creature." In theory, quietism was allegedly a preparatory stage for a quality of outward activity that would glorify God. It was conceived to be a clearing of the decks for God to take over and work His pure will in and through a person. How blessed the thought! One would draw aside into deep contemplation and try to put into repose, quietness, or silence all of his own powers, thoughts, desires, and activities; cease all of his striving; and empty himself of all confidence in his own capabilities. Then, when he was quiet or at rest, God would spontaneously fill the vacuum and cause His grace to flow freely, taking the place of the man's crucified self-style. This grace would urge the person into a right kind of action within God's holy, perfect will. Then the quietist might, in consistency with this deep repose of heart, go out to be "a hundred-horsepower man of deeds." [4] Jones, in a perceptive survey of quietism, points to Fenelon as an example. He, writes Jones, was able to achieve something of a balance. On the one hand was his retreat into the inner citadel

---

[4] Rufus M. Jones, "Quietism," *Harvard Theological Review*. Vol. X, No. 1, Jan., 1917, p. 3. Jones capably demonstrates the elements of appeal in quietism as well as the imbalance in emphasis and its lack of wisdom as he discusses the lives and writings of several of its leading exponents.

of quietness in faith, and on the other was his outward activity. He was a man of deep contemplation before God but also busy with administration, counseling, persecution, and sorrows in a difficult diocese as Archbishop of Cambray in France. Fenelon believed, according to Jones, that we are to seek saintliness not in withdrawal from this world but in the round of daily duties. There we meet pain, care, and other difficulties like getting along with imperfect people and coping with disappointments and defeats. But even in the common activities such as eating, drinking, and necessary toil, we may find God. [5]

These aspects of quietism sound reasonable, but they do not tell the whole story. The movement failed in the eyes not only of the powerful Catholic Church in its own day but also in the sober judgment of many Christians within the historic faith of the New Testament. Characterized often by extreme statements about doing nothing, quietism failed to make practical sense. Many Christians have felt that it distorted and missed the balance of Bible truth as a whole, in most cases at least. Many of its counsels convey the strong impression that the truly spiritual life is in obliterating effort—a fading back into nothingness. The believer, in his bankruptcy in which he can do "nothing without Christ," must blank himself out and let God think, speak, desire, obey, work, and fight through him. God must do everything! All else would be spiritually useless, "nothing." Though there is an element of truth here that the New Testament itself stresses — "Christ liveth in me" (Gal. 2:20) and "without me ye can do nothing" (John 15:5)—the dangers of the system lay along the retreat path into the one-sided emphasis. Jones, commenting on the vagaries and mistakes of quietism, pin-points the underlying fallacy: grace must extinguish and totally replace every spark of our natural life and personality. Of Madame Guyon and Fenelon he says:

> Nothing is more clear than that they succeeded in so far as they retained and ennobled their concrete personalities and their interesting individual characteristics, and that they

[5] *Ibid.*, pp. 48, 49.

failed in so far as they suppressed and annihilated themselves and arrived at abstract love, non-desire, and no-
willing. [6]

Later, Jones exposes the widespread practical failure.

> What they could not succeed in doing, however, was to
> make this "discovery" of theirs work here in this practical
> world. It was so far in to the "centre" of meeting, it was so
> deep down below all consciousness and the experience was
> so completely negative and devoid of content, that the in-
> dividual could bring back nothing in its hands to show for
> its solitary journey. Quietism needed the warm and tender
> objective realities of the Gospel as filling for its abstract
> and empty fervor. It lacked some concrete way of turning
> its moments of fecundity into the permanent stuff of moral
> character and ethical endeavor. It was a noble *mood*, but
> it was too rare and abstract to be translated into real hu-
> man life. [7]

The misconception in the one-sided emphasis of quietism
has made suspect certain other devotional writings since
that time in which spiritual aspirants are urged, in essence,
to "do nothing — just abide." Many are the compelling
catchwords: "Stop trying to live the Christian life," as though
living the Christian life does not involve a trying that is of
true faith; "Relax, just trust the Lord, and let Him do it all,"
as though trusting and doing are always antithetical. The
phrases have a strange power to charm those looking for
easy slogans. One might like to let go and just be swept
away effortlessly in the tide of God's will, but in view of
the legitimate activity we must put forth if we are responsible, faithful, and obedient in doing Christ's will, the quick
formulas turn out to be oversimplified generalizations. Like
the emphases of quietism, they do not give both sides which
are equally parts of a realistic abiding. Repercussions that
sometimes spring from such an extreme can be just as harmful as the opposite extreme, a roll-up-your-sleeves-and-work
philosophy that does not insist that only *Christ*-empowered
effort has value at the throne of God.

What creatures we are of extremes and shortcuts! We

[6] *Ibid.,* p. 50.
[7] *Ibid.,* p. 51.

seem to have a terribly hard time grasping and getting across to others the true *balance of both sides* of abiding as the New Testament teaches it.

If we are to put Christ's words about abiding and bearing fruit in their proper perspective with activity, we need to consider what now follows. It may help to clear away misstatements and provoke us to think seriously about communicating the truth to others in a healthier balance.

DANGER IN REACTIONS AGAINST EFFORT

Certain point-blank emphases which seem to smack of quietistic passivism may be, in reality, just strong reactions to *effort that is legalistic*. That is, they are meant to oppose activity that is wrongly inspired and directed, effort stimulated by the sufficiency of the flesh. Some people never seem to disabuse themselves of the fancy that they can accomplish living a victorious Christian life if they will only give it a harder try next time. They struggle with all their might, and this is just the problem — it is all *their* might. They thresh about furiously in carnal effort to abide, but it all seems as futile as if they were laboring to work their way up a greased rope. They slide back exhausted from trying and sometimes burn out in despair as they slip time and again from their mind's image of what abiding must be. But soon their false optimism in what the flesh can do if rededicated has them rising up out of their own ashes, like the mythical phoenix, to be at the project all over again. Certain devotional writers, who make a strong emphasis against this kind of effort and toward depending upon God for everything, are sincerely seeking to help Christians with such a problem. Their stress against effort is intended to combat this *one* type of activity, not proper activity that is in faith. But the problem in their writings is that sometimes the extreme statements make them seem as though they are absolutely against *all* activity. In reacting, they fail to qualify or explain, and so they pull the truth out of balance in another direction. In the very process of clearing up one misunderstanding about effort, they unwittingly promote another.

For example, G. Campbell Morgan seemed to emphasize

the incompatibility of abiding and effort. Surely he must have been speaking out against false, fleshly effort, since in his total writings he often gave a place to the proper effort of a Christian who works by faith. Notice his exact words at that crucial point:

> First, abiding consists in the cessation of effort. The one thing you do not need in order to abide anywhere is strength. Weakness is the condition of abiding. . . . I have found Christian people strenuously striving to abide in Christ, and by their very effort separating their souls from Him. Rest in Him, abandon yourself to Him, that He may have His way.
>
> To abide means cessation of our effort, and it means the acceptation of His effort, relaxing all the life to the Lord Christ and letting His life have right of way. That is abiding in Him. [8]

In another place, Morgan wrote: "Abiding needs no effort. Effort is made to arrive at a point, not to stay there." Then he illustrated this point. A congregation abides (sits, rests) in a sanctuary without making any effort to do so. When the service has ended, they arise and go out. [9] In the first quote of Morgan, he rightly rejects fleshly effort but simply says we should let God work through us without a word about *our very real personal effort* by faith as we abide, strengthened by His adequacy.

We could multiply statements to the same effect from popular books — books which have much for which we thank the Lord. And, in fairness to them, let it be said that there is a need for an emphasis against legalistic effort. The weakness is that it is easy to get the impression, from such explanations, that abiding is an either/or proposition. It is faith alone with no effort at all on our part (no effort of any kind, it would seem, if the writers do not qualify their statements), or else we are not abiding. For instance, what Morgan has not told us is that Christ's energizing may be *behind and in the effort we ourselves put forth,*

[8] G. Campbell Morgan, *The Westminster Pulpit* (New York: Fleming H. Revell Co., n.d.), 7:271, 272.

[9] G. Campbell Morgan, *The Parables and Metaphors of Our Lord* (New York: Fleming H. Revell Co., 1943), p. 346.

if He controls, stimulates, and imparts true quality (fruitful essence) to it all. The disservice of the particular emphasis by Morgan and certain others is simply this: they portray only half of the picture. We need to hear the other half, too, and so have *the balanced picture all in one unit,* if we are to understand the abiding life as it really is. The fact that many devote themselves to fleshly effort does not invalidate the type of effort we should have in the quality of true faith. Effort is compatible with the abiding and fruit bearing the New Testament talks about. Since Morgan was not against proper effort, he should have made this clear. He has dwelt upon a partial statement which, while serving part of the picture for his purpose at the moment, raises questions in thinking minds about the larger picture.

One aspect of the problem is that some devotional writers, who are quick to tell only the one side (faith without effort) seem unaware that they are creating a problem for some. Yet it is very real to certain new Christians, and all Christians should be sensitive about getting things in balance and not distorting the abiding life even unintentionally. It is refreshing to find a fuller view of the Christian life in K. F. W. Prior's chapter "Faith and Effort" in *The Way of Holiness* (Chicago: Inter-Varsity Press, 1967).

Other writers on the spiritual life have taken certain devotional leaders to task on this very point — that of making the Christian life sound too passive and effortless. B. B. Warfield, for instance, went into great detail criticizing Hannah Whitall Smith's book *The Christian's Secret of a Happy Life* for emphases which to him sounded too much like quietistic passivism popping up in modern dress. One instance is in her illustration of the believer who, like clay in the hands of the potter, is in the hands of God and is *to abide there passively.* [10] Warfield also points out other references where Mrs. Smith uses the analogy of clay and makes the believer seem to be required to exert no effort at all: "The potter must do all the work." "When we have

[10] B. B. Warfield, *Perfectionism* (Philadelphia: Presbyterian and Reformed Publishing Co., 1967), pp. 292, 293; cf. Hannah Whitall Smith, *The Christian's Secret of a Happy Life* (New York: Fleming H. Revell Co., 1941), pp. 30, 31.

put our case in the Lord's hands, our part is simply to 'sit still,' for He will not rest until He has finished the matter." It is not hard to see how such statements left Mrs. Smith's concepts susceptible to criticism. On the other hand, let us say a word on her behalf. Warfield's discussion would have been more objective and fair on this particular point had he given Mrs. Smith a better opportunity to explain herself. She does finally balance this one emphasis, which looks so extreme, by showing *in other places* that she does see the abiding life as one of activity. In another book, she discusses Exodus 14:13, where Moses said to Israel, "Stand still, and see the salvation of the Lord":

> I say, sit still in our hearts, because this stillness of which I am writing is an inward stillness. It may also be an outward stillness as well, and I think the outward stillness often helps the inward. But, on the other hand, it may be accompanied with great outward activity; though never, I think, with bustle or hurry, for "he that believeth maketh not haste." But whether the body is active or still, the attitude of the spirit must always be one of stillness. [11]

She adds:

> There may be storms of hail outside; but within, the "habitation" of the spirit is a "quiet resting-place" in God. This sitting still, therefore, does not interfere with outward activity, but is, in fact, the source of its strength. If I am working at anything outwardly, and am inwardly at rest about it, I shall do it far more successfully than if I fret, and fume, and fuss inwardly. [12]

We may also rightly seek further clarification on what Mrs. Smith meant by quietness from Thomas C. Upham. With her, he wrote much in the same Higher Life movement almost a century ago, and tried in even greater detail to explain its many facets. On inward stillness, or ceasing from self, he taught that we are to cease from all inordinate and selfish outward activity. But "It does not, it will be remembered, exclude an outward activity of the right kind." He added:

[11] Hannah Whitall Smith, *Every-Day Religion* (New York: Fleming H. Revell Co., 1893), p. 205.
[12] *Ibid.*, p. 206.

But some will say, "Is there to be no action? and are we to do nothing?" A person in this state of mind, being at rest in the will of God, and never out of that divine will [?], is operative precisely as God would have him so; moving as God moves, stopping where God stops. He is at rest, but *never idle.* His God forbids idleness. Therefore, he keeps in the line of divine co-operation, and works *with* God. There may be less of vain and noisy pretension, and sometimes less of outward and visible activity; but there is far more wisdom, and far more actual efficiency; for God is with him. [13]

If we are to be objective and impartial, we ought to acknowledge more balance in the overall teaching of a Smith or an Upham than Warfield's criticisms recognized. This is just as true of Keswick teaching, which emphasizes a life of heart rest by faith and so at times is apt to sound as though it is anti-activity. But this same indictment was brought by Catholic writers against Luther. In his emphasis upon faith alone *(sola fide),* he was alleged to teach a sanctification that is idle, against works, giving free rein for sins of the flesh. However, G. C. Berkouwer, in his book *Faith and Sanctification* (chap. 2), has shown that Luther was misunderstood. He taught, in reality, that faith is a sponsor, not a competitor, of good works, and comes before good works. The good person must be there before the good works, for what a man is (his *being)* precedes what he does (his *activity).* Just as Luther's strong emphasis on faith was not inconsistent with *proper* works, so neither is it in the intention of Keswick writers. Fullerton, once a leading voice in Keswick, emphasized that faith in Christ as our very life, and adjustment to Him, is a *preparation for activity.* Speaking of the committal of the soul to God in 1 Peter 4: 19, he said:

But it is not passive. It is the committal of your soul in order that you may be more active than ever . . . you are not going to sit and "sing yourself away to everlasting bliss," as some of our forefathers used to be fond of singing. I hope you will have something else to do! You can sing,

[13] Thomas C. Upham, *Principles of the Interior or Hidden Life* (London: Richard D. Dickinson, 1895), pp. 380, 387.

and you can sit, but you will have to get up in well-doing
— cooperate with God. [14]

He goes on to accentuate being like Christ, who went about
doing good, not only when we have opportunity but going
about *purposefully* to do good.

These are helpful clarifications about what Mrs. Smith
undoubtedly believed when she wrote the unqualified words
which in themselves appear vulnerable. Some who read her
words, however, would have the very practical difficulty of
not realizing how she qualified in other places what she
meant in those one-sided statements. They, like Warfield,
would not comb through another book by her to give her
a chance to fill out the picture. It is also true that even
her explanations on this one question would not be enough
to satisfy Warfield, since his thorough reviews find objections to her system at many other points as well.

Also misleading at certain points was the writing of Robert
Pearsall Smith, husband of Hannah Whitall Smith. Take,
for example, the emphasis he read into (not out of) Philippians 2:13, mentioned also by Warfield: "Is not the promise
worthy of confidence, that God will work in us to will and
to do of His good pleasure, and if He does this, shall we
not have to cease working ourselves?" Smith also said:
"God worketh in you to will and to do; therefore cease
working." [15]

However much we may appreciate some parts of Mrs.
Smith's very influential book and even certain points made
by Robert Smith, what are we to make of his words such
as those just cited? Sometimes, in spite of his sincere intentions, his statements are misleading. Again we can lean over
backwards, give him much benefit of the doubt, and fill out
what he probably meant and should have clarified. Taken
in the context of Higher Life writings, he no doubt meant
that we are to *cease our working* in the sense of making
vain, self-sufficient fleshly effort, depending only on what
we can do, and working only with a human dimension and
in a human framework of things. Like Mrs. Smith and also

---

[14] W. Y. Fullerton, "The Faithful Creator," in H. F. Stevenson, *Keswick's
Triumphant Voice* (London: Marshall, Morgan & Scott, 1963), p. 52.
[15] Warfield, *Perfectionism,* p. 297.

Thomas Upham, Robert Smith held that we depend on God to work by His grace, in which case we cease working in the sense of being self-adequate, but we are able to work in a proper sense. This is most likely what he intended in his comments on Philippians 2:13, yet he misused the verse by reading in what it plainly does not teach. He comes out with only a half-truth and gets the verse out of balance. Paul, by contrast, happily gives both sides: "*You* work out . . . for *God* is at work in you . . ." (Phil. 2:12, 13).

At times these and other devotional writers unfortunately, by devoting their total concentration to one side of the picture, convey to some readers an imbalance or even a misconception about the relationship of things. This is true in Mrs. Smith's words about the clay. At the same time, however, to be fair to a writer, we should realize that he may not intend to say everything about a subject at one point. In charity, we also must remember that few illustrations can perfectly cover all aspects. These writers do not *intend* to give the impression that their words seem to carry, that an abiding Christian need make no effort. But we all would be more helpful to others in the long run if we were more sensitive to guard against allowing our illustrations to leave false impressions.

One of the problems today in witnessing to many on the college campuses is that of moral license. College men and women may have grown up being pampered, having had so many things handed to them. Now, when some respond to the message of salvation in Jesus Christ, they enter into the ranks of Christians transferring their own easy-living image with them. Certain teachings about grace, which finally amount to a cheap grace foreign to the grace the Word of God has in view (see Titus 2:11ff, for example), become like fuel to feed their fires of inner susceptibility toward loose living. So they look on salvation as a sort of "free ride," as one widely-used witness for Christ on the campus put it. They think of it as a nice *addition* to their wild lives, minus any serious responsibility or obedience that might call them to a turnabout from sin. They display their concept of faith without works (or effort) in their permissive morality.

Some writers confuse the reader with inconsistencies. Carron, for instance, gives two different emphases within one writing, not correlating them to explain the apparent inconsistency. He says, "There is no effort in the production of fruit." Later, he writes:

> The question may be raised, how is all this worked out? Since these things are the fruit of the Spirit, do we just remain passive in the hope that the fruit will appear? As indicated in the first paragraph there is conflict between the flesh and the Spirit. In the matter of our initial salvation, we rest in faith on the completed work of Christ to which we can add nothing by our own works. Once launched, however, on the Christian pathway our responsibility enters into the matter. This is clear from the numerous exhortations addressed to us in the Word, but with the exhortations there is the power in the Spirit to carry them out. [16]

One is left wondering how there is no effort in the production of fruit (his earlier statement) if this finally involves active effort (his later statement). He must mean that effort *is* involved — the *right kind* of effort — and therefore the first statement is misleading. Another statement that would have to be modified or qualified considerably is that of Tryon:

> I should say to that branch, "Yes, of course you must produce fruit, but you'll never produce fruit by trying to. It is not the fruit you need to be concerned about, but the *life.* If once you have got *that,* the fruit will come all right." And so I reply to you, Yes, of course you must read your Bible and pray and witness and do good works; of course you must surrender completely to Christ, but don't you see, *all these things are part of the fruit.* You cannot do them by trying to do them, you can only be like a branch tying on artificial fruit, because it does not understand that real fruit must be the result of the vine life within. . . . Apart from Him you can do NOTHING; and prayer and witness and surrender are all included in that "nothing." Every single bit of fruit has to be the result of the life of Christ

in you. It is the life you need to be concerned about, if
you have got *that*, the fruit will surely follow. [17]

Actually, Tryon seems to be against works that are simply of
the flesh and not done in the power of Christ, the Vine life.
We agree that there is no good fruit in that. But his statements, in countering one wrong emphasis, fall into another
by lack of qualification. Let us look at some examples.

He says, "You'll never produce fruit by trying to." Actually, a Christian manifests fruit when he does try, but the
trying is in the energy of the Holy Spirit, whether the activity be in thought, word, or deed. Tryon's wording does
not take account of *this* category.

"It is not the fruit you need to be concerned about, but
the *life*," he writes. But is it not better to see a both/and
situation here, not an either/or? Fruit bearing is not automatic, as if we need not concern ourselves about any works
in the Christian life, but just trust the Lord and be passive,
and the fruit will come without our doing anything. Perhaps Tryon did not mean this, and we hope he did not,
but his emphasis leaves this strong impression.

After he says that such things as Bible reading, praying,
and witnessing are *part of the fruit*, he adds, "You cannot
do them by trying to do them, you can only imitate them,
you can only be like a branch tying on artificial fruit. . . ."
Since Tryon in his context is making a point that all we do
must be by the Vine life enabling us, the above statement
has in view the trying of self-sufficiency. It would help
to have a forthright statement, then, that there can be a
valid effort, a trying that is by faith, in divine adequacy.
It should be said clearly. When he later says that God will
perfect the work in us, he does not add that, according to
the New Testament, we, working in cooperation with God
by faith's dependence, perfect ourselves in holiness (2 Cor.
7:1). There is this human side too, and not just the "God
does it all" emphasis.

These and many other writers say that abiding and fruit
bearing are by no effort, only faith (sort of in the abstract
somehow). Yet it is right at this point that they have

[17] David Tryon, "The Vine and The Branches" (booklet) (Glen Ridge,
New Jersey: Africa Evangelical Fellowship, n.d.), pp. 20-23.

unwittingly wrenched things out of perspective and need a more complete picture that is on our Lord's heart. We go amiss if we carry out the analogy of a natural branch in every last detail. The person has will, intellect, emotion, and, in all normal and healthy cases, much effort. We need to balance our one thesis that abiding is by faith with the legitimate inner activities of the heart and the outward works that are involved in faith. Our Savior said clearly, "If ye keep my commandments, ye shall abide in my love . . ." (John 15:10; see 1 John 3:24). Do we really want to misuse the vine figure to have it say *more* than Christ Himself evidently designed it to teach, especially when this creates a conflict with other aspects of the truth we love in the New Testament?

Christ's words about abiding in John 15, rightly understood, show that He does expect effort in *us*. This effort is harmonious with true faith and with the diligent maintenance of abiding. It will evidently take faith and faith's vital outflow of effort if we are to follow on to know His words by which we go on abiding (v. 7), pray in His will, rise to the vigorous challenges of discipleship (v. 8), demonstrate Christian love (vv. 9-12), do all that He has commanded (v. 14; cf. 14:21), and "go" (v. 16). Paul later helps us catch a vision of balance. He tells us that he "labored" abundantly, "yet not I, but the grace of God which was in me" (1 Cor. 15:10). His exhortation is for believers to be "always abounding in the work of the Lord" (1 Cor. 15:58), and he says he labored, striving "according to His power, which mightily works within me" (Col. 1:29 NASB). He entreats Christians, "Work out your own salvation with fear and trembling" (Phil. 2:12). The fear and trembling do not express doubt about our salvation but an attitude of reverence for our God and His truth. They also reflect the humility involved in realizing the weakness and dangers that reside in ourselves, the perils that beset us, and the awesome need for God to work in us. By working out our salvation he means getting it out into the full expression that is possible in the will of God. But he quickly adds, "For it is God who is at work in you, both to will and to work for His good pleasure" (v. 13). God works *in* the believer but not *in the place of the believer!* G. C. Berkouwer's reminder is apropos: "God's work in salvation, in Paul's view, never absorbs or invalidates man's work, but arouses and stimulates it and gives it meaning." [18] Later in the same Philippian epistle, Paul says triumphantly of his abiding life: "I can do all things," but qualifies this with the words "in him who strengthens me" (Phil. 4:13 RSV). Chalmers gathers up the two sides that are balanced in Philippians 2:12, 13 when he says:

> The relation between the hand that works and the hand by which it is strengthened, furnishes the very strongest, and at the same time most intelligible motive to steady, faithful, and enduring obedience. The man works out his salvation upon the strength of what God has wrought into him; and he does it with fear and trembling, just because most fearfully and tremblingly alive to the thought, that if he does not, God may cease working in him to will any more or to do any more. The doctrine of grace, thus understood, so far from acting as an extinguisher upon human activity, is in truth the very best excitement to it. This dependence between the busy exercise of all your present graces and the supply of new, is the fittest possible tenure on the part of God whereby to hold man to his most constant, most careful, most vigilant obedience. . . . We are aware of the reproach that has been cast on the doctrine of the Spirit's influences; but we trust it will be seen from these views, however imperfectly given, that he who labors in all the present might given, and looks for more, instead of *living in the mystic state of an indolent and expectant quietism,* he of all . . . men is the most awake to every call of duty — the most painstaking and arduous in every performance of it. There is nothing in that mercy which descends upon us from heaven to supersede the activities of men upon earth. Instead of superseding, its very design is to stimulate these activities. When it works in us, its precise outgoing is just to set us working. . . . [19]

---

[18] G. C. Berkouwer, *Faith and Sanctification* (Grand Rapids: Wm. B. Eerdmans Publishing Co., 1952), p. 122.

[19] Cited by Henry A. Boardman, *The "Higher Life" Doctrine of Sanctification, Tried By the Word of God* (Philadelphia: Presbyterian Board of Publication, 1877), pp. 147, 148.

The apostle Peter speaks to us about furnishing various qualities or fruits in a diligent Christian life (2 Peter 1: 3-7). While from one standpoint God provides everything (vv. 3, 4), from another, and in perfect consistency with the first, the believer by faith appropriates and furnishes his life (vv. 5-7). The abiding Christian does engage in various activities of faith. Moule, discussing Peter's words, acknowledges:

> That passage, by the way, may caution us against a disproportionate inference from the precious imagery of "the fruit" in this. The ideas suggested by fruit and fruitbearing are not those of effort and care in the fruitbearing branch; effort and care are the cultivator's part. But St. Peter reminds us that the analogy between the impersonal fruit-tree and the personal believer cannot be in all respects complete. In the conscious and responsible man, as such, there must always be place for "all diligence." Such "diligence" does not create life, or generate it, nor does it in a direct way develop the issues of life. But diligence is the believer's duty in connexion with that development; it means, if done in spirit and in truth, the believer's "laying aside," in the Lord's name, every known thing that hinders the outgrowth and fulness of the fruit. [20]

Moule clarifies, in his context, that from one point of view the Christian's part is "a blessed and wakeful Quietism; a rest, that He may work," yet from another point of view which should be kept in rightful balance with this, his part is to work diligently in the works that true faith inspires. He specifically disavows any agreement with the error often associated with the label "quietism." He realizes that quietism has placed such heavy emphasis upon *one* side (God doing everything) that its idea is far out of balance with the proper sense in which the believer himself is obediently active.

Mickelsen's way of correlating activity with abiding by grace is also helpful:

> Finally, the action of the branches (disciples) themselves is considered. This illustrates the point that allegory com-

[20] Handley C. G. Moule, *Veni Creator* (London: Hodder and Stoughton, 1900), pp. 193, 194.

bines factual experience with elements that do not occur in the earthly reality that is being used for metaphorical purposes. In nature branches do not "act" at all. They may wave in the breeze. They may dry up and wither. But the branches never act on their own — they are simply a part of a tree or vine. In this allegory, however, they "act" volitionally. The disciples are told to "abide (totality of action) in me" (15:4a). Action is also made clear by direct comparison: "As the branch is not able to bear fruit of itself except it constantly abide (pres. tense) in the vine, so neither you (plural) except you (plural) constantly abide (pres. tense) in me" (15:4b). The literal branch abides by being there "positionally." The disciples abide by being there "relationally." In the allegory Jesus warns of the outcome if the disciple does not actively respond: "If anyone does not abide (pres. tense, linear action) in me, he is thrown away (gnomic aorist) as the branch, and it withers and they gather them and cast them into the fire and they are being burned" (John 15:6). Obviously Jesus was not thinking of a mechanical connection. A vital relationship demands a constant activity. Answers to prayer depend on this vital, active relationship (15:7). Fruitbearing, as a sign of this vital relationship, brings glory to God and shows that the one so producing will be Christ's disciple in the future as well as in the present (15:8). In conclusion, obeying Christ's commandments is pictured as evidence that the disciple is abiding in Christ's love (15:9, 10). This allegory dynamically portrays to the reader why he must maintain a fresh, living relationship to Jesus Christ and his Father. This is what discipleship means. [21]

The relationship between God's activity and our own activity in the abiding life was also a theme for Robert Speer:

We shall not go on our way toward the highest unless we trust the indwelling Spirit of God to do His part, that part of which Paul was speaking when he said: "It is no longer I that live, but Christ liveth in me: and that life which I now live in the flesh I live in faith, the faith which is in the Son of God." On the one side it looks natural enough. It is just as when we eat and breathe and exercise in the physical life. These processes are so natural that

[21] A. B. Mickelsen, *Interpreting the Bible* (Grand Rapids: Wm. B. Eerdmans Publishing Co., 1963), pp. 233, 234.

they conceal from us the miracle of life which depends upon them for its sustenance. And so in our higher life we fulfill as we may the conditions set before us, and it seems quite simple; but in reality, back of all that we do, God is doing the real work, ever moving supernaturally upon us and fashioning us into the likeness He hopes some day to see in us. [22]

ILLUSTRATIONS CONTRIBUTE TO MISCONCEPTIONS

G. Campbell Morgan's illustration of *sitting* in a sanctuary does not satisfactorily communicate what is involved in abiding. While a true Christian can never lose his "in me" union with Christ (this never changes!), his daily practical experience of abiding in Him is not realistically conveyed by the image of just sitting. The abiding life is also one of standing, walking, running a race, fighting. All are involved. The very faith itself by which a Christian abides involves the activity of obeying. The multifaceted drama of Christ's will casts the believer in many roles with many things to *do*.

An illustration that goes farther toward describing the *balance* between faith and effort for the abiding man is that of Evan Hopkins who, with Moule, was one of the more careful writers in the Keswick movement. He pictured a situation closely interrelating effort with the rest one may experience by daily faith in Christ. A man caught in the rushing current of a river is close to drowning. His self-efforts are becoming more feeble; he is nearly exhausted from trying. Then he hears a voice, "Lay hold of the boat," and he sees a boat beside him. He grabs and clings. Then he sees another man also struggling in the current and about to be sucked under. He can offer no help that will avail, for then both would go down. The voice now commands, "Get into the boat." This he does, and so he forsakes the experience of clinging for the better one of resting. The boat holds him up in a place of safety, and he is no longer struggling with his own problem. He is himself set free and now in a position to put forth effective effort to help the other man. The improvement of this illustration is that

[22] Robert Speer, *The Marks of a Man* (New York: Hodder and Stoughton, 1907), p. 162.

the man's abiding or resting is not one of simply *sitting* passively, a picture that unfortunately gives the image of being idle, but one of *active effort as he does abide.*[23]

Hopkins, in another place, leaves no doubt about his correlation of two emphases — the no-effort part and the much-effort part — in one consistent picture. Speaking of being filled with the Spirit, which is the abiding life, he writes:

> But someone here will interpose, "I am afraid I shall not be able to keep it up." To which some of us may receive from older Christians the reply, "It is not for you to keep *it* up, but it is He who will keep *you* up." Now this is absolutely true. No amount of self-effort will keep us to the King's Highway of Holiness; only the abiding presence of the King Himself will do that. *But there is a part for us to play. The life of faith is not to be spent in a spiritual armchair. That was the danger against which James was trying to warn those to whom he wrote. We have got to get up and go forward in the spiritual life.*
>
> We need to remember that Jude has told us there is a sense in which we must build up ourselves in the faith, and keep ourselves in the bounds of the love of God. The faith by which we are set free from sin must be fed and nourished if we are to remain victors. Our duty is to keep in vital touch with the One whose very presence spells holiness. And *this* needs as much personal discipline and effort as is required of the athlete training for a race. [24] (italics mine)

This is a helpful emphasis on both sides at the same time. But now let us return to the illustration of the man in the boat being free from effort to stay afloat but able to carry on activity in ministering to others. The picture, while graphic to depict what Hopkins intends, is still not as fully analogous to spiritual abiding as it might be. As such, it is like many other illustrations which help us on certain single facets of the Christian life but do not portray *the overall balance in abiding.* Of course, we realize that no one illustration is absolutely perfect to cover all points. For

[23] Cited by Steven Barabas, *So Great Salvation* (Westwood, New Jersey: Fleming H. Revell Co., 1952), pp. 149, 150.

[24] Evan Hopkins, *Henceforth* (London: The Inter-Varsity Fellowship. Fourth Ed., 1957), pp. 44, 45.

example, Moule related resting in Christ to the matter of effort by picturing a great wheel greased at the center and so able to run its swiftest, smoothest round. That teaches *one* point: being well-greased (i.e., resting in faith) causes one to be effective in his actions (i.e., the work of faith). [25] Yet a wheel is inanimate and impersonal. It has no will, intellect, and emotions which can be involved in a struggle of faith even while abiding. So, like the vine, the wheel cannot take us into all analogies with the abiding life of a *person*, who does have intellect, will, and emotion. Or consider the illustration of stepping into an elevator in a high-rise building. You exert no effort to climb; the elevator does it all! This might be used to picture one's faith in the all-sufficiency of Christ to help him overcome the gravitational pull of the sinful nature within him, and to bring into effect the law (principle) of the Spirit of life by which there is victory (Rom. 8:2). But since he just rides the elevator while he himself is passive and idle, there is nothing really analogous to the struggle which every abiding man experiences daily. Life is not really quite so easy and automatic. The illustrations of overcoming gravitational pull by the law of aerodynamics or by the tube on which one floats in a swimming pool are similar in relation to Romans 8:2. Yet in all of these pictures — those of the wheel, the elevator, the airplane, and the tube — we have beautiful analogies for certain aspects of the Christian life, but no broad tie-in with what abiding is like. Most of them involve the idea of passivity and idleness. Hopkins avoided that by having his man *active* from the boat. But there is still another difficulty. All of the illustrations picture what we could call "abiding" ("resting" evidently has the same idea for most devotional writers) by relating a person to some *object* or *machine* by which he has sufficiency. The object or machine, of course, represents the Lord. And even though in Hopkins' picture the man is active, the relationship in which a boat holds a man up from the rushing current does not convey the personal involvement and struggle of faith which realistically occurs daily in the person who

[25] Handley C. G. Moule, cited by W. H. Griffith-Thomas, "The Victorious Life," *Bibliotheca Sacra,* July, 1919, pp. 278, 279.

seeks to abide. This all leads one to ask, Are we not unwise in pressing one illustration (such as that of the vine) to teach us the *whole* Christian life?

Certainly we acknowledge that the vine illustration is ideal to show the deep richness of intimacy with Christ, and that we receive His life by faith. But not all the aspects of the total Christian life (and there are many facets!) emerge naturally out of the one figure. So, to say that abiding in Christ involves no effort, or to contend that there is no effort in bearing fruit is an unwise and arbitrary conclusion to make from the illustration in John 15. No one illustration, be it in the Bible or conceived by Bible teachers today, is adequate to take care of all points of the spiritual experience. How wise it has been of our great God to give us not one but *many* illustrations. These supplement one another and give us balance, whereas if we had but one, we would almost certainly wander off on certain points not intended by the analogy. For example, the picture of being members of one body (1 Cor. 12) supplements that of the vine and fills out the idea of what abiding involves. Although we may see these to some extent also in the vine, the analogy of the body (e.g., in Ephesians 4) really underscores certain truths particularly, such as the relationship with other believers, an interinvolvement of lives, a cooperating spirit of love, and gracious understanding of how greatly we need others and they need us. Still another illustration that supplements what is involved in abiding is that of marriage. The wife is married to the husband and so will be "in" union with him as long as the marriage endures (Rom. 7:1-4). This is analogous to what Christ means by His words "in me." Yet the wife's daily experience of this is a different matter. That is, her own personal involvement in abiding with her husband is distinct from the wonderful fact of the union itself. She can trust her husband, rest in his loving care for her, and have her joy in him. She lives a life of loyalty and dedicatedly *relating* to him and to his cherished goals. This may grow deeper, richer, and more complete as their abiding lasts. She also may live a life of *rejecting* attitudes, interests, and actions in which her husband cannot share in true sympathy, and which, if she followed them, would cause her to be unfaithful to him. And she is not only giving herself to him but also *receiving* from him, keeping the lines of communication open. To be "in him" in marriage involves no effort; it has already been a fact since the day she became "Mrs. Prince Charming." But in this relationship she has hundreds of outward acts (related to inward attitudes) that please him. He also delights in her as they share in the glad-hearted effort of love, the effort so intimately flavored by love that it is difficult to distinguish between the love and the love-effort. In one sense her love-effort is a result (fruit, Rom. 7:4) of abiding. In yet another, without inconsistency, it leads to further abiding. For her, abiding fosters abiding, just as success encourages success.

Now let us return to Christ's words in John 15:5: "Without me ye can do nothing." In conclusion, we may rightly say that when we do not depend upon His life, all that we do is vain in the sense of being unfruitful in His evaluation. A very busy life of an unsaved person goes down as "nothing," and this quality of "nothingness" is also true of the Christian to the degree that he lives only by self-sufficiency, leaving Christ out of the consideration. But the opposite is also true, that with Christ we can do something! A life of abiding and bearing fruit will be one of effort. To the degree that we really depend upon Chirst to live His vine life in and through us in all the effort of our lives, we will be fruitful. Fruit bearing in John 15, then, correlates with great activity in those who respond by faith to the many exhortations of the New Testament.

LET'S PUT IT ALL TOGETHER

Abide in me (John 15:4).
Walk in newness of life (Rom. 6:4).
Walk in the Spirit (Gal. 5:16).
Walk as children of light (Eph. 5:8).

Often when the writer has given the message of abiding and has afterward encouraged discussion, Christians have been ready with certain questions. It is the purpose of this chapter to discuss three of these questions and then correlate abiding in Christ with other New Testament key terms for the spiritual life. Here, then, are some of the questions Christians have often wondered about.

Beginning to abide. How do I begin to abide? Every truly saved person, in the overall thrust of his life, does abide in Christ. By this it is meant that he continues in his new life in Christ. The difference between Christians is in the matter of the consistency, degree, depth, and richness of intimacy with the Lord. This relates to the *quality* aspect in abiding. If, then, you are a genuine Christian, you have been abiding *to some degree* in that you have related your life to Christ, rejected certain attitudes with which He could have no fellowship, and received His refreshing influence by true faith, be it ever so small. This abiding may have been erratic and inconsistent in your experience. Your problem is one of coming to live in a greater, deeper, richer, more daily and hourly sense of your privilege of being "in Christ." However shabby your experience of this union may be right at the moment, apply more persistently the principles of relating your life (all of it!) to Him and to His purposes revealed in the Word, rejecting contrary attitudes, and receiving Him into all things that concern you. As you keep on letting His Word be the spiritual food of your life and His grace your enablement, you will discover that the quality of your abiding is enhanced more and more.

Perhaps at this point you are young in the Lord and inept in working with Him to make the changeover to His new style of living. If so, you will no doubt feel somewhat awkward in the first steps of growing in Him. For you, beginning to abide may be much like learning to drive a car. Remember what it was like when you first got behind the wheel? Or, if you have not yet learned to drive, imagine what it is like. It seems as though you have a hundred things to remember to do all in close coordination. You should be sure to fasten your seat belt, make sure the shift lever is in "Park" or "Neutral," turn the ignition key to start the car, and give the engine a little gas by the accelerator pedal. But that isn't half of it. If you are parked at the curb, you need to look behind you to make sure no traffic is coming, shift to "Drive," flick on the left-turn signal to indicate that you are pulling out into the lane, and feed the car a bit more gas, not too much and not too little. Oh, yes, and for goodness' sake, be more careful how you are steering because you almost sideswiped that parked car you were pulling around back there. You must give yourself more clearance! And get your foot on the brake or you may not stop in time to let that boy on the bike pass over at the crosswalk. On and on it goes in learning to drive a car, and it may be quite complicated at first because so many new things are coming at you so fast. But, then, as you keep on applying what you are learning, it really does not take very long before you are doing in a rather natural, coordinated unity of action what seemed to be a hundred different acts before. Now, too, your mind is increasingly free to get on with other thoughts, since much of the mechanical aspect of driving is being executed competently with a degree of spontaneity because you are not directly aware of a concentration upon just this matter.

Learning to abide in Christ is somewhat analogous to this. In a sense, it can all seem rather complex, since there are many details to put into action in this matter of living and keeping in view the provisions of grace. But you are simply to trust Christ and do what you know to do in obedient faith. As you continue to learn and to do His will, receiving the grace for this out of His own sufficiency, the total involvement of living a Christian life will open up to you more and more. The measure of your day-by-day consistency and degree of involvement in the matters we have emphasized — relating, rejecting, and receiving — will determine the measure of your progress.

Knowing very little. But, someone will say, "I know so little about abiding. Does this consign me to failure?" Let us consider the young, growing Christian.

A young Christian, a "babe," may be truly abiding in Christ even though he has had very little time to grow in his Lord. Of course, he does not yet know much about what the Bible says, as a more learned believer might skillfully explain it. He just has a simple faith in his Lord with the small amount of knowledge, but he puts his faith and knowledge to work in a childlike spirit of dependence. Although he cannot systematically explain the mechanics of the Christian life with the precision of a theologian, he does experience much of the meaningful reality, the crux of it all.

But it is also true that with greater knowledge of the Word (1 Peter 2:2, 3; 2 Peter 3:18) and trusting application, he grows. Erroneous and shallow concepts that his own ignorance has led him to assume, or which he has picked up from the background of his spiritual bankruptcy of the past, are corrected as he grasps truth new to him and puts it into practice. He lives in the prosperity of an expanding knowledge!

If only those with perfect knowledge could really abide, we would all be disqualified. God accomodates Himself to our finite limitations and works with us patiently and realistically. His relationship with us may be compared with that of a human father who has an intimate relationship with his child even though the child still has blind spots about many things. God looks on the heart and takes note of the *motive* even where the believer is in need of vast improvement. The Christian may, without realizing it, be working against himself and his Lord. When new light is afforded him, he may rebel out of foolish pride and refuse to change, insisting on doing or teaching in his own way. If he does this, he is sinning, and God may deal with him in a way that appears harsh at the moment. Actually, however, His great love is behind the discipline: He is seeking to cleanse the believer so that he might yet bear more fruit.

Being conscious of Christ's presence. Must I be aware of Christ's presence with me every moment? Yes and no. The answer is yes in the sense that when I look over my life in a panoramic sweep, I can be aware that His faithful presence was constantly with me as He promised. The answer is no, however, in the sense that when actual moments come I may be necessarily occupied with thoughts that are directly and immediately upon other matters. It seems wisest to understand this as we generally understand "pray without ceasing" to refer basically to an attitude in which we do not knowingly tolerate interruptions in our dependence upon the Lord. It would be ridiculous, of course, to insist upon prayer twenty-four hours a day every day to fulfill the spirit of the statement. G. Campbell Morgan tells of the blessed relationship he enjoyed with his wife, Annie, and how he always thought lovingly of her. But he could not, in the responsible involvements of each full day's work in ministering God's Word, be thinking directly of Annie. The abiding Christian is like this in his relationship to Christ. He is not a person with a faraway gleam in his eye or a daydreamer's detachment from reality — a person so preoccupied with "heavenly" thoughts that he is of no earthly good. His life-beat may be one with that of Christ in that he has learned, by spiritual reflex, to relate whatever he does all the day long to Him and to His purpose. That is the set of his heart. Yet he must be employed through much of each day with thinking that concentrates squarely upon the specific issues of his work, service, problems, and so on. But because of the heart-set that profoundly shapes his life-style, the moment he is disengaged from these things his mind may quite spontaneously fly to his primary focus of loving interest — Christ! And even in the thick of all those activities, his life is permeated by Christ so that he often thinks of Him, communes with Him in the heart's affections, prays for guidance, lives for His glory. He learns that the busy work of the day need not intrude a hair's breadth between him and Christ but may itself be filled with Christ with whom he may share everything in life.

Relating abiding to other concepts. What is the interrelationship between "abiding" and other terminology the New Testament uses for the spiritual life? Each Christian is to "be filled with the Spirit" (Eph. 5:18), "walk in the Spirit" (Gal. 5:16), "walk in the light" (1 John 1:7), grow toward being "perfect" or mature (1 Cor. 2:6; Phil. 3:15; Heb. 5:14), and grow toward being "he that is spiritual" (1 Cor. 2:15).

In answering the above question, let us begin with the Spirit-filled life and the concept of fruit which we bring forth when we abide. This fruit is the fruit of the Vine, Jesus Christ (John 15; Phil. 1:11). But it is also called "the fruit of light" (Eph. 5:9 RSV) — a phrase which emphasizes the essence or character of God as light; and "the fruit of the Spirit" (Gal. 5:22) — a description which stresses the Person who is the source in union and in cooperation with Christ. The Holy Spirit is responsible for the life-flow within the spiritual branch or believer. To the same extent of the capacity to which He fills (and this means He controls and empowers), the Christian is abiding. A young, immature Christian and an older, mature Christian may both be abiding and filled with the Spirit, yet the latter has a greater capacity. The Spirit controls to that capacity. This does not mean that the Christian of greater maturity has more of the Spirit than the less mature. It simply means that the Spirit has more of him, that is, a greater capacity within him with which to work freely. As the Christian grows up in Christ, more areas of his life are effectively touched and transformed by the Spirit "from glory to glory" (2 Cor. 3:18), or from one growth-stage of reflecting God's beauties to a more developed one. The Spirit makes a difference where previously the believer might not even have imagined there could be a difference. The Christian's capacity expands. Even in those aspects that the Spirit already controlled at his earlier level of growth there can yet be a deeper, richer, fuller, more seasoned manifestation of Christlikeness in attitude, word, and action.

What is the status of Christians who are not at the moment filled with the Spirit? Are they abiding? They are persons who abide in some degree in the overall sweep of their many-faceted lives, according to New Testament terminology on abiding. And, in the long-range view, they have some of the Spirit's control (Rom. 8:2-17; Gal. 5:16-23; 6:8, et al.). But they may not at the precise moment, day, or week be living in the good of this abiding as they might be, or be controlled by the Spirit in the sense of direct yieldedness to Him in particular details of life. This inconsistency does not rule out the overall thrust of the life of the genuinely saved person.

But someone will no doubt say, "What about a Christian who, in his usual pattern, is not filled?" Should we say (and some have labeled this answer as an easy way out) that he is really not saved, after all? It is possible, but not necessarily so. Of course, a person whose pattern is one of fleshly living may never have been authentically saved and so is not really "in the Spirit" (Rom. 8:8, 9). But it is also a fact that a young Christian, a "babe," may in his first days, weeks, or months be what Paul designates as "carnal" (1 Cor. 3:1). In practical experience, as he does not know and apply much of the Word to his total sphere of life, he has not yet laid aside many of the old habits of attitude and conduct that characterized him in his days as the unsaved, merely natural man of 1 Corinthians 2:14. In the horticultural imagery that James seems to have in mind, the new Christian has not laid aside much of the foul, rank growth that is now like dead wood, and has not received with meekness very much of the Word planted on the inside of his life (James 1:21). He may be quite predominantly inconsistent with what really ought to be true in his daily experience. For him, at least at this time, being controlled by the Spirit appears to be a rather on-and-off, start-and-stop, erratic kind of life. And yet it is true that God has by His own operation set a new life principle within him — the "law of the Spirit of life in Christ Jesus" — and it is a fact that he, like everyone else who has been justified, will be sanctified (Rom. 6 - 8). Eventually, the carnal Christian's life should get straightened out so that he more noticeably and consistently reflects the Spirit's control, both in abiding and in bearing fruit. Even in the time that is more predominantly one of carnality for him, there can be *some* spasmodic fruit that manifests in a degree the life of Christ that is really in him.

It is also true that a person may profess to know Christ and yet remain for an abnormally long period in the "baby" stage, rather markedly characterized by carnal thinking, speaking, and acting. Paul has this in view when he says of some of the Corinthians: "You are still fleshly. For since there is jealousy and strife among you, are you not fleshly, and are you not walking according to man?" (1 Cor. 3:3, *translation mine*). There are three parts of this statement that should be specially studied.

First, Paul plainly said that the Corinthians were *still* fleshly. In other words, whereas they had understandably been babes in Christ and had displayed fleshly characteristics when he had been among them four to five years before, the tragedy was that *they had not changed!* They had not been culpable for acting like babes when they *were* babes, but they had had time to grow and take on spiritual characteristics in place of the fleshly. Now they were blameworthy.

Second, he said that they were "carnal" or "fleshly," but he used a different Greek word than that translated "fleshly" in verse one. Earlier, he stated that they were carnal, using the Greek word *sarkinos;* now he said they were carnal, using *sarkikos.* A distinction in emphasis between these two words is recognized by many scholars. *Sarkinos* places emphasis upon the idea that they are "fleshen," or "made of the material or substance of flesh." As Christ said in John 3: "That which is born of the flesh is flesh; and that which is born of the Spirit is spirit." These Corinthian believers had been born of the flesh, had lived in the flesh as unsaved people, and now as Christians they were still in the flesh and of the flesh. The wonder was that they had been also born of the Spirit and so had entered into the privileges of this dimension of life which they had not had before when they were *only* of the flesh. As baby Christians, they were fleshen in the sense that they were composed of the material of flesh as before and reflected a type of living that was much the same as when they had been unsaved. The old flesh life still showed noticeably. Then, after the passing of those few years, Paul said they were *sarkikos*, a word which concentrates on the character, tendency, or disposition. In other words, the Corinthian believers were following the characteristics or tendencies of the flesh on a rather predominant scale even a long time after they had become Christians.

Third, Paul tells us that they were "walking according to man." The translation "according to man" is from the Greek word *kata* (according to) and the word *anthropon* (man) in the accusative case, meaning that "man" is the object of the preposition. This type of combination, using *kata* plus the accusative, places emphasis upon the *norm* or *standard* of whatever is in view. Here, then, Paul is saying that they were walking (conducting their lives) according to the norm or standard of unsaved men who are *only* in the flesh, and denying the new life in the Spirit which was available to them as Christians. In Romans 8: 8, 9, he speaks of those who are "in the flesh" *(en sarki)*, meaning the unsaved, who are "in the flesh *only*," and of those who are "in the Spirit" *(en pneumati)*, meaning the saved. The latter are still in the flesh until death or the return of Christ, but they are *also* in the new realm of the Spirit with all the privilege and potential involved in this. If a person is "in the Spirit," Paul expects him to begin to walk consistently in a manner that reflects this. He is thinking of this when he speaks of those who do not "walk according to the flesh but according to the Spirit" (Rom. 8: 4, 5). Again, with the *kata* (according to) and the accusative (flesh, Spirit), he is stressing norm or standard. He has patterns of life in mind. On the one hand, it is sadly possible for a saved person to revert back to, lapse into, or show forth the earlier fleshly life, acting out of character with the spiritual potential of the new life within. There is still a propensity toward corrupt fruit in thoughts, words, and acts. That is, he still has a capacity to walk "according to the flesh." But, on the other hand, by virtue of "the law (principle) of the Spirit of life" now within him, he has been set free from "the law (principle) of sin and death" which always used to be a dead weight pulling him down (Rom. 8:2). He has been liberated from its tyranny in the sense that there need no longer be an enslavement to sin. The doors of his life have swung open and the Liberator Himself, Christ, has come within. The believer need not continue in sin and has no excuse to do so. So Paul expects, and so should we, that the person truly justified will come to reflect a life that is "according to the norm or standard of the Spirit." Some manifestation, some degree of this will be there, for the Lord definitely expects "fruit" in the one who has eternal life (Rom. 6:22) and indicates that a true son of God will be led by the Spirit (Rom. 8:14).

It would appear that the phrase "walk according to the flesh" in Romans is equivalent to "walk according to man" in Corinthians. Either walking according to the flesh or walking according to the Spirit is possible for the Christian, but the latter is to become his life norm as soon as possible. The degree to which he walks according to the Spirit, whether little or much, determines the quality of his abiding. Again, the difference among Christians is in the matter of depth, richness, degree, or extent in harmony with their receptivity toward God and their particular stage of growth.

When Paul speaks of those who walk not according to the flesh but according to the Spirit (Rom. 8), he has reference to overall, general life-patterns that characterize the unsaved and the saved. Although a saved person, such as one recently converted (1 Cor. 3:1) or one persistently disobedient for some time (1 Cor. 3:3, 4), may walk according to the flesh or according to man, Paul does not expect this to be the general rule of his life, for there is a sense in which he contrasts saved and unsaved along this very line (Rom. 8:13, 14; Gal. 6:8).

Often, thinking Christians ask how walking in the light (1 John 1:5) relates to walking in the Spirit. They are equivalent in the sense that the believer who is doing the one is doing the other. They are distinct only in the sense that these are two different ways of describing the same reality. Walking in the light emphasizes the sphere of the essence or character of God who is Light, while walking in the Spirit focuses upon the actual Person of the Godhead who is predominant over this sphere of life. This is by the same principle that "fruit of light," stressing essence, is the same as "fruit of the Spirit," directing attention to the Person. Other emphases with the word "walk" which are also true in the normal Christian life appear in such exhortations as "walk in love" (Eph. 5:2), "walk circumspectly" or carefully (Eph. 5:15), and "walk in wisdom" (Col. 4:5).

How, then, does abiding relate to walking in the light? They are the same. They are simply two distinct figures: a vine and a light. Start again with the idea of fruit. From the standpoint of one picture, we yield the fruit of abiding in the vine. To be consistent when we use the other figure, we call it the fruit of light. The fruit of abiding equals the fruit of Christ in Philippians 1:11, which equals the fruit of light in Ephesians 5:9 (RSV), which equals the fruit of the Spirit in Galatians 5:22, 23. *Abiding* stresses relationship and continuance; *light* looks at essential character; and *the Spirit* emphasizes the Person of God.

Are we also to correlate a Christian's abiding with his knowledge of the Word and maturity? Yes. Recall from chapter eleven that abiding involves two main things: *time* and *quality*. The time you have been a Christian plus your knowledge of the Word (breadth, depth of insight) plus the degree or vital quality aspect of your abiding determines your level of growth and maturity. The quality aspect, as shown before, has in view your actual application of the Word in a life of relating to Christ and His purpose, rejecting sin, and receiving from Christ. The time factor involves not only how long you have been a Christian but the question of how consistent you are in the time you spend in richer communication that is possible with the Lord experientially. It also concerns whether there are few or many deviations that retard progress and to what extent these are prolonged. Here Christians differ. Some are "born running," so to speak, in the sense that they get off to a fast start and go on to grow in spiritual health by leaps and bounds. Theirs is a tremendous hunger for the Word, a vital intake of it, and a vigorous obedience to it. Others, however, are very slow. They have more setbacks, periods of disobedience, and dragging of their spiritual feet. Let every Christian who reads this say, "By the grace of God, may my response be of the first type!"

Is the person who abides the same as the Christian who is "perfect" (1 Cor. 2:6)? He may be; yet there is a valid distinction. The believer who is "perfect" (Gr. *teleios*) is the one who by his receptivity to the divine viewpoint of life (the Word) has reached a measure of maturity or completeness. This term is suitable for him in the sense that he has come to live in the norm or standard of it as his actual daily experience or life-style. This is what is true of him predominantly enough to categorize or label him. That is, it is a steady and consistent way of life for him. This man who is "perfect" or mature is abiding in Christ, and the quality of his abiding is deep, rich, and thoroughgoing. But we must distinguish between abiding and maturity in that even a person who has only recently become a Christian may to some degree of quality be abiding. He is not yet perfect or mature.

Are we then to distinguish being filled with the Spirit from being a spiritual person? Yes, though they are quite closely related. A Christian may be filled with the Spirit to his capacity of the moment the very day he is saved, or at any time, and yet be intermittent or inconsistent in his experience of abiding. The spiritual Christian is the one for whom the "walk in newness of life" (Rom. 6:4), a life controlled by the Spirit rather than the flesh, has come to be the steady, stable, and regular norm. "He that is

In the following chart various aspects of the spiritual life as pictured in John 15 are correlated with those aspects as they are indicated by other terminology in the New Testament.

JOHN 15 RELATED TO OTHER PASSAGES

John 15	Romans	Galatians	Ephesians	James	Peter
1. Abide (meno) means "to continue"; continuing in Christ is a positive activity.	"Shall we continue in sin?" (6:1). "Continue" (epimeno) adds the prefix to meno for a more intensive idea. We are not to continue in sin, the negative side of abiding in John 15.	"Christ liveth in me" (2:20) = ". . . and I in you" (John 15:4).		Continuing (para-meno) in the law of liberty (1:25) = meno with prefix. He who has this relationship with the Word abides in Christ.	
2. Branches draw from life in the vine (15:4,5).	". . . walk in newness of life" (6:4).	"Christ liveth in me" (2:20; 5:25).	We are "strengthened . . . by His Spirit in the inner man" (3:16) "that Christ may dwell . . ." (3:17).	We are given "wisdom that is from above" (3:17, 18; cf. 1:21, the implanted Word).	We are called to be "partakers of the divine nature" (2 Pet. 1:4).
3. Branches are united together intimately in the vine.	We have "grown together" in the likeness of Christ's death (6:5), a figure from horticulture showing closeness, intimacy.		We are united in one temple (2:19-22) and body (3:5, 6; 4:1-16).		We are united as stones joined in a temple (1 Pet. 2:4-9).
4. More than servants, we are friends of God	We are servants given over to a new master; not				We are servants who recognize Christ as Master

5. We obey and delight in the Word (15:2b, 3, 7, 10; 14:21).	We obey and delight in the Word (6:17; 7:22).	We are those who "sow to the Spirit" (6:8).	Obedience is implied in the phrase "imitators of God" (5:1).	We must be doers and not hearers only (1:21-27).	We are to be obedient children (1 Pet. 1:14, 22, 23; 2:2, 3).
6. Fruit is the product (15:5, 8).	The Christian bears fruit (6:21, 22; 7:4, 5).	The Christian has the fruit of the Spirit (5:22, 23).	We bear the fruit of light (5:9 rsv).	We bear the fruit of righteousness (James 3:17, 18).	The Christian is fruitful (2 Pet. 1:8).
7. Death is a consequence of sin (15:4-6).	Death is a consequence of sin (6:21, 23; 8:6, 10).	One who sows to the flesh will reap corruption (6:8).		Death is a consequence of sin (1:15; 5:20).	
8. The Holy Spirit is the enabler (14:16, 17, 26; 15:26).	The Spirit is the enabler (8:1-17).	The Spirit has been provided to us (3:5; 5:16).	The Spirit strengthens the inner man (3:16; 5:18).	The Spirit works in us (4:5, 6).	Preachers of the Gospel are enabled by the Spirit (1 Pet. 1:12).
9. Without Christ we can do nothing (15:5).	In himself, man is carnal, needing Christ's power (7:14).	In himself, one would produce works of the flesh; he needs Christ's life (2:20; 5:19-21).	In himself, one is sinful (4:22-24) and needs Christ's power (6:10-13).	In himself, man is sinful (1:21; 3:14, 15; 4:1), but God gives grace (1:19; 4:6).	In himself, man is sinful (1 Pet. 2:1) and needs the strength God supplies (4:11).
10. When we are genuinely saved, we live in the will of God, characteristically (15:2b, 3, 7).	We walk according to the Spirit, led by the Spirit (6:1; 8:4, 14).	We do not do the works of the flesh as a life pattern, nor "sow to the flesh" (5:21; 6:8).	Sons of disobedience (the unsaved) do not obey, but sons of God do (cf. 5:5, 8).	True faith produces works in God's will (1:22-27; 2:14-26).	Divine life within one results in good fruit (2 Pet. 1:5-11).

spiritual" (1 Cor. 2:15), then, is, in Paul's terminology in the context, the very same person whom he designated earlier as "perfect" (2:6). Being "perfect" is potentially but not yet experientially true of every saved person, for he is, as stated before, not simply "in the flesh" only but also "in the Spirit." In the Christian life that Paul teaches, "if we live in the Spirit, let us also walk in the Spirit" (Gal. 5:25). That is, let it become our actual practice to live as fully as possible in the good of what is now possible in this new realm.

Another correlation in terms is in the matter of our faith. It has been helpful to many Christians when we have spelled out more definitely what abiding is by using words like relating, rejecting, and receiving. These are intended as faith-words. They mean, in essence, what Paul is getting at in Romans 6: "*Reckon* . . . yourselves dead indeed unto sin, but alive unto God" (v. 11), and "Yield . . . your members as instruments of righteousness unto God" (v. 13). He does not mean that the Christian must *make* it so, as though by our simply thinking hard enough it will begin to come true. He has already shown that it is a *fact* that we have died and risen, and now it is our good privilege simply to believe it is so. "Reckon" (Gr. *logizo*) is a word used in accounting. Imagine a man who has 100 million dollars in the bank. He can put it down in his records as the fact it is and go out and live according to his extraordinary wealth. He can wear expensive clothing, enjoy relaxing cruises on a yacht, dine in whatever exquisite restaurants he desires, and on and on. And the Christian, who has died to sin and risen united in resurrection life with Christ the Vine, can reckon on the incalculable wealth of this and live like the man it privileges him to be. He can count on the fact that sin's penalty has been paid to its uttermost extremity in the death of Christ, and life in its uttermost potentiality opens before him in the resurrection life of Christ. And so to some degree, with more growth always yet possible (even for the very mature!), he reckons himself dead to sin and places himself at the disposal of Christ. In terms of John 15, he lives like a branch in the vine. The result is fruit (Rom. 6:22; 7:4).

GOD'S JUDGMENT ON A PROFESSING BELIEVER

Every branch in me that beareth
not fruit he taketh away (John 15:2a).

How diverse have been the interpretations of these words of our Lord! Some have held that the first part of verse two teaches that a person may be "in" Christ in a saving sense and yet lose that salvation. He may be "taken away" from salvation. Others have rightly answered that such a teaching would contradict various statements in Scripture, including strong statements by Christ to the effect that a man once truly saved is saved forever (John 6:37-40; 10: 27, 28). There are ways of harmonizing 15:2a with other biblical teaching when that verse is understood in its proper sense. These we will consider in this chapter and the next two, with a preference for the second of the views given below. The two main proposals are:

(1) The branch "in me" represents a person truly saved but temporarily not bearing fruit, whom the Father "takes away" to heaven in discipline. Having once been saved by grace, he is forever saved on that basis. His lack of fruit, or works, which do not merit salvation in any degree, cannot later cause him to forfeit it.

(2) The branch "in me" but with no fruit represents a person who has only nominally or seemingly had a relationship to Christ. Fruit cannot help a person gain salvation and it cannot keep him saved. But fruit is a mark of the truly saved and, since this person has none, he has never been actually regenerated.

Those who oversimplify Christ's allegory in John 15 are fond of emphases like these: "The passage is talking about bearing fruit and so has nothing to do with having salvation or not having it. It must relate to Christians only." "Communion, and not union, is in view. Christ takes union for granted as already true. Communion is the particular matter that receives the emphasis." "Christ is speaking only to saved men — the eleven — since Judas Iscariot has departed (13:30). Therefore, every detail that He mentions must apply strictly to the saved." Thomas Lowe has stated it as clearly as anyone:

> Remember the matter under discussion is fruit bearing. Our salvation, oneness with Christ, eternal safety as being part of His body, are not under discussion, and these expressions [evidently he means vv. 2a, 6], which seem to relate to these subjects, must be held down to the particular subject matter; otherwise they would conflict with other portions of this same gospel, John x. 28. This is by a rule of construction good in any court. The warning is addressed to believers, and the penalty is such as may be inflicted on them. Nothing can destroy their eternal life. This penalty is therefore one which is not inimical to this, and relates to life in this world. [1]

An unwarranted assumption that seems to underlie these conclusions is that when Christ is addressing saved men, no words having reference to men not truly saved would be relevant. It is assumed that Jesus would not include words about judgment upon an unsaved person when those in His audience are definitely saved.

But the statements above, while catchy and partly true, oversimplify the picture, causing some to miss certain aspects of what our Lord has in view. They would have to be somewhat qualified in order to agree with the fuller implications of the New Testament. In actuality, the passage speaks of both union and communion but, as most expositors realize from thinking through on the issues, the union may be either genuine or spurious in nature. The subject really is fruit bearing that relates to authentic salvation. The fact is that Christ can, even while giving instructions or privileges to the saved, intermingle with these certain warnings which He speaks directly to them ("ye") but which

[1] Thomas Lowe, *The Truth Magazine,* 11:505, 506.

can happen only to the unsaved. He does this, for example, in Matthew 10:31-39 and 18:1-35 (see the second point of chapter sixteen in our discussion of John 15:6). The epistles also, while speaking directly to saved people, often weave into passages that refer to the Christian life and the bearing of fruit (Rom. 6:21-23; 8:12, 13; Gal. 5:21b; 6:8; Eph. 5: 5-7, et al.) certain statements pertaining to those not saved.

We must be careful not to interpret John 15 according to certain pat formulas that restrict it to what we would have it mean. We should be willing to test even the ideas that are popular and widely accepted in some circles by a patient study of the words, phrases, and other features in the context. This we ought to do in the light of all the issues that bear upon the passage in the Old and New Testaments.

Some say, correctly, "Fruit bearing *follows* conversion, and is not a *means* of salvation." The point is certainly right in countering false teaching that would posit works or fruit as somehow being the basis of salvation. One problem, however, is that some cloud the issue by making it appear that if we say fruit is necessary in the Christian life, we are then subtly teaching a salvation by performance rather than by grace. Their emphasis is relevant against a works-salvation system, but it is a "straw man" if used against the view taken in this chapter. It springs from misunderstanding or else misrepresentation of what the view actually is. Fruit is not simply nice; it is necessary. It does not merit salvation, but does manifest it once it really is there. It does not earn it, but does express it; it does not secure it, but is a sign of it; it is not a condition of conversion, but a consequence of it.

Certain expositors, reacting to the false teaching of salvation by works, overstate the case in the other direction by inaccurate emphases like this: "If a person never has any fruit at all in his entire Christian life, he is still saved, for salvation is by grace alone." Certainly salvation is by grace alone, but if that statement is to be made true to the Bible's concept of saving grace and its practical effects, it must be qualified and modified. Paul argues in Romans 5:12ff that we are justified on the basis of the one act of Christ's death and not by any acts of our own; however, he goes on to show in Romans 6:1ff that the genuinely saved are not to continue in sin but are to bring forth fruit in a life of sanctification. If a person has really been saved by the grace of God, then that grace working in him will result in fruit somewhere, sometime, in some form, and to some degree (Eph. 2:10; Titus 2:11ff). When we rightly understand the epistle of James, we see that men are not saved by their works but by grace — through faith that shows forth its reality in works.

It is our sincere hope that this clears the air of misunderstanding. If so, we will be able to look at John 15:2a on its own merits to see what it means. Attention now focuses upon reasons why it is best to interpret the branch that is without fruit as a *professor* but not a *possessor* of salvation.

The branch has no fruit. This is a plain fact. It is in direct contrast to the branch in the same verse that is bearing fruit, a clear reference to a saved person. Its declared status of having no fruit indicates that Christ is not speaking of a real Christian. A number of truths about fruit seem to bear this out.

Think first of Christ's concept. To Him, the saved are like trees bearing good fruit and the unsaved are like trees bearing bad fruit (Matt. 7:16-20; 12:33). His forerunner, John, spoke similarly (Matt. 3:7-12). Our Lord implied in Matthew 21:43 that Israel as a nation had not yielded fruit as evidence of faith that would make men ready for His kingdom. Lack of fruit on a national scale demonstrated lack of faith and salvation on a national scale. Only a remnant of individuals within Israel had appropriated salvation by faith, and this was bound to issue in fruit that would reflect the reality of grace in them.

This is the concept not only of Christ but also of John the apostle. In his first epistle, John makes it clear that a person who is truly saved does commit acts of sin and needs forgiveness and cleansing (1:9; 2:1, 2; 3:3). But it would be inconceivable in John's way of thinking to characterize a saved person in any point-blank way as bearing "no fruit." Suppose a man has no love, for example, and love is the chief feature of the fruit. In John's thought, the man who does not love his brother is right now abiding in eternal death and does not have eternal life abiding in him (1 John 3:14, 15). He is not describing one episode in the man's life only, but his life as a whole, by which he can label him. It is evident to John that "every man" who is authentically born of God and destined to be like his Lord *some day* (1 John 3:2, 3) will manifest at least some life-movement toward becoming pure like Christ *now*. That involves the bearing of some fruit. John shows by his categorical clarity, when the natural import of his words is not explained away, that he could not tolerate a person's claim to be a child of God if there is no fruit of that life in him.

Paul agrees. He shows in Romans 6 that for the one truly justified (justification is the big subject in Romans 3 - 5) and converted from a life empty of good fruit (vv. 20, 21) it would be incongruous, inconceivable, inadmissible, and intolerable to continue in sin. He is now to have "fruit unto [or with respect to] holiness" (v. 22). He is to walk by the Spirit, and, indeed, "as many as are led by the Spirit of God, they are the sons of God" (8:2-4, 14). The person who is led by the Spirit will surely have fruit of the Spirit. Even though a Christian may have only some fruit and be far from the greater fruitfulness yet possible later in his life, he is different from the man who bears "no fruit." Paul also has the concept that the truly saved will persevere through the preserving grace of God, as in Colossians 1:23: "If ye continue [Gr. *epimeno*, intensive form of *meno* used in John 15] in the faith. . . ." The "if" introduces one of several types of "if" clauses in the Greek New Testament. In this instance, the "if" introduces what is called a first-class condition. So it means, "If you continue, and I assume that you will. . . ." Paul, discerning the mind of Christ, felt that where genuine faith in the Word of God is present, that Word works effectually in the believer (1 Thess. 2:13). Where the grace of God in truth is known, fruit and growth follow (Col. 1:6).

Peter joins in this idea too. Writing specifically of fruit, he is constrained to flash a red light of warning for his readers. Some, taking for granted that they are saved, may be assuming what is not a reality for them (2 Peter 1:5-11).

He counsels, "Give diligence to make your calling and election sure" — that is, a genuinely confirmed certainty. From God's side, calling and election are by grace and are sealed in grace. From the believer's side, there is a sense in which proper assurance of this can come from various matters, including, for example, God-given fruit. Peter has referred to this fruit in the context. It is evidence of the real thing.

In addition to the concept of Christ, John, Paul, and Peter, there is the principle in John 15:2a itself. Christ's way of saying what He says here is significant. The action of the Father toward the branch with no fruit appears to be *final*, not provisional as in the case of the branch which bears fruit. In the latter case, there is His *further activity* toward the branch so that it may bear even "more fruit." For the branch bearing no fruit, however, the only act in view is *removal*. There is a finality about that (cf. also v. 6). As the passage stands, Christ does not anticipate or hint at even a possibility of this branch beginning to bear.

Look at it this way. If the person pictured here is without fruit, then he is without love (vv. 9-14, 17), joy (v. 11), or peace (14:27). These are specifics of the fruit mentioned in the context itself and in Galatians 5:22, 23. And since the characteristic pattern of the branch is in view (see the discussion under "John's present tenses characterize men," p. 206), and not just an isolated time such as when a true Christian is temporarily living quite carnally, it is questionable whether this can speak of a truly saved person.

The contrast our Lord draws between the two branches is itself interesting. He sets forth a similar distinction between some production and none at all in His parables of the talents (Matt. 25:14-30) and the pounds (Luke 19:12-27). In the case of the talents, the distinction is between the one who produces *nothing* with his talent and those (in two separate classes) who produce *something*. Christ later interprets the distinction as clearly that of the saved and the unsaved (Matt. 25:30). In the example of the pounds, the one man out of three who produces *nothing* is finally stripped of his pound (Luke 19:24). His status as saved or unsaved is not clearly indicated. While the enemies of the nobleman in the story are sentenced to death (v. 30), no detail is put down about this non-producer's destiny. However, in view of the almost identical nature of the two parables, it is highly probable that this person would face the same destiny as the other person who produces nothing. Clear detail stated in the other, closely related parable indicates what is most likely the case here. He is the same kind of person, a man never truly saved.

While we are considering this fact that the branch in question bears no fruit, it is appropriate to hear the words of two beloved Bible teachers. Dr. Harry Ironside says:

> There are a great many believers who bear *very little fruit* for God, but all bear *some* fruit for Him. There are many people in the Vine (and the Vine speaks of profession here on earth) who bear *no fruit* for Him, and will eventually be cut out altogether when Jesus comes. There will be no place with Him because there is no union with Him. We are grafted in by faith. I do not know much about grafting, but I do know that it is one thing to put a graft in, and it is another thing for a graft to strike. It is one thing for a person to be outwardly linked with Him, and quite another for that person to have life in Christ. What is the test that proves whether he is really in the vine? If he bears fruit. *All who have life bear some fruit for God. If there is no fruit, you can be sure there is no life, no real union with Christ* [italics mine]. [2]

And Dr. Arno C. Gaebelein emphasizes:

> The evidence of being a true believer, a true branch in the vine, is fruit bearing. Those who claim to be Christians, also to be branches in the vine, and bear no fruit prove thereby that their profession is a false profession. These professing Christians, by saying that they are branches also in the vine, cannot abide in Christ, bear no fruit, and will be treated as dead branches. [3]
>
> Whenever a person takes upon himself the profession of a Christian, he claims by that outward profession to take the place, the position, the privileges and responsibility of a believer in Christ. He is in his profession a follower of

---

[2] H. A. Ironside, *The Eternal Security of the Believer* (New York: Loizeaux Brothers, Inc., 1934), pp. 47, 48.

[3] Arno C. Gaebelein, "Question Box," *Our Hope*, Vol. XLIV, No. 9, 1938, p. 63.

Christ, a separated one and also a branch in the vine. But while his profession in church membership indicates all this, in reality this person is only nominally a follower of Christ, only nominally a branch in the vine, only nominally identified with Christ. He has not the reality of it, he does not possess what he has taken upon himself in profession, for he was never born again. As a result there is no fruit, because there is no life. . . . That there are thousands upon thousands of such branches, dead and unfruitful in the professing church, does not need any demonstration. It is only too evident. Such will be taken away in judgment. But the real branches are purged (or cleansed) by the Father, to bring forth more fruit. The evidence of being a living branch in the vine is the fruitage. [4]

Now we will turn to the next reason why we believe the unfruitful branch represents one who only professes and not one who possesses salvation.

Only the saved are cleansed. Here the point is to compare John 13:10, 11 with 15:2b, 3. In chapter thirteen, Christ emphasizes a direct contrast between the *eleven* who are surely saved or chosen (v. 18) and *Judas* who is not saved. He speaks of the eleven as "clean" (Gr. *katharoi*), but in a direct way excludes Judas, a professing but not a genuine believer. Then, in 15:3, He teaches that "ye" (the eleven are "clean" *(katharoi* again). He must mean that they are clean in the sense that they have been justified by faith. This explains why the Father goes on to cleanse them in a different sense — sanctifying them by faith (v. 2b). The clear-cut contrast in verse two suggests that the branch which is *removed* is in a different category from the branch which is *improved* by cleansing. The contrast in 13:10, 11 is evidently the contrast here also. The principle of interpretation is this: Christ's differentiation in the clear passage (chap. 13) provides a background that defines His contrast when a little later He uses the same terms in a verse that is not as clear. Judas is not cleansed, but the eleven are; the branch with no fruit is not said to be clean, but the eleven disciples are.

[4] *Ibid., The Gospel of John* (New York: Publication Office, *Our Hope,* 1936), pp. 296, 297.

Some resist this truth by reasoning that Judas himself was once saved but afterward rejected salvation. Therefore, they say, the branch in 15:2a could represent a person once saved but now lost. However, upon careful consideration, verses generally counted on to teach that Judas was at first saved do not teach this. John 17:12 is sometimes cited to show that Judas must have been saved once because the Father had given him to Christ. Our Lord says, "those that thou gavest me I have kept, and none of them is lost, but the son of perdition." What the verse actually is saying is this: "Those that thou gavest me I have kept, and none of them perished. But (by contrast) the son of perdition did perish." The word "but" or "except" (Gr. *ei mē*) is used in an abbreviated expression, as in Matthew 12:4 and Luke 4:26, 27. For example, in Matthew 12:4 the consecrated bread in the tabernacle was not for David or those with him, "except" for the priests. This does not mean that the priests were among those with David. It means that the bread was not for David or those with him, but it was for the priests serving in the tabernacle. In John 17:12 Judas is in a category different from the eleven, just as in John 13:10, 11. The same is true in John 6:70 where Christ says, "Have not I chosen you twelve and one of you is a devil?" Judas, though chosen as one of the apostles, was not chosen to salvation (John 13:18). He never was a genuine disciple, and Christ knew that all along. John says in 12:6 that Judas was a thief. Judas, at heart, was evidently the type of person to whom Christ referred in Matthew 7:22, 23. Many will claim that in His name they have prophesied, cast out demons, and done many wonderful works. Yet the Lord will say to them finally: "I never knew you: depart from me, ye that work iniquity." He will not say, "I *once* knew you, but *now* I do not," but, "I *never* knew you," never at any time in the past, despite what might be argued to the contrary. It comes down to a matter of reality, and Judas never had real salvation to lose.

The point here stands. The branch without fruit represents a person who has only a nominal relationship with Christ, and Judas in the context is an example.

The taking away means judgment upon an unsaved man.
The point here focuses upon the fact that the Father
"takes away" (Gr. *airei*) the unfruitful branch. The word
is from the root verb *airo*, which the New Testament uses
more than a hundred times. A proper interpretation depends upon what the word itself can mean and what is
most likely its meaning in the connection here. Some say
that this passage means that the Father graciously "lifts up"
a believer who is weak and fruitless to help him on toward
beginning to bear fruit. It is true that *airo* often does mean
"to lift up." (We will consider this idea at length in chapter
seventeen.) However, most expositors, whether regarding
the unfruitful branch as representative of a saved or an unsaved person, prefer the translation "he takes away."

In the lexicons, the verb often has the thought of *removal.*
There are vivid examples in the New Testament and in
the Greek translation of the Old Testament (Septuagint).
A man takes away another's cloak (Luke 6:29); a stronger
man overpowers a strong man and takes his weapons from
him (Luke 11:22); a member of a local church is removed
or excommunicated for immorality (1 Cor. 5:2); a man is
taken away in death (Matt. 24:39; John 19:15); the devil
takes away the Word of God sown in a person's life (Luke
8:12, 18); our "certificate of debt consisting of decrees" is
taken away by Christ (Col. 2:14 NASB) who is the Lamb
of God that takes away the sins of the world (John 1:29);
members of the bodies belonging to Christ are taken away
from one sphere — sanctification — and devoted to sinful
use in another sphere — immorality with a harlot (1 Cor.
6:15); Jacob told his household to put away other gods
(Gen. 35:2); the Lord denounces the wicked, who take
away the rights of those who are in the right (Isa. 5:23);
the dominion of Christ in His Kingdom shall not be taken
away (Dan. 7:14); saved persons are not generally taken
out of this world by God but left here to serve Him (John
17:15). There are many other examples. Liddell and Scott
also point out an extrabiblical source in which the word
is used of clearing away dinner. [5]

[5] Henry G. Liddell and Robert Scott, *A Greek-English Lexicon,* new ed.
revised by H. S. Jones (Oxford: The Clarendon Press, 1940), p. 27.

Some link the removal idea with the claim that the unfruitful person is saved. They believe that Christ means a believer is taken home to heaven early, and they point to cases in which God took men away in death. Sometimes these were saved men. He took unbelievers, as the ungodly of Noah's day, the firstborn of Egypt, the forces of Pharaoh at the Red Sea, those destroyed by fiery serpents (Num. 21:4-9), those in the plague at Midian (Num. 25), and many more. But He also judged believers; e.g., Moses (Deut. 34), who disobeyed Him in striking the rock in Horeb and was removed before Israel entered Canaan (Num. 20); and Samson, who, though a man of faith (Heb. 11:32), nevertheless wasted much of his life in unfruitful compromise and was finally put to death when he might yet have had many good years (Judg. 13 - 16). A prime New Testament example involves those who sin at the Lord's table and are judged, resulting in weakness, sickness, and death (1 Cor. 11:30, 31).

It is true that these are good examples to show that God sometimes takes away the saved. But still it is more likely that in this specific passage the unfruitful branch represents an unsaved person. Why is this so? First, the specific imagery of the vine has an Old Testament background. The vine which God removed and burned with fire was largely an *unsaved* Israelite nation (Isa. 5:1-7, 24; Ps. 80: 16; Ezek. 15). It is more likely, then, that in a similar picture of removal and burning (John 15:2a, 6) those judged are unsaved. [6] Second, it is more fitting to relate the words

[6] Some would question using the figure of *corporate* Israel being removed as evidence that an *individual* branch in John 15 which is removed is likely referring to an unsaved person. But the point seems to be valid. We have shown earlier that the Old Testament vine is the background for Christ's allegory. The vine that was judged in the Old Testament was predominantly made up of unsaved people in the particular generation living at the time of judgment. Though some righteous persons (part of a godly remnant) suffered death (Ezek. 21:3, 4), exile (Dan. 1), or scattering (Jer. 43 - 45) along with the wicked, this does not erase the fact that the calamity was brought on by widespread and rampant disobedience. Had God's indignation not been trifled with more and more until judgment was absolutely inevitable, He would not have broken off the branches of the vine and burned it. The breaking and burning in the Old Testament are said to be because of the sin of the ungodly (Isa. 5:24; Jer. 11:17; Hosea 10:1, context). While the righteous often suffer like-

"takes away" to similar horticultural imagery in the olive tree illustration of Romans 11:16-24 than to passages where no such specific picture is in view. In Paul's analogy of the tree, Israelites with only an *external* connection (opportunity of a privileged relationship to God in the Abrahamic Covenant of Genesis 12:1-3) but with no true, inner union, are branches depicted as having been removed (Rom. 11: 17, 19, 20). If they were broken off, and yet a saved person cannot lose his salvation, then it is apparent that their previous contact in the place of blessing must be understood in some way other than in a vital, saving sense. As McClain says:

> Abraham is the root, for through him and his seed the favor of God has flowed into the world. The natural branches are Jewish, because "salvation is of the Jews." But on account of unbelief certain of the natural branches were broken out, and wild Gentile branches were grafted in. This does not mean that all Jewish branches were saved. As a matter of fact, they were not saved, or they would not have been broken out. But it does mean that during the present age the Gentile is enjoying a place of favor which properly belongs to the Jew. [7]

The fact is that in this place of privilege those with true faith persevere (they stand by faith, v. 20), while those possessed by unbelief do not. Continuance by genuine faith is a mark of those really saved, as in Colossians 1:23, where it is assumed that they will continue. Salvation,

wise in a physical devastation that touches all in general as a fire sweeps through the green and the dry (Ezek. 20:47), the judgment is not basically against them. Also, main New Testament passages that use Israel as a corporate example of ungodliness leave the impression that the Israelites were predominantly unsaved (Heb. 3:14-19; Jude 5-7). It is true that Israel as a people with continuity through the centuries may be described as once relatively pure, centuries later degenerated (Isa. 1:21; Jer. 2:21; Ezek. 16; Hosea 10:1), but destined yet to be fruitful again in Messianic times (Hosea 14). Yet the generation at the time the vine was judged was, as a whole, enmeshed in gross wickedness. And, for that matter, even the Israelites living in the Egyptian sojourn were rather widely polluted with sin, according to some descriptions in Scripture (Ezek. 23:3; 1 Sam. 8:8). Therefore, in view of the predominantly unsaved condition of Israel, the vine that God burned, it is legitimate to say that Christ could be speaking of an unfruitful branch as representing an unsaved person.

[7] Alva J. McClain, *The Jewish Problem and the Divine Solution* (Winona Lake, Indiana: The Brethren Missionary Herald Company, 1944), p. 26.

then, finally is involved in this picture of the place of privilege or blessing.

If what we have said is true in the similar horticultural figure of Romans 11, then the removal of unfruitful branches in John 15:2a can also have in view those who are not really saved.

Third, the unfruitful branch must represent an unsaved person because the removal is in itself a problem for those who hold the view that this branch represents the believer. While it is true that a saved person may be taken to heaven in discipline as in 1 Corinthians 11:30, 31, he is not removed from Christ the Vine but still is in union with Him. It is difficult to conceive of our Lord as using this picture of clear-cut removal from the vine if He had a saved man in view.

The question of *when* the Father takes away the unfruitful person is to receive consideration later in a discussion of verse six, which is closely related to the first part of verse two in the context.

The meaning of "in me." This is a very crucial point. Arminian writers, believing that we may forfeit salvation, and many Calvinists, not believing so (along with all Calvinists), insist that Christ's words "every branch in me" speak only of a vital union. This can be none else but a saved man. So it is easy to see why this is a big point on which some Arminians rely for their doctrine. They like to think they have an argument that is airtight and unanswerable. [8] An Arminian often says, with a ring of finality, "See, he

[8] The Arminian view here includes such sources as: Joseph Benson, *The New Testament of Our Lord and Saviour Jesus Christ, Matthew to the Acts of the Apostles* (New York: T. Carlton and J. Porter, n.d.), 1:633; Adam Clarke, *The New Testament of Our Lord and Saviour Jesus Christ, The Gospels and Acts* (New York: Eaton and Mains, 1884), 5:381, 382; George P. Eckman, *Studies in The Gospel of John* (New York: The Methodist Book Concern, 1907), Part II, pp. 127, 128; C. E. Luthardt, *St. John's Gospel* (Edinburgh: T. & T. Clarke, 1878), 3:145; M. F. Sadler, *The Gospel According to St. John* (London: George Bell & Sons, 1899), p. 369; Robert Shank, *Life in the Son* [the most detailed discussion] (Springfield, Mo.: Westcott Publishers, 1960), pp. 40-48; and John Wesley, in *One Volume New Testament Commentary,* by John Wesley, Adam Clarke, Matthew Henry et al. (Grand Rapids: Baker Book House, 1957), on John 15:5.

was *in* Christ!" Or he insists, "It is self-evident, the natural meaning, all very simple and straightforward." And some Calvinists also emphasize the words "in me," but interpret the Father's removing action as involving a saved person whom He disciplines or else blesses.

A good friend, much used of God in leading people to Christ, came to visit me one day. One of the subjects in the Word that came up was abiding and bearing fruit according to John 15. This provoked a question about the first part of verse two, and he exclaimed with great certainty, "It is talking about a saved man; it has to be!" But on further consideration he decided that he, like many, had drawn this conclusion because of what he thought was sure on the surface, without inquiring very far about the possibilities.

Some Arminians have said to me that no interpreter would entertain any other explanation if he were not hard-pressed to force John 15 into conformity with his theological presuppositions. But this is subjective and may be turned against the Arminian also. He, too, will interpret passages such as John 6:37-40 and 10:27, 28 so as to bring them into conformity with his "theological presuppositions," making sure they come out right. Surely, both the Calvinist and the Arminian may do so in a sincere, honest attempt to harmonize Scripture responsibly. So let us be done with uncharitable words and seek to look at the matter on other bases.

Let it be understood first that the principle of taking words at their face value is generally sound in Bible study. Yet it is subject to frequent problems in verses where other factors show valid cause for a different sense than the meaning that seems to be apparent at the outset. Interpretation is not always cut-and-dried. Even Arminian interpreters often find it necessary, without feeling they are being inconsistent, to explain certain verses with qualifications that allow other factors in the total picture to modify what a statement appears to be saying. For example, problems arise in the strict wording of such verses as these: Genesis 6:6, God repented; Jeremiah 36:30, Jehoiakim had no one to sit on the throne after him, but, in fact, his son

Jehoiachin did reign for three months; Matthew 8:22, allow the dead to bury their own dead; Matthew 27:9, Jeremiah is mentioned as having made a statement, and we must decide in what sense Jeremiah may rightly be considered to have said it; John 5:31, where Christ says, "If I bear witness of myself, my witness is not true"; Acts 19:2, the disciples of John the Baptist at Ephesus say that they have not heard so much as whether there is any Holy Spirit, which sounds at first as though they are not even aware that He exists; and Romans 13:8, "Owe no man anything but to love one another," which could at first be taken as forbidding any time payments. We must explain the *proper sense* in which these statements are true. If we fall back upon the convenient but easily challenged slogan "Take it just as it is," we are not being aware and responsible."

Now let us look first at how one may use the words "in me" to argue that this refers to a saved man. First, he says that "in me" speaks of union as directly and clearly as words can express the idea. Second, he may emphasize that the verse does not speak of every branch that is "supposed to be in the vine, according to the opinion of men," as Calvin and others have filled out the sense interpretively. To add words in this way, he argues, is an unwarranted tampering with the text that does not draw out what it says but imports what our imagination thinks. Third, he can point out that the phrase "in me" always refers, in the gospel of John, to an authentic union (6:56; 10:38; 14:10, 11, 20, 30; 15:4, 5, 6, 7; 17:21 ["in me" and "in us"], 23). So he insists that it must certainly have the same meaning in 15:2. It is not likely that Christ would risk confusing His disciples by shifting to a sense so opposite that it refers to a professor rather than a possessor.

But even in light of the above there must be reasons why many of the great writers on the gospel of John have finally concluded that a professor and not a possessor must be in view, after all. It is essentially in this way that the first part of verse two is explained by Barclay, Barnes, Barrett, Bernard, Calvin, Dods, Erdman, Godet, Grosheide, Hendriksen, Hengstenberg, Hunter, Hutcheson, Jacobus, Lampe, Lange, Macgregor, Maclaren, H. A. W. Meyer,

F. B. Meyer, Morgan, Morris, Andrew Murray, Milligan,
Plummer, Reith, Ryle, Spurgeon, Stott, Tenney, Tholuck,
B. Weiss,[9] and many of the better-known dispensational
writers. Among the latter group are Keith L. Brooks, A. C.
Gaebelein, F. W. Grant, Ironside, Kelly, Strombeck, and
Vine.[10] Of course, a count of heads of such an imposing
number does not in itself prove the view. Yet it is a sobering fact that so many of the most thoroughly capable
scholars and expositors from a wide range of theological
convictions interpret the phrase in this sense. This in itself should beget within a person a spirit of willingness
to rethink the matter with an open mind and a teachable
heart. They may be right after all.

We should clarify that, gramatically, those who hold the
professor view may interpret "in me" in two different ways,
as Godet says.[11] The great majority connect "in me" with
"branch" and read it as "every branch in me that bears not
fruit." But some such as Grosheide and Romaine[12] have
favored linking "in me" with "bears" and translating it as
"every branch that bears no fruit in me." This second
translation clears the way to say that the branch in the
first part of verse two is in some *other* vine. Naturally,
then, such a branch does not and indeed cannot bear fruit

[9] The viewpoints of all these writers are found in their commentaries or
works discussing John 15, except for Spurgeon, whose interpretation appears in a sermon, "A Sharp Knife For the Vine-Branches," in the *Metropolitan Tabernacle Pulpit* (London: Passmore and Alabaster, n.d.), 13:
553-564 (1867); also John R. W. Stott, whose comments are in *Christ
the Liberator* (Downers Grove, Illinois: Inter-Varsity Press, 1971), pp.
53, 54.

[10] These viewpoints appear in the writers' commentaries on John, with
these exceptions: Brooks, *Son of God* (Los Angeles: American Prophetic
League, Inc., n.d.), p. 57; Ironside, *Eternal Security;* J. F. Strombeck,
Shall Never Perish (Chicago: Moody Press, 1966), pp. 118, 119; and W.
E. Vine, *Expository Dictionary of New Testament Words* (London: Oli-
phants Ltd., 1959), 4:106. A very capable, detailed discussion recently
from this viewpoint by a dispensationalist is that of Charles R. Smith, "The
Unfruitful Branches in John 15," *Grace Journal*, Spring, 1963, pp. 3-22.

[11] F. L. Godet, *Commentary on the Gospel of John* (Grand Rapids: Zondervan Publishing House, reprint of 3rd edition, 1893), 2:294.

[12] F. W. Grosheide, *Het Heilig Evangelie Volgens Johannes* (in Kom-
mentaar op het Nieuwe Testament). (Amsterdam, 1950), 11:335; William
Romaine, "A Treatise Upon the Walk of Faith," *The Whole Works of the
Late Reverend William Romaine* (Edinburgh: Tenelson, 1844), p. 287.

in Christ even though it may in certain outward ways *seem* to be in Him. God knows the truth: it actually bears only false fruit in the false vine. By contrast, however, the branch of which Christ speaks in the latter part of verse two really does bear fruit in Him, the Vine, and is in Him. But the second translation, as Hendriksen recognizes, makes the matter too complicated and is evidently not Christ's point.

> If that were the meaning, then besides the branches that bear good fruit there would also be those that do not bear such fruit, and these would again be divided into two categories: a. *some* do not bear good fruit because they belong to a different vine; *others*, because they do not remain in the vine, Christ. Verses 4 and 6 seem to teach clearly enough that the reason (the *only* reason as far as this allegory is concerned) why some branches do not bear fruit is that they do not *remain* in *the* vine (Christ). [13]

There is also another reason for rejecting the view just mentioned. "In me," in John's writings, always refers to a person being in another person. Therefore, it is better to understand the first translation as the sense Christ intended, though scholars favoring both translations agree on our main point that He was speaking of a professor who is not a possessor.

What evidence, then, shows that Christ is referring to a person without genuine salvation?

First, a man could in one sense be of Israel and yet in another sense not be of Israel (Rom. 9:6-8; cf. 2:28, 29). Since Israel as the vine (Isa. 5) is the background for the allegory here, this consideration is relevant. A man could in one sense be in Christ the Vine and yet in a deeper and more determinative sense not be in Him. The Israelites illustrate the principle. They might be Jews outwardly but not Jews inwardly; they might be in Israel and yet not in Israel; they might be circumcised by the outward rite but not circumcised within the heart and spirit (Rom. 2:28, 29; cf. Deut. 10:16). They were not of Israel in the more profound, qualified sense. They did not constitute spiritual

---

[13] William Hendriksen, *The Gospel of John* (Grand Rapids: Baker Book House, 1953), pp. 298, 299.

seed whom God acknowledged as walking in the vital, by-faith reality of Abraham, and so they were not truly saved. Since it is plain that there are two different senses of being a Jew or an Israelite, it is also possible that Christ saw two different classes of men professing to be "in me."

Second, Christ Himself recognizes that there is a type of person who may profess for a time to be related to Him and "seem to have" but not actually have spiritual reality (Luke 8:18). What he seems to have for a time, and which men without God's unerring discernment are ready to credit him with having because of his profession, is not at any time a real, saving relationship. Christ and His apostles teach the sobering fact that one's *profession* of a saving relation to Christ must be subject to spiritual inventory. It may be suspect and even spurious. In the parable of the soils, the four soils on which the seed fell represent categories of men who hear the Word. Christ distinguishes between the fourth class which was fruitful and the three classes which were unfruitful. The three, though differing in experience, are alike in that none are really saved.

Third, as stated earlier, one could be *in* the olive tree and yet not be saved (Rom. 11:16-24). There were Israelites in that tree whom Paul regards as being at one time branches (to serve the illustration). Yet they were broken off because of unbelief. Their in-out relationship does not mean that they once were saved but then lost that salvation. It simply denotes that they were "in" only in the apparent sense, not in the vital sense. Now, since this is true in Romans 11, it may also be true in John 15:2a where the illustration is similar.

Fourth, the Bible can use terms in different senses in different passages. For example, when Peter says that heretical teachers deny the Lord who "redeemed" them (2 Peter 2:1), he uses the Greek word *agorazō*, to buy or redeem. But he does not mean that redemption has been actually applied to these false teachers in the sense that they are saved. He means, rather, that the Lord redeemed them in the sense that He rendered them "savable" by paying the price for a salvation that is available to them. Exactly the same word used for saved men is used for them, but because of other details in the context we are wise to relate the word to them in a different way. There are many places in Scripture where the true meaning is not what the literal wording of a particular phrase might at first seem to suggest.

Fifth, the apostles often show that one may be long thought of as a Christian among Christians and yet all the while have only a superficial relationship with Christ, empty of actual salvation. So is the teaching of Paul (2 Cor. 13:5) and John (1 John 2:19). John recognizes that what one "says" (professes) about knowing Christ in reality may be subject to question or repudiation if his life does not manifest the fruit of obedience to what Christ taught (1 John 2:4). He clarifies that one who "says" he abides in Christ ought to walk as Christ walked (2:6). James, too, speaks of a man who "says" he has faith but has no works, and he asks, "Can that faith (the definite article before "faith" particularizes the faith as the one he professes to have) save him?" (James 2:14 NASB). He shows in the context that it cannot, for it is spurious and not genuine faith, after all.

Evidently the early fellowships of Christians had the same problem we face today in the mixing of the mere professors with the true possessors of salvation. In practical terms, a man's true colors were not always immediately apparent, just as now. If one mingles with Christians, claiming with the usual phraseology to be one of them and going through many of the same activities, others in the fellowship charitably credit him with being what he says he is. Often, however, time will tell. Its pressures and situations cause the governing force of the life to emerge. Then as well as now (for John's words are just as relevant to our situation), Christians would have to confess: "We thought they were Christians, but they went out that it might be manifest that they really were not. How wrong we were about them!"

Sixth, the context of John 15:2a favors the professor view. In what way? The sharp contrast between 15:2a and 2b, 3, in view of the clear statement in 13:10, 11, shows the professor-possessor distinction. Also, there is the categorical type of black-white contrast which John consistently uses when he has in view a saved-unsaved situation. There is the example of the abiding man and the nonabiding man, to be discussed at length later. Then there are a number of reasons for explaining verse six as referring to an unsaved person and then relating this to the first part of verse two in the context.

Seventh, this view is really in harmony with the way John uses the words "in me" elsewhere. This point, of course, is crucial. It is acknowledged that the phrase refers to a vital relationship with Christ. But it is possible for our Lord to use it here even to include professors. In such a case He uses "in me," not of what He Himself knows absolutely to be the branch's real status but from the standpoint of that branch (person) and other men among whom this allegory must become meaningful in practical church situations. Professors only seem (or profess) to have the real union. In giving His illustration of a vine, it is natural for Him to refer to such branches as being "in" the vine, in contact, though only apparently. Christ Himself knows unerringly the ones to whom this apparent relationship is authentic and the ones to whom it is not. Believers view all who profess this relationship as having it, unless they have God-given discernment rather immediately (cf. Peter in the case of Simon in Acts 8) or detect phoniness later on.

But there are still other considerations which make it clear that the branch in 15:2a represents only a professor.

John emphasizes two groups, not three. It is a feature in John's writings to state truth in exclusive terms. He chooses blacks and whites and looks at the broad sweep without going into the question of categories that lie between. He refers to the general, overall characteristic bent of a person's life that marks him as belonging either in one exclusive group or in the other. It is only after thinking carefully through his tendencies in using words and setting up contrasts that we become sensitive to this trait in his style. We become impressed, for example, with the sharp distinctions between the saved and unsaved in his writings. When he is writing or giving us the words of Christ, he usually has these two groups before him and not the three or four or more we list today, including the unsaved, the spiritual Christian, and the carnal Christian. Paul specifically distinguishes three and quite plausibly even four types in 1 Corinthians 2:12 - 3:4: the natural man (and there are different types here), the spiritual man, the carnal Christian who was only recently converted, and the carnal Christian who has been saved for some time but is *yet* carnal and wilfully so. But John's classifications are broader, as in these examples:

TEXT	SAVED	UNSAVED
3:18	he that believeth	he that believeth not
3:20, 21	he that doeth truth	(he) that doeth evil
3:36	he that believeth on the Son	he that believeth not the Son
4:13, 14	Whosoever drinketh of the water that I shall give him shall never thirst.	Whosoever drinketh of this water shall thirst again.
5:29	they that have done good	they that have done evil
6:53, 54	Whoso eateth my flesh, and drinketh my blood, hath eternal life.	Except ye eat the flesh of the Son of man, and drink his blood, ye have no life in you.
8:31	If ye continue in my word, then ye are my disciples indeed.	If ye do not continue, ye are not my disciples (implied).
10:27	My sheep hear my voice . . . and they follow me.	Those who are not my sheep do not hear and follow me (implied).
12:23-26	If (a grain of wheat) die, it bringeth forth much fruit. . . . He that hateth his life in this world shall keep it unto life eternal.	Unless a grain of wheat . . . dies, it remains alone. . . . He who loves his life loses it (RSV).
13:10, 11	Ye are clean,	but not all (i.e., Judas Iscariot was not clean).
14:21, 22	He that hath my commandments, and keepeth them . . . I will love him, and will manifest myself to him.	He who is of the world (v. 22) does not keep my commandments nor love me, and I do not love him (in the sense meant here) and manifest myself to him (implied).

The contrast we usually see, significantly, is not between two classifications of truly saved men, the spiritual and the carnal. Rather, it is between believer and unbeliever, saved and unsaved. It is true, of course, that when Christ introduces the vine illustration He has in view at this particular time only the sphere of profession. That is, He excludes from the field of consideration, at the moment, the vast host of the unsaved, those of the world who make no profession at all to be in Him, who even persecute Him (15:18-25). And He does not include here those who are outright followers of some faith other than Christianity. We could, of course, make three, four, or many more groups, but at least three. But even here, Christ's contrast as John gives it is still between the genuinely saved and those who profess to be but actually are not so, as is evident in that they bear no fruit. In John's way of putting things, the one who walks in the light following Christ is the genuine believer, whereas the one who walks in darkness is not saved (8:12; cf. also 1 John 1:6, 7). With this persistent pattern in view from the larger framework of the gospel of John, it is fitting to understand the contrast in 15:2 to be that of a mere professor and a possessor. And this relates to the next point.

John's present tenses characterize men. In Jesus' statement "every branch in me not bearing fruit. . .," the word "bearing" (Gr. *pheron*) is a present-tense participle. It is possible to view it as what Greek grammar labels an adjectival participle in its ascriptive use. This simply means that the word "bearing" functions as an adjective and, with the word "not," ascribes to the "branch," which it modifies, the *quality* or *characteristic* of bearing no fruit. Christ's thought would then be that it is a characteristic pattern or persistent habit of this type of branch not to yield fruit.

But it also makes sense to understand the participle "bearing" as expressing a verbal idea. As such, it could be *causal* in its idea: "because it is not bearing fruit (that is, under conditions brought out in the context)"; or as *conditional:* "if it is not bearing fruit"; or as *temporal:* "when it is not bearing fruit." In any of these senses, however, the present tense would still reflect what is habitually or characteristically true of the branch.

Some understand the present tense here as meaning no more than that the branch is not bearing fruit *right now*, "at a given time." [14] This leaves the possibility that it may have borne fruit at some time in the past, but now has not done so for some years, months, weeks, days, or hours. This is said in the conviction that the person referred to is saved, though carnal or, in the usual terminology, "out of fellowship," just at this precise time in question. In their reasoning this makes sense when we realize that almost every child of God may bear no fruit at one time or another — even many times. In response to this view, we acknowledge that the saved do certainly have their "ups and downs," and the downs may be very sad ones. The Bible tells us of Abraham's lying (Gen. 20), David's committing adultery (2 Sam. 11, 12), Jonah's pouting (Jonah 4), Peter's denying Jesus three times (Luke 22:54-62), and John Mark's deserting Paul (Acts 13:13; 15:37, 38). But is Christ at this point addressing Himself to *this particular problem* in the life of a saved man? Those who say He is also usually believe the passage teaches that God takes the believer away to heaven early, though there are other views also, which will be considered later. But this explanation has difficulty, among other things, with the obstinate word "every." Neither the Bible nor experience indicates that God removes *every* child of His who is not right now bearing fruit. Certainly He does take some (1 Cor. 11:30, 31). But the word "every" *is* true in the case of professors who never trust Christ genuinely. The Father will take away every one of these absolutely, in His own time.

It is best, then, to explain the words "not bearing" as speaking of what is the characteristic of the person in his life-thrust generally. The focus is not simply upon one week, day, or hour of his life. Christ's concept here is like that in His present tense verb "followeth" in 8:12. It is the same as John's present tenses for the one who "keeps" or "does not keep" His commandments, or who "practices

[14] Lewis S. Chafer, *Systematic Theology* (Dallas, Texas: Dallas Seminary Press, 1953), 7:4.

righteousness," where his contrast is between saved and
unsaved and the rule, norm, or pattern of the life is in
view (1 John 2:29; 3:23; 5:2, 3; et al.). When John writes
of a person who "commits sin" (1 John 3:4-10; 5:18), he
is talking about one whose life as a whole has been shaped
by sin. Paul, likewise, states his conviction that a comprehensive pattern in a life shows up its real character. If one
is characterized by a habitual practice of sin, he warns that
the person will not inherit the kingdom of God (1 Cor. 6:9,
10; Gal. 5:21; 6:8; Eph. 5:5, 6).

But there is one other factor in John 15 which suggests that
the branch without fruit represents a person not really saved.

Fruit bearing demonstrates genuine discipleship.   Christ
tells us that in bearing much fruit men who claim adherence
actually prove to be His disciples (John 15:8). The word
"disciple" does not distinguish a special, spiritual, or committed type of saved man from an unspiritual saved man,
but refers to any saved man. A man's bearing of fruit does
not in any degree *save* him or *make* him a disciple, yet the
presence or absence of fruit does *manifest* the nature of his
professed allegiance to Christ, whether he is a true disciple
or a phony. Judas Iscariot, who was said to be a "disciple"
but was actually unsaved all the time (John 6:70; 12:4),
was never a fruit bearer.

"Disciple," meaning basically a learner or follower of another's teachings (as John also had disciples, John 3:25),
has a rather wide range of references in the New Testament.
When referring to disciples of Christ, it can mean: (1) Any
or all of His twelve disciples (Matt. 10:1; 21:1); (2) some
individual even outside the twelve, as Joseph of Arimathaea
(John 19:38) or Ananias (Acts 9:10); (3) a wider band of
disciples than the twelve, such as the one hundred and
twenty (Acts 1:15); (4) any *apparent* follower of Christ,
though he might later prove not to have been genuinely
saved and persevering (John 6:66).

It does not appear satisfactory to make the distinction
some make in which a disciple is a saved man who is
committed, as opposed to a saved man who is not a disciple
but carnal. "Disciple" is another word that speaks of what

a truly saved person is. There are, however, varying degrees of faithfulness as a disciple and even inconsistencies or sinful failures when a disciple does not act like a disciple. Think, for example, of the twelve disciples selfishly bickering over who were to have the highest positions in Christ's kingdom (Luke 22:24-30). Yet disciples do not suddenly become nondisciples. There are differences in depth, richness, and intimacy of discipleship just as there are differences in abiding, following, keeping the commandments, mortifying the flesh, serving, looking for Christ's appearing, etc. It is not that one becomes a disciple in order to gain salvation in any sense by merit or works; it is simply that when one is really saved by grace through faith, he is a true disciple of Christ. Discipleship, among many other things like servanthood or following, is what a saved man has entered into, the life upon which he has embarked.

That "disciple" is meant to designate any saved person is shown by several considerations. First, in the early church "disciple" came to be equated with any Christian in general (Acts 11:26; cf. also 6:1, 2, 7; 14:20, 22, 28; 15:10). So in the Great Commission the verb "disciple," or "'disciplize,'" speaks of what is to be done to every convert or Christian (Matt. 28:19). Second, John 12:25 gives a point-blank contrast between an unsaved person (he who loves his life loses it) and a saved person (he who hates his life in this world shall keep it to life eternal). This same contrast is in view in Luke 14:26, 27, which speaks of discipleship (cf. also Luke 18:22), and John must intend the same categories as Luke. Here, the principle of interpretation is that a clear passage helps to show the real idea intended in one that may seem unclear. Matthew 10:37-39 is a parallel passage whose context clearly emphasizes the *unsaved* person (v. 33). Other statements there, worded similarly to those in Luke 14:26, 27, must also refer to a person not truly saved, not simply to one who is saved but carnal. Luke 9:23-26 also bears this out. Third, Christ clearly teaches that abiding (perseverance) in His Word is a mark of genuine discipleship (John 8:31). Here, *abiding* is an evidence that one is authentically a disciple, just as *love* is an indication in John 13:35 and *fruit* in 15:8.

In the light of the implication in the word "disciple," it seems best to conclude that the person without fruit in John 15:2a is not really saved, not actually a disciple in truth. This line of consideration fits with all the others of this chapter in pointing to the conclusion that Christ was speaking of one who merely professes and not of one who possesses a real relationship with Himself.

THE MAN WHO DOES NOT ABIDE

If any man abide not in me he is
cast forth as a branch (John 15:6a).

It is not simply the *positive* matter of abiding and bearing fruit that our Lord emphasizes. He also sounds a negative note throughout this allegory. This He develops more in the vivid detail of verse six. "If any man abide not in me, he is cast forth as a branch and is withered; and they gather them, and cast them into the fire, and it is burned" (literal translation).

Whatever is our interpretation of the unfruitful branch in verse two, we must relate verse six to it in some way that is consistent. Some distinguish the two verses so that they do not refer to the same type of person, but most expositors unite them. It is convenient to chart the six basic ways this writer has seen for relating the two verses.

VERSE 2a	VERSE 6
(1) saved but carnal	(1) same
(2) saved but carnal	(2) professing but unsaved
(3) saved but carnal	(3) not even professing
(4) professing but unsaved	(4) saved but carnal
(5) professing but unsaved	(5) not even professing
(6) professing but unsaved	(6) same

In views (3) and (5) on verse six, the man could be *any* person who does not abide in Christ, for what is said is true of all who do not experience His life, within or outside the realm of profession. It is possible, however, to hold that Christ basically had number (6) in mind, with the sphere of profession included. But the same principle would also apply in essence to the wider group of *all* the unsaved. They, like the branch apart from living contact, are dead.

The explanation preferred here is (6) qualified so as also to see the application of (3) and (5) in verse six to all outside the life of Christ. In effect, then, it is a combination, recognizing that verse six can refer to the same man as indicated in the first part of verse two but can also be even wider in application. The discussion that now follows will develop the connection of the two verses along these lines. As we think back to the preceding chapter, where the focus was on the first part of verse two, the logic is this: if verses two and six basically refer to the same type of person, then, of course, verse six is directly relevant in explaining with more detail the meaning of verse two.

First we will look at the connection between the two verses. Later, it will be our purpose to consider the meaning of each separate part of verse six.

The connection with verse two. Several factors show that it is best to connect the verses.

(1) Natural flow of the context. Most students unite the two as speaking of the same type of person because of the natural sequence of thought in Christ's illustration. Verses four to six evidently expand the same basic contrast we see in the whole of verse two, which has application both to the saved and the unsaved. In both verses two and six, Christ is explaining what happens to a branch that bears no fruit. Note the comparison:

VERSE 2a	VERSE 6
General statement: The Father takes the branch away.	Specific statement: The Father takes the branch away (e.g., by means of angels).
Branch not bearing fruit; obviously it is not abiding.	Branch not abiding; obviously it is not bearing fruit.

Though the concentration of the two verses is not exactly the same, they supplement each other by looking at two closely related, but different, sides of one total picture.

(2) Common emphasis upon removal. In verse two, the Father removes the branch, while in verse six the branch is removed *and* is described in terms of what happens when a branch is removed from a natural vine. When two verses so close together in the same allegory emphasize the same point (removal) about a branch that is unfruitful, it is strained and unnatural to say they picture two different types of people. The burden of proof is on those who want to differentiate.

(3) Common emphasis on one who is without true union. Some propose that the first part of verse two speaks of a person who is saved though not bearing fruit, but that verse six speaks of a person who is unsaved. In line with this, one suggestion is that we could write over the former the words "in me" (authentic union) and over the latter the words "not in me" (only apparent union, now severed). But this seems rather arbitrary and artificial when we see the implications of the passage. More naturally, the two verses relate to the same type of person basically. Verse two speaks of a man who bears no fruit and so must not be an abiding man according to verses four and five. His "in me" relationship to Christ is only seemingly valid for reasons already shown. Verse six conceives of a man who does not abide in Christ, and who therefore has no true union and no fruit. Again, it is more likely that two verses so close together, having complementary lines of emphasis, are telling us about the same kind of person.

(4) Common relation to background passages. In the Old Testament imagery of a vine, which forms a background to help us interpret Christ's picture here, the persons who bear no fruit (as in v. 2a) are the same persons later removed in judgment or burned (as in v. 6; cf. Isa. 5:1-7, 24; Ps. 80:16; Ezek. 15; cf. Jer. 11:16).

For the reasons given above, then, it is best to relate the first part of verse two and verse six as having in view the same type of person.

The meaning of verse six. It will help to summarize at the outset what Christ means, then examine various details of the verse to show that the explanation is correct.

Christ, more likely having in view the sphere of those who make some profession of union as in the context (vv. 2-5), speaks of a person whose characteristic pattern of life is that of not abiding in Him. He has never been really saved, whatever his seeming relation to the Lord at any time outwardly. He lives apart from life in Christ (he is cast forth) and withers in a process throughout life on earth until the final corruption of physical death comes. After this, he will be gathered with other unsaved people by God's angels at the future judgment and cast into the "lake of fire."

Now we are ready for the details.

(1) *The man does not abide.* Earlier we showed that when the word "abide" occurs in its spiritual sense in John's writings, it refers to a continuing relationship of intimacy. It characterizes a person and indicates that he possesses or does not possess genuine life in Christ. The person who does not abide in Christ (the life pattern being in view) is not really saved. This is put solidly beyond doubt by other examples John furnishes. Let us look at some of these.

His use of the word "abide" in John 6:54-56 helps clarify the meaning. Christ, who is the bread of life for men, says, "He that eateth my flesh, and drinketh my blood, dwelleth in me, and I in him" (v. 56). Our Lord has perfect discernment and knows the person who truly eats, drinks, and abides, and the one who does not. But He is clear, in His own terms of limitation, that it is the person who abides who is actually saved. It is he who (a) has eternal life and (b) will be raised up at the last day to share ultimate life in Christ (v. 54). The one who, according to John 15:6, does not abide, is a person who, in Christ's words about abiding, does not "eat my flesh and drink my blood" and therefore does not have eternal life and will not be raised up among the righteous at the last day. In the more immediate context, he is the type of man in whom Christ's *words* are not abiding (15:7).

John shows in other black-white descriptions that one's abiding in the word or having it abiding in him is closely associated with the reality of salvation (5:38; 8:31; 15:8; 1 John 2:14; 3:24; 2 John 2, 9). The John 8:31 passage links a person's abiding in the word with the genuineness of his alleged discipleship. The statement of 1 John 2:14 vitally associates abiding in the word with overcoming the evil one — Satan. This is significant in the light of John's customary way of putting matters. To him, the overcomer (that is, the person who receives this designation because it is his overall, general life-style) is the one who is truly saved (1 John 4:4; 5:4, 5; Rev. 2:7, 11, 17, 26; 3:5, 12, 21; 21:7). He is not simply a victorious Christian in contrast to one who lives in defeat. Every saved person is an overcomer, by faith. The difference between one saved person and another is in the *measure, degree,* or *extent* of the overcoming.

It is good to state this concept in a way directly relevant to the point of John 15:6. The person John describes as having the word of Christ abiding in him is the saved person. Since the contrast of verses six and seven is directly between the person who abides in Christ (and has Christ's words abiding in him) and the person who does not, the conclusion is hard to avoid. The man who does not abide (v. 6) is not saved. It is just as true here as in 1 John 3: 14b, where it is said that the man who does not abide in love abides in death.

The same basic kind of contrast between the saved and unsaved, using sweeping characterizations, appears in John 12:24-26. "Verily, verily, I say unto you, Except a corn of wheat fall into the ground and die, it abideth alone: but if it die, it bringeth forth much fruit. He that loveth his life shall lose it; and he that hateth his life in this world shall keep it unto life eternal. If any man serve me, let him follow me; and where I am, there shall also my servant be: if any man serve me, him will my Father honour." Mark the contrasts:

UNFRUITFUL (UNSAVED)	FRUITFUL (SAVED)
Does not die.	Does die.
Abides alone (just himself, with no fruit).	Brings forth much fruit.
Loves his life in this world.	Hates his life in this world.
Does not serve Christ (implied, v. 26).	Serves Christ.
Does not follow Christ (implied, v. 26).	Follows Christ.
Is not honored by the Father.	Is honored by the Father.
Does not keep his life unto life eternal.	Keeps his life unto life eternal.

The conclusion is evident. The person who is abiding and fruitful is really saved and has eternal life. The man who does not abide and bear fruit is not saved and does not have eternal life.

It must be the mind of Christ, then, to view the man who does not abide (15:6) as actually unsaved. As in other sweeping descriptions when He is summarily contrasting men, our Lord has in view the whole general life of the man who does not abide. He is not speaking of a small segment of his life as though his abiding is only temporary.

(2) *The subject changes from "ye" to "a man (anyone)."* Some writers, such as Grant,[1] have sought to prove too much from Christ's changes in His use of pronouns in these verses. He changes from "ye" (vv. 3-5) to "a man," "he," "them" and "it" (v. 6), and then back to "ye" (vv. 7ff). Grant, referring verse six to judgment upon an unsaved person, says on verse seven:

> The Lord would not have it supposed that it might be possible for those truly His to be thus cast forth and to perish: therefore His altered speech. He returns, immediately now, to His former direct address: "If *ye* abide in Me, . . ."

But when we put this theory to the test, it turns out to be arbitrary.

[1] F. W. Grant, *The Numerical Bible: The Gospels* (New York: Loizeaux Brothers, 1899), 5:588.

First, Christ has switched pronouns twice already before verse six. He refers to the branch in the third person, "it," in verse two, even in the part which definitely speaks of the saved. Yet He comes back to the second person "ye" in verse three. Then, in verse five, He alters His words from "ye" to "he" and "the same," and finally returns again to the second person plural in His words "ye are not able to do anything."

Second, Grant is mistaken in assuming that Christ avoids saying "ye" to the disciples in any warning relating to the unsaved. Grant obviously feels that such a warning would have no relevance at all to saved men. But our Lord does speak in a direct way to His disciples in such a context. For example, He uses "ye" often in Matthew 18 (vv. 3, 8, 35), speaking specifically to the disciples, even when He is warning that a man may miss the kingdom and go into eternal fire instead. Another instance is Matthew 10:31-39, where He switches from the second person plural "ye" (v. 31) to the indefinite "whosoever" (vv. 32, 33), then back to the "ye" (v. 34), then again to the indefinite "a man" (v. 35) and "he" (vv. 37-39). The fact is, then, that Christ does give direct warnings even in the audience of the disciples ("ye").

But how can this be if they are saved by grace through faith and will certainly never fall back into condemnation? The answer is in stressing not only the eternal security of the true saint but also the perseverance of the saint. Those who are truly saved *will* abide, just as they *will* hear the Shepherd's voice and follow Him (John 10:27), and just as they *will* walk in the light (8:12; 1 John 1:5ff). The same kind of truth occurs in the epistles. In Romans 6:16 Paul says that the person who yields to God is a servant "of obedience unto righteousness," but he who yields to sin is a servant "of sin unto death." A life pattern of slavery is in view, either to God or to sin. Romans 6:13 exhorts the believer to do what verse sixteen assumes he will do: "Neither yield ye your members . . . unto sin: but yield yourselves unto God." A person who has eternal life by grace through faith *does* live the kind of life he is exhorted to live. Similarly, those who are really sons of God walk

in and are led by the Holy Spirit (Rom. 8:2-4, 14; Gal. 6:
8), yet they are exhorted to walk this way (Gal. 5:16, 25).
Again, the saved will follow Christ (John 10:27), yet they
are exhorted to "be followers of God" (Eph. 5:1).

We may draw a conclusion to resolve the problem, then.
The warnings and exhortations are there, it is true, but those
who are really Christ's will heed them by faith. True faith
by which men are justified is a living faith that fosters
works, obedience, and perseverance. Men of faith are abiding men; other men are not.

Christ anticipates and assumes that the eleven, and others
like them who do have His life, will manifest the spiritual
trait of living by an orientation which He calls "abiding."
It is inconceivable that one truly sharing Christ's life should
give no valid expression of this in fruit whatever. However,
it is also true on the practical level that we can break
down the general, categorical terms of John's gospel and
epistles and consider fruitfulness during certain specific
periods of time. In this sense, any saved person's experience
in some particular attitude, word, or act may not express
the essence of Christ's fruit-yielding life. In the words of
verse five, it may be "nothing" as opposed to "fruit," which
has eternal value and worthwhileness. This is because the
Christian has, for a time, depended upon himself. He has
tolerated sin in some way rather than relating properly to
Christ. But the present view makes this distinction. Christians do sometimes suffer heartbreaking setbacks in which
they squander away opportunities for "nothing." Nevertheless, they also manifest to *some* distinguishable degree, by
some fruit at *some* point or many points along the way,
the reality of having been "born anew to a living hope"
(1 Peter 1:3).

But there is also a second reason why Christ spoke warnings even to truly saved men. He was preparing them for
a realistic and sensitive ministry among others after He
had departed. All their lives His people will face the hard
fact that the spurious are mingled among the genuine in
the Christian fellowships. Even though they themselves,
in hearing His warnings, may have faith's assurance that
by the grace of God they are personally safe forever from

condemnation, they must emphasize the other side too. They must teach others of the intimate privileges of abiding, but sometimes, in the same breath (like a preacher today!), also relate what is true for the person who does not abide.

(3) *The branch is cast forth.*   There have been various ideas of what the word "cast forth" (Gr. *ekballo)* means here.

Some see in it a picture of excommunication from a local church fellowship. Arndt and Gingrich say it can mean "expel" [2] Ignatius seemed to be referring to this type of action when he wrote: "He . . . that does not assemble with the Church, has even by this manifested his pride, and condemned himself." [3] Moule translates Ignatius' phrase "condemned himself" as "excommunicates himself." [4] In line with this view, Macgregor points to John 9:34 where the same word, *ekballo,* is used to depict the Jews expelling the blind man Christ had healed. They "put him out" (NASB) of their synagogue. [5] Other New Testament usage might also suggest it as a picturesque word for excommunication. It is the term used also for casting out worthless salt (Matt. 5:13; Luke 14:35), bad fish (Matt. 13:48), and fear (1 John 4:18). In Revelation 6:13, the verb used of a tree's casting forth its fruit when it is violently shaken is translated "let fall," a picture similar to the casting forth of a branch in John 15. Another indication that it might mean excommunication comes from the fact that most men who think this is the idea in 15:6 see it also in verse two. And, in verse two, the verb *airo* for "takes away" is the same as in 1 Corinthians 5:2 where excommunication is clearly meant and applied to a professing believer. In

[2] William Arndt and F. W. Gingrich, *A Greek-English Lexicon of the New Testament and Other Early Christian Literature* (Chicago: Chicago Press, 1957), pp. 236, 237.

[3] Cited by C. F. D. Moule, *An Idiom Book of New Testament Greek* (Cambridge, England: University Press, 1953), pp. 12, 13, from Ignatius' *Epistle to the Ephesians,* 5:3.

[4] *Ibid.*

[5] G. H. C. Macgregor, *The Gospel of John* (London: Hodder and Stoughton, 1938), p. 288. Macgregor feels, then, that the word means excommunication here. He cites 1 John 2:19 with the words: "He has proved himself to be in no true sense one of Jesus' 'own' . . . and therefore is excluded from the guarantee that none of Jesus' own shall be lost (6:39, 10:28f.) . . ."

1 Corinthians 5:13, the compound form *ekairo* (*ek* plus *airo*) intensifies the idea.

Others do not believe that Christ is referring to excommunication publicly. He is, they feel, simply giving a graphic description of a believer being estranged from spiritual intimacy with Himself, though he is still saved. The issue is personal abiding in Christ, and when a person ceases to abide, the reality of his being cast forth occurs in the spiritual realm of his relationship with Christ. This, they hold, is true whether men around him know about it at the moment or not. Often, however, discerning believers will either begin to suspect something is amiss or know it with certainty because of his telltale attitudes, words, or actions.

What, then, does the phrase "cast forth" mean? It is possible that the type of person Christ has in view might experience public excommunication at the hands of men, but we cannot limit the casting forth to that alone even if we assume that they are instruments of God in this. Lenski evidently recognized this when he wrote: "The actuality of the divine act is hidden from us, but it usually appears in the outward separation from the church, except in the case of hypocrites who, though outwardly in the church, are no longer of the church." [6] What Christ is describing seems to be true of *any* man who does not abide. If so, there is much possibility that many such persons will not be cast forth by other *men*, even though they do not possess true salvation with their profession. Only God Himself, directly, and not man, is unerring and absolute in such a matter. It is more likely that the "cast forth" relates to that fact which *God* knows about such a man. Whatever his standing may be in the eyes of men in the church group or Christian fellowship, God knows his true status and casts him forth. He has no real, inner abiding relationship with Christ. In fact, if we are correct in saying that his lack of abiding and of fruit shows him to be only a professor, he *never* was in Christ in the genuine sense. As we have seen in relation to verse two, the "in me" union for him was

[6] R. C. H. Lenski, *The Interpretation of St. John's Gospel* (Minneapolis: Augsburg Publishing House, 1943), p. 1038.

only apparent and not actual. For the one who has genuinely come to Christ, the sure promise of Christ is, "I will in no wise cast out" (John 6:37), and that word "cast out" is the same as the word used in 15:6.

Some no doubt will have the problem that a preacher — a friend of mine — expressed. "If he was a branch," he reasoned, "he must have had *greenness* at one time. This means that there was real life there, so he has to be a saved man." It is natural to make this observation, yet it is based upon a misunderstanding. The fact that according to this allegory a person was conceived of as a "branch" at one time does no more indicate that he was a saved man, necessarily, than it does those branches broken off the olive tree (Rom. 11). Few illustrations exactly match spiritual realities in every point of detail. Those who *seem* to be true branches in Christ but are not really so can show forth seeming gifts and graces, and their performances may appear to have the "greenness" of life, as in the case of Judas Iscariot.

The person who is "cast forth" is, by analogy, like a *branch* that is cast forth. This is in the sense that he has no living connection with Christ. His qualifications for any authentic experience of God's life in this nonabiding state are no more promising than those of a branch out of contact.

May he yet be saved? Yes, as long as he lives in the present life, the possibility remains. The branch depicts a man, and a man may yet believe. By faith before physical death he may be joined to Christ, this time in reality, just as branches joined to the olive tree by grafting refer to people who are really saved (Rom. 11:17).

(4) *The branch is withered.* Christ means simply that the branch is "dried up." We must answer two key questions here. First, in the light of verses in Scripture which refer to withering, is it more likely that this branch pictures a saved or an unsaved person? Second, when does the withering take place?

We will look at the first question now. Withering in the Bible is applied to different groups but it predominantly describes the unsaved. All men in the flesh wither like the grass, with age, due to the process of deterioration toward corruption in death because of sin (1 Peter 1:24; Rom. 5: 12). However, since this is true of both the saved and the unsaved, it does not settle the question in verse six. Ezekiel predicted that Israel nationally, pictured as a vine, would wither in the judgment of God upon her people, land, and city in 587/586 B.C., (17:9, 10). The fig tree, representing Israel, withered after Jesus found no fruit on it and cursed it (Matt. 21:19). Neither is this figure helpful since it depicts a *national* withering and, although it is true that most of those in Israel were unsaved, some were saved. Then there is a passage in which withering is shown to be the experience of a saved man (Ps. 102:3, 11). The psalmist, amidst painful suffering because of God's heavy discipline (v. 10), describes his experience in vivid pictures. He is in trouble (v. 2), his bones burned as a hearth (v. 3), his heart withered like grass (v. 4). He is oppressed by an overwhelming aloneness, like a sparrow alone upon a housetop (v. 7), is reproached by enemies (v. 8), weeps (v. 9), his life seems to be declining away, and he is withered like grass (v. 11). Since this is a believer who is withered, one could argue that a believer is the one withered in John 15:6. But still the majority of passages about withering refer to the unsaved (Ps. 37:2; 129:6; cf. 1:3; Isa. 40: 7, 8, 24; Matt. 13:6; possibly James 1:11). One of the most vivid instances is in the teaching of Christ. He tells of seed that fell upon stony soil (depicting a *person* hearing His word), and the plant that sprang up had no root and withered (Matt. 13:6). This is a picture of a person who hears the good news of Christ's word, gets off to a start as a professing believer, but fades out when difficulties come. He does not persevere (vv. 20, 21) as the truly saved person does (Col. 1:23). It is evident that he had no true fruit. The faith he claimed for a time is shown in the long run not to have been genuine.

In biblical description, then, withering can be true of a saved man, but in most cases it relates to the unsaved. Therefore the latter is more likely the idea Christ intended in John 15:6. This meaning, of course, fits with many other evidences that point in the same direction.

The second question asks when the withering occurs. One writer suggests that withering here "may well be taken as a graphic picture of what happens to the unbeliever's body during the period between his death and the resurrection of his body that it may be cast into hell." [7] He evidently means the lake of fire (Rev. 20:11-15). In evaluating this possibility, we observe that withering is never in Scripture likened specifically to the process of physical corruption after death. Also, the body of even the saved man would wither (suffer corruption) physically after his death, whereas the withering in 15:6 appears to be true of only a *specific* type of person. At the same time, however, we might ask: is not physical corruption after death the end of, and part of, that process of withering which is due to sin? That is, would not withering finally come to this? For the unbeliever, physical death would be without remedy, for his lack of abiding in his life before this would be irreversible or irrevocable. Therefore, while it is true that the saved man would also die physically, his future is to be bright in union with Christ forever. The unsaved person's corruption, however, only precipitates him on to an awful destiny. This is described in verse six in the events that follow the fact that he is "withered."

It is admittedly difficult to determine just what the withering represents. In biblical description, unsaved men wither throughout the entire process of life, and the end of that process is reached in physical corruption. But if the withering process of an unsaved person is to be kept distinct from that which is true also of a Christian, it undoubtedly also involves a drying up of his inner life which might have been spiritually oriented with God. Potentially he might have been privileged with knowledge (light) about the life God offers, but actually he never appropriated this in true faith. Even the faculties and perceptions which are his by that grace of God common to all men are withered and lost to usefulness toward God, and this is finally, irrevocably sealed in physical death.

[7] Charles R. Smith, "The Unfruitful Branches in John 15," *Grace Journal,* Spring, 1968, p. 15.

The Greek tenses of the verbs in verse six are important in deciding the meaning, although there are different possibilities from the standpoint of grammar alone. First, the verb "abide" ("if any person abide not") is in the present tense (menē). Certain ancient manuscripts had it in the aorist tense (meinē), as shown by textual footnotes in Greek Testaments. But the present tense is the better attested reading in the evaluation of most textual authorities and is the reading favored here. Either possibility in this case, however, would be consistent with the overall explanation being given to the verse. After this, the aorist tense is used for both the verbs "cast" and "withered," but then there is a change to the present tense for "gather," "cast," and "are burned." The two verbs in the aorist are viewed by many authorities (among whom are Blass and Chamberlain) as examples of the "gnomic aorist," a type of aorist tense that expresses some fact so generally, universally, or timelessly true that it is an axiom. [8] In accordance with this idea here, it is an axiom in natural law that a branch which does not abide in a vine *is* "cast forth" and *does* wither. Analogously, this is also axiomatic in the spiritual sphere for the man who does not abide in Christ. The gnomic idea is possible, but it is a more rare type of aorist usage in the New Testament, where even many of the alleged examples are open to other explanation, according to Moule. [9] Here, the two aorists make good sense if taken simply as emphasizing past acts (a more normal aorist idea), acts which are the consequence of not abiding. The emphasis would be upon the instantaneousness or suddenness of these acts. This could be so with either the usual Greek aorist or even an aorist influenced by Old Testament Hebrew thought. Abbott, an authority on the grammar in John's writings, is inclined toward the Hebraic idea:

> In xv. 6 (lit.) "If a man be not abiding (μένη) in me —
> [behold] *he was cast* (ἐβλήθη) outside . . . and was with-

---

[8] F. W. Blass, *Grammar of New Testament Greek* (London: Macmillan and Co., 1911), p. 194; W. D. Chamberlain, *An Exegetical Grammar of the Greek New Testament* (New York: The Macmillan Company, 1941), pp. 77, 78.

[9] Moule, *New Testament Greek,* pp. 12, 13.

ered," the reader is asked as it were to pause after the statement of the conditional "not abiding." Then he looks back and — the branch "has been cast out." This is not like the Greek instantaneous aorists above mentioned (2443c), *all of which are in the first person*. Probably it springs from Hebrew literature, which regards the sweeping away of things evil as an act of Jehovah so speedy that it is past before there is time to speak of it as future or present: "A thousand years in thy sight *are but as yesterday when it is past, and as a watch in the night. Thou hast carried them away as with a flood*." The most conspicuous instance of this is in Isaiah's prophecy (Is. xl. 6-8 LXX, [lit.]) "All flesh [is as] grass . . . the grass *was dried up* and the flower *fell away* . . . but the word of our God *abideth* for ever," which has been reproduced in the Epistle of St. James with aorists thus, "Like the flower of the grass he shall pass away. For the sun *rose up* (ἀνέτειλεν) with the scorching wind and *dried up* (ἐξήρανεν) the grass and its flower *fell away* and the fair show of its countenance *perished* (ἀπώλετο)." In the light of these passages, and of the above-mentioned (2443) instances of Hebrew influence on Johannine tense construction, ἐβλήθη appears to be a Hebraic, not a Greek, instantaneous aorist. [10]

While Abbott understands the aorists in 15:6 to be instantaneous, he later states concerning "cast forth" that it "may not be Hebraic, though it is in accordance with Hebraic Greek." [11] So it still emphasizes the suddenness of a past act in 15:6, as Moule also believes. [12]

Another possibility in verse six is favored by Meyer and Alford. [13] They conceive of Christ as using what happens to branches to project His thought to a future standpoint in regard to a *person*. Then, looking back upon a life that did not abide, He vividly depicts the consequences, telling what *has* occurred (two aorist tenses) and what *is* trans-

[10] Edwin A. Abbott, *Johannine Grammar* (London: Adam and Charles Black, 1906), p. 327, No. 2445.

[11] *Ibid.*, p. 586, No. 2755.

[12] Moule, *New Testament Greek*, pp. 12, 13.

[13] H. A. W. Meyer, *Critical and Exegetical Hand-Book to the Gospel of John* (New York: Funk & Wagnalls, Publishers, 1884), p. 431; Henry Alford, *The Greek Testament*. Vol. I, The Four Gospels (New York: Harper & Brothers, Publishers, 1859), p. 777.

piring (three present tenses). He is describing the scene from the vantage point of the future judgment when the unsaved will be consigned to their destiny. Meyer writes:

> Jesus places Himself *at the point of time of the excution of the last judgment,* when those who have fallen away from Him are gathered together and cast into the fire, after they have been previously already cast out of His church, and become withered (having completely lost the higher true ζωή [sic., one who thus fell away would never have had the true life to lose; his possession of it would only have been a seeming one]). Hence the graphic lively change of tense: *In case any one shall not have abided in me; he has been cast out like the branch, and is withered* (already before the judgment), and (now what *takes place at the last day itself) they gather them together,* etc. (italics his).

This leads us to ask what the distinction between the two aorists and the three presents would be. Why does the verse switch to the present tenses? One possibility is to view the presents as "aoristic" presents. As such, they would look at the facts as *now* occurring (at one specific point), without describing a process transpiring. Were that the idea, the three present tenses would be much like the two aorists preceding them. However, since there is a change to the present tenses, it would appear better to understand some difference between the tenses that would explain the change. As stated earlier, the aorists could emphasize the instantaneousness with which a branch was cast forth and withered, then the presents could be examples of what Dana and Mantey call the "customary present" tense. [14] Viewed in this way, the three verbs describe what customarily occurs or is reasonably expected to happen to dead branches in a vineyard: "They gather them, and cast (them) into the fire, and it is burned." Our Lord evidently intended what happens to literal branches to picture vividly what finally happens to a man who does not abide in Him.

A word also needs to be said about the "if" aspect in verse six. From the standpoint of Greek grammar, the con-

[14] H. E. Dana and Julius R. Mantey, *A Manual Grammar of the Greek New Testament* (New York: The Macmillan Company, 1958), p. 183, no. 173.

struction could be understood in especially two different ways. Greek students find four and sometimes five types of conditional "if" clauses in the New Testament. A. T. Robertson, seeing four, categorizes John 15:6 as a third-class condition. So the "if" *(ean)* expresses, with the word "abide" in the subjunctive mood, an element of uncertainty but yet expectation that the man in view will not abide. Maybe he will, maybe he will not, but the subjunctive with "not" brings the possibility that he will not into the realm of likelihood. [15] The last part of the verse then tells what is always true in such a case of not abiding. While many (probably most) would explain the construction as a third-class "if," following Robertson, as this writer has been inclined to do, some feel that the phenomena of the verse meet all the specifications of a fifth-class condition. This is the present general condition described by Smyth and by Chase and Phillips. [16] In the present general, "if" *(ean)* appears with a verb in the subjunctive mood, and the last part of the sentence may utilize the present tense indicative or its equivalent. Here, the three present tenses could complete or round out such a condition and, taken as customary present tenses, would fit well with the idea of the present general. This type of construction states a general fact (one always true in the estimation of the one speaking), such as "if Bill Walton plays, UCLA's basketball team wins."

Now let us summarize the essence of Christ's teaching in the first part of verse six. He is referring to a person who is never truly saved and who will be severed from all potential relationship with Him. But, for further consideration of this man's destiny, we go on to the next statement.

(5) *They gather them together.* Christ's word here, *sunago,* means "to gather together." In its noun form, as in our English word "synagogue," it means "a gathering place," such as the Jewish centers of worship. Our Lord

---

[15] A. T. Robertson, *A Grammar of the Greek New Testament in the Light of Historical Research* (Nashville, Tennessee: Broadman Press, 1934), p. 1020.

[16] H. W. Smyth, *Greek Grammar* (Cambridge: Harvard University Press, 1959), p. 528; A. H. Chase and Henry Phillips, Jr., *A New Introduction to Greek* (Cambridge: Harvard University Press, 1962), p. 78.

actually says, ". . . *they* gather," not ". . . *men* gather," as in some translations. He is referring not to men finally but to angels who, as agents fulfilling God's will, are to gather "them" (the unsaved) to consign them to their eternal destiny. We will give reasons for this interpretation shortly.

Who is doing the gathering? In Palestinian vineyards, the gatherers would be *men*, the vinedresser's servants or members of his family. As stated before, Christ says "they," not "men." The word "they" is the translation of the third person plural form of the verbs "gather" (*sunagousin*) and "cast" (*ballousin*). We do not know strictly from the verbs themselves who the "they" refers to. However, the answer is fairly obvious in the imagery, as in Luke 14:35, where the same indefinite "they" occurs in the third person plural of the verb "to cast" (*ballo*): "they cast it out." Both in Luke 14:35 and John 15:6 Christ is speaking of the action taken by those directly involved. Men who have salt that has lost its savor throw it out as worthless; men who work in a vineyard gather dead branches and cast them into a fire. The one passage describes a man as *unfit*, the other looks at him as *unfruitful*. In the spiritual realm, which the pictures of salt and branches illustrate, the identification of "they" can be made only by other considerations. Here, in 15:6, it is best to explain the actions as those of angels and not men. In a debated illustration involving judgment, we are wise if we are sensitive to other illustrations about judgment which are notably similar. These help us to see the correct meaning here. In Matthew 13, Christ Himself pictures *angels* as gathering up tares (representing the unsaved) to separate them from wheat (believers) at the end of the present age (vv. 28-30, 40, 41). Later, in verses forty-nine to fifty, He describes the same fact by visualizing *angels* as gathering good fish (believers) into containers (the kingdom) and discarding bad fish (unbelievers). John the Baptist portrayed the same scene by the figure of a farmer using his winnowing fork to separate the grain into one pile destined for his barn and the chaff into another heap destined to be burned (Matt. 3:10-12). In all of these instances, the idea of judgment is similar to that pictured in John 15:6.

It is also significant that the word "gather" occurs a number of times. In the New Testament, at least three of the verbs which mean "to gather" are used for gathering a harvest. These become vivid figures for gathering men in judgment (*sunago*, Matt. 13:30; *sullego*, Matt. 13:28, 29, 30, 40; *trugao*, Rev. 14:18). Such imagery, applied to men, always elsewhere depicts a gathering of the unsaved for judgment. In view of this, it would seem to be the most evident idea of the gathering in John 15:6 also. At the same time, there is no illustration in the Bible which uses "gather" in relation to the judgment of a saved but carnal person. Nor is it said that *men* gather other men in some type of spiritual judgment. In several places, however, it is clear that *angels* gather men.

One other matter is important to notice before going on. Why does the thought change suddenly from one man ("he") in the first two verbs to the pronoun "them" (Gr. *auta*, third plural)? This is natural because: (1) the plural emphasizes the collective group of which the singular branch (person) is only one representative case; (2) the plural fits with the third person plural verbs "they gather" and "they cast." It is more natural to speak of gathering "them" (a number, in a group) than simply one branch or person.

(6) *They cast them into the fire.* The imagery used here for the disposing of branches is much like that used by Christ when He said that "the grass of the field . . . is cast into the oven" (Matt. 6:30). The reference, as before, is more naturally to unsaved than saved people. Why is this so? First, there are the similar illustrations, already pointed out, where angels cast the unsaved into fire. Second, in close connection with this, there are many other passages which actually speak either of a *place* or a *state* of fire in which the unsaved will be punished (Isa. 30:33; Jer. 7: 31; Matt. 5:22; 18:8, 9; 23:33; 25:41; Mark 9:43, 48; 2 Thess. 1:7, 8; Heb. 10:27; Jude 7; Rev. 20:15). This, of course, is to include those who professed a genuine union with Christ but never in fact possessed it, as well as those who never even made the profession.

Some, we realize, contend that the saved are in view

here. And it is true that the symbol of fire sometimes relates to believers. However, the view we are taking can be held even in light of this. For example, fire graphically depicts the intensity and pain of the believer's sufferings which God uses to purify him (Ps. 66:12; Isa. 43:2; 1 Peter 1:6,7; 4:12). Messiah's purifying of the "sons of Levi" at His second advent to qualify them for a worshipful ministry as priests in the messianic Kingdom is likened to the refining of silver and gold by fire (Mal. 3:2,3). Messiah will also refine a remnant of Israel as they pass through the fire of tribulation before the beginning of His future kingdom on earth (Zech. 13:8,9). But these passages do not appear to be speaking of the same truth that John 15:6 has in view. The preponderance of references to fire as connected with judgment upon the unsaved favors the explanation that this verse also refers to the unsaved.

(7) *It is burned.* The burning, as already shown, is that of the eternal state where the unsaved are. The verb for "burned" here is actually in the singular form: "*it* is burned," not "*they* are burned." This raises a question. Why is there a change in the third person singular verbal suffix ("it") rather than a retention of the third person plural ("they")? There are various explanations. First, a marginal reading of some ancient manuscripts has "they gather it, and cast (it) into the fire, and it is burned," referring to a single branch throughout. But this reading is not as well attested. Second, the change may be resolved with the reading in the Nestle text. The figure involves the burning of vine branches. The process of gathering and throwing would form a *unit* or *pile* of branches which Christ could conceive of in a corporate sense. From this standpoint He could say, "*It* is burned." Third, the singular form of the verb "burned" could be translated, "*They* are burned," since it follows and fits with the word "them" *(auta)*, a neuter plural form. A fourth explanation could be that Christ made the earlier change from the singular "he" to the plural "them" simply to accomodate the plural idea in the words "they gather," then reverted to the previous emphasis upon the *individual* representative branch in question. So He

said, "*It* is burned." In other words, it is burned along with other branches like it.

A dubious interpretation is sometimes proposed by the view that this is the judgment of a carnal Christian. The "it" allegedly refers to *works* (all that is of the flesh-life only, conceived of as a unit) produced by the believer, not the *branch* itself. Such men as Arthur W. Pink, Everett Harrison, and Raymond Saxe argue for the view. Pink sees a change in verse six from "a man" to "them" and feels that "them" refers to works which burn. He says:

> The "them" and the "they" are what *issues from* the one who has been cast forth "as a branch." And *what* is it that issues forth from such a one — what but dead works — "wood, hay, stubble!" And what is to become of his "dead works"? 1 Cor. 3:15 tells us: "If a man's works shall be burned (the very word used in John 15:6), he shall suffer loss, but he himself shall be saved, yet so as by fire." [17]

Harrison, taking this view, says: "Since the subject is the bearing of fruit and not eternal life, the burning is a judgment upon fruitlessness, not an abandonment to eternal destruction. The branch is the potential of possible fruit-bearing, not the person himself. It speaks here of unfruitful works (cf. 1 Cor. 3:15)." [18] A Christian worker looked at John 15:6 and exclaimed in my hearing: "Isn't it wonderful that it is the works that are burned, not the person! It is the branches that burn, not the believers themselves." Another spoke of it in a similar way, as follows. Some Christians produce "branches" which will not pass God's judgment. Their "branches," or the service they have rendered, will be burned at the judgment seat of Christ. These will all come to nothing, and the believers will receive no rewards from them. [19]

[17] Arthur W. Pink, *Exposition of the Gospel of John* (Grand Rapids: Zondervan Publishing House, 1956), 2:408.

[18] Everett F. Harrison, "The Gospel According to John," *The Wycliffe Bible Commentary*, ed. Charles Pfeiffer and Everett Harrison (Chicago: Moody Press, 1962), p. 1107; cf. also Raymond H. Saxe, "Security for Eternity," dissertation for a doctor's degree in theology, Dallas Theological Seminary, Dallas, Texas, 1954, pp. 239-241.

[19] William W. Orr, *Will God Keep His Own?* (Pasadena, California: Radio School of the Bible, n.d.), p. 22.

This view strains under the difficulty of injecting into John 15:6 an idea which is not only foreign to it but opposed to its direct teaching. The passage is actually speaking in a direct way of what happens to the branches which bear no fruit, and branches represent *persons* themselves (vv. 2, 5). Christ says, "I am the vine, ye are the branches." In verse five it is the *person* who is a branch (not his works); it is the *person* who either abides in Christ or does not; it is the *person* who is not able to do anything apart from Christ. The person and the fruit he bears are two distinct things. In the Old Testament passages that are the background for John 15, the vine and the branches refer to people, not works. When the fire burned the vine, it burned people — Israelites. That branches refer to people, not works, is confirmed also by the somewhat similar picture of branches in Romans 11:16-24.

In making verse six a text parallel to 1 Cor. 3:15, the view fails to recognize a basic difference. In John, it is clear from Christ's contrast that some branches (those abiding) do not even get into the fire. In the judgment of which Corinthians speaks, *every believer* will face the test of fire. Evidently a different phase of judgment (fire) and a different purpose are in view in the two cases. John speaks of the unsaved, Paul of the saved.

Right at this point we should mention that some (not all) who think John 15:6 speaks of a saved person have sought to prove it partly on the basis of the word translated "it is burned." This argument, which the writer has heard but has not seen in print, proposes that the word *kaietai*, from the root *kaio*, speaks of a less intensive burning than another verb, the compound word *katakaio*. The latter word could have been used by Christ if He had an unsaved person in mind. *Katakaio* appears, for instance, in Acts 19: 19, where those at Ephesus who had practiced magic brought their evil books to a bonfire and began burning them up — utterly consuming them. *Katakaio* means "to burn down," but we mean the same thing when we say "to burn up" (in smoke). In the Septuagint translation of Exodus 3:2, Moses watched the bush while it burned *(kaietai)* but was not consumed *(katekaieto)*. But the big point the present argument wants to make is from 1 Corinthians 3:15, where the believer's *work* is burned up *(katakaio)* but he himself, though judged as by fire, is saved through it and not consumed. So, both in John 15:6 and 1 Corinthians 3:15, a saved man burns but does not utterly burn up.

This argument is not convincing. Even *kaio* can mean to burn up, denoting an intense burning. It is so used here and in Isaiah 5:24 (Greek) since, when natural branches are burned, they burn up intensely, not mildly or partially. The compound word, *katakaio,* would not be necessary but superfluous here to convey the obvious idea, a severe burning. Also, we must not make too much of the distinction in Exodus 3:2 to gain a point in John 15:6, for as the *Expositor's Greek Testament* says of the bush: "This only shows that without the miraculous interposition it would have been consumed." [20] In addition to this, we need to realize again the difference between John 15:6 and 1 Corinthians 3:15 as pointed out above. And one would have to face all of the evidence from the entire phraseology in verse six that points more toward an unsaved person. Then, too, even if a legitimate distinction between *kaio* and *katakaio* were to be brought into force in verse six, the idea would not necessarily show that a *saved* man's judgment is in view here. It could be used just as well to argue that a man who does not abide and who will go into the lake of fire will not be annihilated or consumed absolutely (as natural branches are) but will suffer eternally (cf. Matt. 25:41; Rev. 20:10).

Still another interpretation of verse six understands the last three verbs as describing the spurning reaction of *men* to a professing Christian whose life testimony contradicts the claim of his lips. [21] The writer has seen this view stated by men who hold that the person is a hypocrite, an unsaved

[20] Marcus Dods, *The Gospel of St. John,* Vol. I, The Expositor's Greek Testament, ed. Robertson Nicoll (New York: George H. Doran Co., n.d.), pp. 829, 830.

[21] Lewis S. Chafer, *Systematic Theology* (Dallas, Texas: Dallas Seminary Press, 1953), 3:300; J. F. Strombeck, *Shall Never Perish* (Chicago: Moody Press, 1966), p. 123; Frank C. Torrey, "Fruit-Bearing," *Moody Monthly,* April, 1940, p. 421.

person who claims to be a Christian. He has noted that it has also been held by men who are sure that the person is saved and bound for glory, though not abiding in Christ.

One argument for this idea, from the plural number in "they gather," is that the judgment must be by men (plural) and not by God (singular). But this is very arbitrary. First, "they" can represent those who carry out the judgment of God, namely angels (plural). Even in the culture of vineyards, the work of servants ("they") in gathering dead branches was, in a real sense, the work of the owner whose servants they were. The Bible ascribes to angels the work of gathering men, whereas it nowhere represents men as "gathering" men for a judgment of their spiritual lives. The advocate of the present view might react to this by pointing out that he emphasizes only the *general* point of the three verbs and does not need to match all three details with spiritual analogies. But the fact remains that every detail *does* match with the angel view, according to much Scripture. And since Christ means particular things by other details of the allegory, why not here?

Second, casting into the fire (spiritually) is nowhere else in Scripture said to be the work of men, but rather of angels. There is the added significance that even the same verb for "cast" *(ballo)*, used here, is employed to designate the activity of angels (Matt. 13:42, 50; Rev. 14:19). *Ballo* is also used in reference to the unsaved being cast into the fire of future judgment, the same type of picture as here, though angels are not mentioned specifically as the agents (Matt. 3:10; 5:29; 7:19; 18:9; Luke 3:9).

Third, fire (burning) in the sense of judgment is related to the judgment of God through His agents. It is true that in the Old Testament God's fire was brought on the vine (Israel) through human instruments such as the Babylonians (Ezek. 20:45-48), who spurned Israel and her God (36:23). But in company with such words as "gathering" and "casting," which are associated with angels so often in the New Testament, the fire is more likely the future judgment into which angels will cast all who are without Christ.

A sober examination of Scripture, then, places the burden

of proof upon those who explain the judgment as that of *men* spurning a professing Christian (either carnal or unsaved), whose life is a mockery. Certainly it is true that men do have contempt for such inconsistency, as Lot lost his testimony in Sodom (Gen. 19) and as David gave occasion to the enemies of the Lord to blaspheme (2 Sam. 12:14). But that does not appear to be what Christ means in John 15:6.

There is still another view of verse six that we may consider. Some believe that a saved man is in view both in the first part of verse two and in verse six and say that verse six emphasizes not judgment but *uselessness* for bearing fruit. [22] Actually, this view and the one immediately above are very much alike except that the claim here is that the saved man is laid aside as good for nothing. The logic is as follows. Verse six, fitted squarely into its context, quite naturally appears to be a direct alternative to verses five and seven. It is both preceded and followed immediately by possibilities for a person who is unequivocally saved. Therefore, with such a connection in the flow of thought, it makes sense to say that it speaks of the consequences that follow when a *saved* man does not abide. Christ has made the point-blank statement in the foregoing clause that "without me ye can do *nothing*" (referring to the eleven, all saved men). Is it not completely logical to say that a *saved* person may experience the nothingness that Christ goes on to illustrate in the very next breath? Quite smoothly, then, according to this view, verse six presents a vivid case in particular of the results when a Christian does exactly what verse five has established as conceivable for him to do — "nothing." In his nonabiding situation, he is spiritually as useless as a vine branch that is severed — now dried and brittle, and unable to fulfill its intended purpose. It is fit only to be burned. In the illustration, the central idea is that of being useless, specifically with regard to doing the one basic thing branches (or Christians) are supposed to do — bear fruit. And how do those

[22] The writer has not seen in print the specific developments of this view as explained in the discussion, but has heard them in messages and has on file correspondence that deals with verse six in this way.

who hold this view explain the burning? They usually conceive of it in one of two ways. Either they say that the Lord is talking only about the *natural* branches burning, without carrying this detail of the picture over to the spiritual realm, or they give another explanation. The burning is simply one vivid detail, admittedly the most extreme in the picture, by which Christ can most effectively communicate His point. After making His strong statement about accomplishing *nothing*, He backs it up with a strong picture. A master teacher, He uses the powerful device of *antithesis* in His analogy, stating the utter impossibility of the bearing of fruit by men who do not abide. In this way He impresses upon the eleven that it is absolutely imperative to abide in order to bear fruit. As His comparison dramatizes what happens to natural branches out of contact with a vine, He goes quickly to the utter extreme — the nth degree — of the situation, the most drastic picture of uselessness: branches burning. The point is not that saved, though unfruitful, men will be lost at last and burn in eternal fire. It is rather that their efforts are empty to the point of nothingness in doing the great thing that is the emphasis in the context itself: bearing fruit.

But this explanation is too general. It does not go far enough. Certainly Christ is focusing upon uselessness for fruit bearing in one who does not abide. However, the burning is more likely to mean something specific that will actually occur as a consequence for spiritual branches that are out of contact. Other details in the context have specific actions to depict, such as the removal in the first part of verse two and the purging in the latter part. Further, the view is rather quick to withdraw the burning from any close relationship to other very similar biblical references where fire in plant life does illustrate judgment upon the unsaved. We have already adduced a number of reasons to show that John 15:2a and 6 have in focus men who do not truly possess a vital, saving identification with Christ.

One other comment should be made before we leave the verse. Although there is an analogy between what happens to dead branches and what happens to men who do not abide, we should not try to make the two agree at every point. For example, the burning of branches and the judgment of unsaved men is not the same absolutely. Burned branches are consumed so that they lose all identity and have vanished. Men who burn in the fire of eternal judgment retain their identity as persons and go on suffering punishment. Only in a general sense does the analogy hold here — that of perishing or coming into ruin.

What a tragic loss not to abide and therefore to come to such nothingness! What an indescribable blessing to believe on the Lord Jesus Christ and be saved by grace through faith. What a privilege to share His life forever, and, in the present expression of the reality of this, to abide in Him and bear fruit!

DOES THE FATHER
"LIFT UP" BRANCHES?

Every branch in me that beareth not
fruit He taketh away . . . (John 15:2a).

We come now to a view of the unfruitful branch (v. 2a)
that is popular among some Bible teachers, pastors, and
other Christian workers. It has such appeal that some professors in seminaries, Bible colleges and institutes, and other
Christian organizations are sure that it is right. It seems,
from a rather extensive check, that most of these have not
stated their convictions in published form. Here and there
some have put down their thoughts in small booklets that
are not widely known. But the view is evidently more
broadly disseminated than the scarcity of printed matter
might suggest. Among those who hold this view and are
known to many readers in the Christian audience are E. W.
Bullinger, Arthur W. Pink, and Ivor Powell. [1]

[1] E. W. Bullinger, *The Companion Bible: The Gospels,* or Part V (New
York: Oxford University Press, n.d.), p. 1557; see also his *Figures of Speech
Used in the Bible: Explained and Illustrated* (New York: E. and J. B.
Young and Company, 1898), p. 13 and footnote on p. 305; also Arthur
W. Pink, *Exposition of the Gospel of John* (Grand Rapids: Zondervan
Publishing House, 1945), 3:337; and Ivor Powell, *John's Wonderful
Gospel* (London: Marshall, Morgan and Scott, 1962). It is difficult to
find many statements of this "lift up" view in print, at least in works
known very widely even among evangelicals and fundamentalists. However,
it seems to be far more popular than this scarcity would indicate. When
this writer corresponded with a number of teachers and pastors in very
responsible positions across the United States not long ago, he received
several letters reflecting the "lift up" interpretation. A number of professors
in seminaries, Bible colleges and institutes, as well as many pastors and
Bible conference speakers, teach it. Many who are under their ministry
undoubtedly repeat it after them. It is difficult to locate the actual rise
of the view, but this writer is inclined to think that it is not much earlier
than Bullinger, i.e., within the past century.

Here is the way the view interprets the first part of verse two. It speaks of a person who is truly saved but not bearing fruit right at the time. The Father, in His wonderful graciousness, cares for this "branch" as a faithful husbandman. Imagine a husbandman who goes out to look at his vines and sees a branch trailing down in the dust. There it is not receiving the good of the sun's energizing rays. He reaches down and lifts it up from the ground rather than taking it away. One Bible teacher phrased this as God the Father "stooping down in overalls" to help the believer. The husbandman then stretches the branch on a trellis-wire or ties it to a stake that will support it. There it is exposed to the sun's rays which will have a wholesome effect so that it can begin to bear fruit. The Father, in the analogous spiritual realm, condescends to "lift up" (Gr. *airei*) a Christian who is not presently bearing any fruit. He ministers in various ways to place that believer in positions and situations in which he may *begin* to be fruitful. His dealings are with infinite grace, patience, and tenderness. His great desire is that the "branch" may yet become very usable to Him.

A friend whom the writer appreciates very much commented on the view in a letter this way: "This branch often has it easy, so to speak, while the fruitful branch (verse 2b) receives the rough treatment of pruning which is conceived to make it even more fruitful. This is because our wise Father knows just how to deal with each of His own in a way that is sensitive to what the person is prepared to bear. He deals individually because each Christian's needs are different. But with each varying type of loving ministry He chooses, His desire is that every branch should bear fruit."

If this interpretation is taken in verse two, how is verse six related? Those who so explain verse two have different ideas here. Some believe that the man in verse six is not "in me" (so not saved), while the man in the first part of verse two is. Others feel that both verses speak of a saved but carnal person, though there is a difference. Here, some propose that a Christian who has no fruit may be lifted up and established to bear some fruit (v. 2a). But when such a Christian goes on not yielding his life to the Lord, not abiding, then he must face the spurning judgment and merciless condemnation of men who reject his Christian profession as a mockery (v. 6). Or, in another view of verse six, the judgment is not by men but eventually by God Himself at the judgment seat of Christ (as in 1 Cor. 3:15). There are even other variations, so many in fact that some are not to be dealt with here (but see the earlier discussion of verse six itself in chapter sixteen).

Two points are crucial to this position on verse two. One is the premise that the branch without fruit is a saved person. The other is that the verb *airei* (from *airo*) means "he lifts up," without the idea of removal to another place. There is, however, another view that the branch means a saved person and that the verb means "He lifts up," yet the branch is lifted up out of its place to heaven in a premature disciplinary death because of persistent unfaithfulness (cf. 1 Cor. 11:30; 1 John 5:16). [2] We saw this earlier while considering verse six and so will not discuss it again here. It is our purpose at the moment to look at the other "lift up" view that leaves the branch on earth that it might *begin* to produce or *return* to fruit bearing that it has had in the past. Since only the second of the two points above is unique to this view, we will consider it alone. We have already seen reasons why some argue that the person in view is saved and have noted answers to these.

There seem to be two main reasons why some expositors insist on the view we are considering and the particular translation "He lifts up."

The basic Greek meaning. Bullinger, for example, says that *airo* is used 102 times in the New Testament and is translated "take up, lift up" in more than 40 of these. He views "lift up" as the basic, primary meaning of the word, says that "take away" is only a secondary sense, and suggests that his readers "see the lexicons." He lists a number of verses supporting the "lift up" meaning, and there are

[2] Lewis S. Chafer, *Systematic Theology* (Dallas: Dallas Seminary Press, 1953), 3:299, 300.

also others sometimes pointed out for this view (Matt. 4:6; 16:24; Luke 17:13; John 5:8-12; 8:59; 11:41; Acts 4:24; Rev. 10:5). [3] A point from the Liddell and Scott *Greek-English Lexicon* could also be used here, for they show that the word *airo* was employed outside the New Testament for the idea of hoisting a sail or even raising a cheer. [4]

Let us look at some of the instances in the New Testament itself, and we shall see that some do not bear out the view in John 15:2a convincingly while others could possibly be so understood.

Luke 17:13 says, "They lifted up their voices." In John 11:41 we read that Jesus "lifted up his eyes" to the Father. Christ bids the impotent man in John 5:8: "Take up thy pallet, and walk." The word *airo* is repeated with the same idea in verses nine, eleven, and twelve. In John 8:59, the Jews "picked up" stones to throw at Jesus. Now in these cases it is true that the "lift up" idea is present. But the strong accompanying sense of lifting up to *take away* or *remove* raises a question about the clear-cut nature of the evidence. For example, when the impotent man was to lift up his pallet, it was not simply to elevate it but to transport or carry it away to a different place, evidently to his home. The Jews who lifted up stones did so not simply to raise them to a higher level but to remove them in the direction of Christ. But then there are some of the examples which would be more analogous to the idea that the Father lifts up a branch that remains in the vine. For instance, when men lift up their voices, it is true that they elevate them to a higher pitch though they still belong to the same persons. This is a possible comparison with a branch lifted up from a low place to a higher place but not actually removed from the plant. And when Jesus lifted up His eyes, looking to heaven, His vision was elevated and His physical eyes were raised also. But His physical eyes did not leave His body. This might be conceived of as analogous to lift-

[3] Bullinger, *The Companion Bible*, p. 1557.

[4] Henry G. Liddell and Robert Scott, *A Greek-English Lexicon*. New edition, revised and augmented by H. S. Jones (Oxford: The Clarendon Press, 1940), p. 27.

ing up a branch from the ground to a trellis. When the angel in the vision John saw in Revelation 10:5 lifted up his right hand to heaven, the removal was only in the sense of elevation while his hand was still related to the body and not away from the body to which it was attached. And Moulton and Milligan point out a magical formula of the third century giving instructions to take twenty-nine palm leaves [this comes close to the picture of lifting up branches] and "lift them up two by two." [5]

In addition to the New Testament idea of "lift up," the Old Testament has many examples in which *airo* is the Greek (Septuagint) word translating such Hebrew words as *nasa* (to lift) and *netal* (to raise up). The chief baker, in telling Joseph his dream, said, "I thought I lifted up three baskets of mealy food on my head" (Gen. 40:16 *translation mine*). Ruth, having gleaned about an ephah of barley, "took it up, and went into the city" (Ruth 2:18). The psalmist said, "To thee, O Lord, do I lift up my soul" (Ps. 25:1). Jonah told the sailors, "Take me up and throw me into the sea" (1:12 RSV). In other instances, men lift up their hands (Ps. 28:2); those hating the psalmist lifted up their heads, meaning that they exalted themselves (83:2); the psalmist lifted up his eyes to the hills (121:1); and the lion representing the empire of Babylonia in Daniel's vision was lifted up from the ground and made to stand on two feet like a man (Dan. 7:4). *Airo*, then, is used often in the Greek version of the Old Testament (part of the background for John 15:2) to mean "lift up."

But besides this, the Old Testament also has other words which express the concept that God does lift up believers who are down and in need. One Hebrew term is *qum* (to rise, set up, establish), as in Psalm 41:10: "Be merciful unto me, and raise me up," and Psalm 113:7: "He raiseth up the poor out of the dust." Another word is *zaqaph* (to lift, comfort, raise up), as in Psalm 146:8: "The Lord raiseth them that are bowed down."

---

[5] James H. Moulton and George Milligan, *The Vocabulary of the Greek Testament.* Illustrated from the Papyri and Other Non-Literary Sources (Grand Rapids: Wm. B. Eerdmans Publishing Co., 1963), p. 14.

In seeking to be fair, we can say that some of the examples of *airo* do clearly mean a lifting up. From this it would make sense to say Christ means that the Father lifts up a weak, unfruitful person to support him.

But is this what John 15:2a really means, then? No, for although it is possible, it is still not the more likely meaning, since we must decide finally from even wider evidence that bears on the question.

(1) It remains true that in many cases *airo* means an actual, clear-cut removal or taking away. Even the better examples for the "lift up" view do not sufficiently offset that.

(2) The specific Old Testament background that is directly relevant for the illustration of a vine itself does not have a "lift up" idea in prospect for branches bearing no good fruit. Instead, the prospect is judgment (Isa. 5:1-7, 24; Ps. 80:16; Ezek. 15; cf. also the similar prospect for the fig tree without fruit, Luke 13:6-9).

(3) The fact that branches are *broken off* in the similar horticultural picture of the olive tree (Rom. 11:16-24) gives more support to the sense "he takes away" than "he lifts up." Jeremiah 11:16 connects closely together the *breaking* of the olive branches and the *burning* of them.

(4) The silence in John 15:2a after the word for "he takes away" makes any gracious purpose of the husbandman, while possible, only conjecture in the final analysis. There seems to be a finality about the Father's act in the word *airei,* for we do not read after this the words "that it might begin to bear fruit." This, of course, is in direct contrast to what the verse does specifically tell us of the branch that is bearing some fruit. The latter is pruned (i.e., a person is cleansed) "that it might bear more fruit."

(5) There is the point-blank statement that the branch bears no fruit at all as far as the text itself is concerned. This, in view of John's customary way of sharply drawing his contrasts between the saved and the unsaved in black-white categories according to the overall character, is more easily resolved with the view that this symbolizes one who merely professes to be in Christ.

(6) Many saved men who are not bearing fruit at the moment would not require a tender, gracious ministry of the Father (for they may be carnally resisting that at the time) so much as a seemingly harsh work that will bring them back to their spiritual senses. They would need to be jarred from the deceitful delights of sin by which they are now being enticed and brought back to the will of God.

But there is a second reason why the "lift up" interpretation is sometimes favored in 15:2a.

The culture of actual vines.   One might stick to his convictions that the "lift up" view is right by pointing out that a husbandman *does* lift up branches. He might vividly describe a visit he made to a vineyard and the wide-scale trellising he observed there. This would seem rather convincing for the "lift up" idea. For some it would put the interpretation out of the range of doubt, if they did not think it through carefully. But it is not that easy to settle. If one brings vine culture itself into the picture, it is also possible for the word *airo* to have the meaning "takes away." Grape farmers *remove* branches, too! As a matter of fact, the writer has heard experts in viticulture say that it is far more customary for branches that have no fruit to be removed than to be lifted out of the dust. It is arbitrary to argue an advantage for the "lift up" view on the basis of horticultural practice when there is another custom that suits the meaning of a word even better.

In conclusion, it seems best to agree with Harrison, who has stated that the "lift up" idea, though attractive to many, is not as likely here as is often assumed. [6] But while what is said in support of the view is not the point in John 15:2a specifically, it is still true in the Christian life that the Father does lift up those who are bowed down. Let us rejoice that our Father certainly does watch over us with a faithful care beyond that of all other husbandmen! Let us be glad that He does surely see us in those times when He knows and we know that we are right down in the dust as was the

[6] Everett F. Harrison, *John, A Brief Commentary* (Chicago: Moody Press, 1962), p. 90. He says: "It is a dubious interpretation which gives to *taketh away* the force of 'lifts up' (from an unhealthy state). . . ."

psalmist (119:25), even when we are not at the moment bearing the precious fruit for which He yearns. And thank God He does pick us up and hold us! He brings us into the sunshine of His grace, we get a new lease on life, and we go on to bear "fruit unto holiness." He knows that we are truly His, branches in reality, as in the latter part of verse two, and He has found in us *some* fruit which is the expression of His own imparted life. He prunes or cleanses us so that we may bear even more fruit!

JOHN 15:1-6 IN A NUTSHELL

Now that we have looked at various ways of explaining John 15:2a and 6, it is helpful to draw together what we believe Christ was really saying in the passage as a whole.

Our Lord spoke the allegory out of a rich sensitivity to the images His listeners would know so vividly from their Old Testament, the intertestamental days, their Temple, and the culture of vines. Israel was the vine of the Lord according to their Scriptures, and the vine had been an emblem of Israel on Maccabean coins as well as on the gate of Herod's Temple. Now Christ Himself was "the true vine," meaning the ideal and ultimate vine.

Christ, in using the picture of a vine, was primarily focusing attention on the thought of union and communion men might have with Him, and also His great desire to see fruit in His people. With the rejection of Him by Israel as a nation now sealed and His death, resurrection, and ascension looming imminently before Him, His people would be the members of the Church He had said He would build (Matt. 16:18). They would include both Jews and Gentiles who would believe on Him as did the eleven disciples who were listening to Him in the upper room. With these people (branches), He would have union and communion; in them He would expect fruit.

Fruit is so important in one of Christ's branches that He emphasizes the subject immediately (v. 2) and mentions it eight times in the passage. He draws a point-blank contrast between two types of branches (persons). The first does not bear fruit, but the second does.

It has been concluded that in speaking of the person with no fruit Christ means one who is not really saved to begin with. Such a person therefore does not show forth the fruit that will in some measure be manifested when a relationship with the living Christ is authentic. This conception of the person has come from a thorough attempt to weigh various relevant factors that bear upon the meaning and let the evidence of Scripture speak for itself. The crux of the problem involving this person is that our Lord speaks of him as being "in me." To some it seems a natural meaning that this absolutely must mean only a saved man. They assume it to be an open-and-shut case and, as they often say, they "take the words as they are" and go no farther. Robert Shank even sees any view different from his own — that one may lose salvation — as characterized by the words he saw over an ironsmith's shop: "All kinds of fancy twistings and turnings done here." [1] This type of statement could be used against any view with which one disagrees and so settles nothing. What Shank views as a job of twisting or turning may be the correct interpretation of Christ's meaning, which he has failed to recognize because he has not given other factors of Scripture their proper sense and correlation with other details. The question has to be carried farther than some are willing to take it if a view they *think* is right is to be tested by all the checkpoints of careful interpretation. We dare not make a quick assumption before looking at many matters that have a real bearing on the interpretation. It is the mind of Christ we seek, and not what might at first strike us as the meaning.

In this study, we have put the words "in me" under a probing searchlight and also inquired along a number of lines of Scripture that construct a fuller context in which to decide with confidence what Christ means. We honestly concluded that the realm of professing persons is in view as being "in me." Some persons under this designation are indeed genuine, others are only seemingly so or claim to be so. This is the most satisfactory interpretation, not be-

[1] Robert Shank, *Life in the Son* (Springfield, Missouri: Westcott Publishers, 1961), p. 44.

cause of one point but because it has much more in its favor than any other explanation. Some of the reasons are summarized now.

(1) The person bears no fruit at all as far as the verse itself describes him. This does not easily identify him with the truly saved who in most other Scriptures are thought of as bearing *some* fruit.

(2) The sharp contrast in verse two between two types of persons is consistent with an overall pattern of contrasts in the gospel of John where the distinction is between unsaved and saved. Verse two fits within a larger picture, then.

(3) When Christ views Himself as the ideal Vine, the true Israel, it is natural for Him to speak even of those who merely profess a relationship to Him as being "in me" (in a sense). The Old Testament background to which we ought to look for help in explaining Christ's meaning shows that mere *professors* were mingled in with *possessors* in the vine of the Lord, Israel.

(4) When the Father takes away the unfruitful person, *removal* is the most likely meaning of the verb *airo* from the standpoint of word usage, the Old Testament background of judging Israel the vine, and vine culture itself.

(5) Christ's contrast in 15:2a and 2b, 3 appears to be the same type as in 13:10, 11, where He clearly distinguishes Judas (unclean, unsaved) from the eleven disciples (clean, saved).

(6) Removal of the branch not bearing fruit is very similar to the picture of removing branches from the olive tree in Romans 11:16-24. There, certain Israelites were "in" the tree and yet they were such in a sense in which they were unsaved all the while. Those removed were "in" in a different sense than those not removed.

(7) The first part of verse two which speaks about the branch being taken away seems in context to be referring to the same type of judgment later described in greater detail in verse six. Significantly, this would tie together quite naturally the same ideas we find in the Old Testa-

ment passages about the vine — the vine with its *branches, removal,* and *burning.*

(8) The "in me" relationship for some could be understood in the way in which many Jews were in the covenant bond by outward circumcision (one sense) but not by inward circumcision of the heart (another sense).

(9) Christ shows elsewhere that there must be a distinction between what a man really *has* and what he may *seem to have* for a while (Luke 8:18).

For these and added reasons we feel that we have gathered up the true perspective of verse two. The branch that bears no fruit represents a person who prefesses to be in a genuine relationship with Christ just as others for whom this profession is real. Christ, for the sake of the contrasts in the illustration, conceives of him for the time being as related even though for him it is only nominal, of course. His failure to abide and bear fruit shows his actual status. In reality, he is not saved and never has been.

In view of the reasons given, this explanation is not an easy way out of the problem as some who misunderstand the case have claimed. Such a view meets the demands of the many factors in the large sweep of Scripture as well as standing the test of careful exegesis in individual verses that relate to the perseverance of the saints. The view also stands strongly against loose living or license tolerated under the auspices of teachings that misconstrue the grace the New Testament itself emphasizes. It looks, as the New Testament does, for the fruit of that genuine grace that brings salvation, which is "instructing us to deny ungodliness and worldly desires and to live sensibly, righteously and godly in the present age, looking for the blessed hope and the appearing of the glory of our great God and Savior, Christ Jesus . . ." (Titus 2:11, 12 NASB).

Christ's point about such a branch without fruit is that it is taken away. But what does this mean, more specifically? It could possibly mean that the Father takes such a person away through excommunication from the local church fellowship, a judgment reflecting His will but carried out by responsible spiritual persons. Yet if that is even in view it is only a prelude to the Father's ultimate removing of the unfruitful person after his life on earth and in the final judgment. The taking away, then, is a terse statement of the same thing that verse six portrays in much greater detail.

Our Lord moves on, in the latter part of verse two, to describe a branch that *does* bear fruit, and *all* agree that this represents a saved person. He bears fruit (and that could even be very little, though it will be at least *some*), and the Father cleanses him in a process of his living day by day so that he may bear *more* fruit. He effects this cleansing by the ministry of the Holy Spirit using His Word as the instrument to "set apart" the believer more and more (John 15:3; 17:17; 1 Thess. 4:1-8). The Christian experiences this reality when he interacts with the Word and welcomes it into his situations with the desire to obey it by faith and by God's gracious enablement. Confessing sin that he has tolerated and seeking to forsake it by the help of the Lord (Prov. 28:13; 1 John 1:9) is part of the cleansing process also. Sometimes, too, the Father cleanses His child and increases his fruit bearing by bringing trials into his life. In such times, the Christian may see more of his own inadequacy to cope with life's situations and learn to rely more wholly upon his Lord as the Vine. He seeks God's ways more devotedly. His life is purified and he grows more like the Lord, bearing fruit.

What, then, is this fruit Christ talks about? We have seen that the passage itself emphasizes fruit in the sense of inner attitudes such as love, joy, and peace. This is in harmony with the "fruit of the Spirit" in Galatians 5:22, 23. But we have also discovered from other verses in the New Testament that fruit may have a wider range of meaning for the Christian. The inner virtues themselves are closely related to, and find concrete expression in, good works, good words, and even people led to the Lord. These, also, are fruit according to the way the Bible uses its terminology.

In verses four and five, Christ underscores the idea that good fruit is the product of a life that abides in Him. "I am the vine, ye are the branches." Those genuinely "in me" are to "abide in me" in experience. He contrasts the person who does abide in Him (v. 5a) with one who does not (v. 6). The abiding man bears *fruit* and *more* fruit and *much* fruit. He is, to be consistent with the picture of the vine, a green and prospering branch bearing a lush cluster of grapes. By contrast, the man who does not abide is like a branch that is severed from the vine, dried up, and eventually fit for nothing but to be burned.

What goes into a life that does "abide"? What does abiding include? First, "abide" has the concept of *time,* of continuing. All who are genuinely saved, those who have the Son and His life as in 1 John 5:11, 12 (not just apparently so by outward connections), will continue or persevere. Going on with the Lord is for them a characteristic way of life. When a saved person veers temporarily off on a tangent and is sadly inconsistent with his claim to belong to Christ, this does not alter the fact that his relationship with Christ is real and not spurious. Looked at over the entire sweep of time, his life will have some signs of life in Christ, of abiding, in terms of fruit.

Second, in addition to a *time* idea, "abide" also includes some degree or depth of *quality* involvement with Christ. Abiding is not simply a matter of time but also of the quality that fills that time. Here, various Christians are at different stages of growth in relation to the degree, depth, or consistency of their fellowship with Christ the Vine. The abiding of one person may be of a quality that is far richer than that of another. Any Christian also may grow so that his abiding, at a given time, is of much greater quality than it was some weeks, months, or years before. In chapter fourteen, entitled "Let's Put It All Together," one may see how this understanding of abiding correlates consistently with what Paul says by different terminology (perfect, spiritual, carnal) in 1 Corinthians chapters two and three.

So we see that abiding relates to both *time* and *quality.* Let us summarize this matter of quality. When we speak of quality-involvement with Christ, we mean what has been spelled out under three words: relating, rejecting, and receiving.

First, the person who is abiding is in some measure vitally *relating* his life to Christ — to His Person (what and who He is) and to His purpose (what He is seeking to do). Gradually in this matter of maturing, he is coming to desire more and more, through the Word he appropriates as his spiritual food, to live in harmony with Christ as a Person. He beholds the glories in Him and cries out, "Oh, to be like Him!" or "Let the beauty of Jesus be seen in me, all His wonderful passion and purity." Joined intimately with this desire to relate himself to Christ as a Person is his longing to be more and more one with Him in purpose. In this sense it is very meaningful for him to sing, "Only to do what He wants me to do, every moment of every day." And in the measure in which he becomes vitally involved with Christ Himself through His Word, he also becomes increasingly committed to His purpose and conformed to it (John 15:7).

Second, the person who is abiding is *rejecting* various attitudes, interests, and motives with which he realizes Christ cannot sympathize. These are things whose character is wholly opposite to the fruit he is to bear. Christ cannot condone these because of His very Person and purpose as made known in the Word. In every saint on this side of glory there is inconsistency (sin) here, and he must ever be learning and applying Christlikeness. The quality with which he does abide at any point is the degree of his progressive sanctification (negatively from sin, positively to the will of God). It is also the measure in which he is an overcomer of whom John writes (1 John 5:4, 5).

Third, the person who is abiding is *receiving* the adequacy of Christ with which to meet the issues of life. He receives the Word of Christ to dwell richly in him, receives the testings God uses to prune or cleanse him, and receives Christ's presence and power made real by the Holy Spirit. Here again, Christians differ widely in the degree of quality involvement, and one Christian's quality can vary greatly at different stages in his own process of growth. But the quality of his abiding will be in the degree that he truly receives the adequacy of Christ for all that life offers and all that he can offer to life.

Failure to be all that we might be at a given point does enter into this experience. In the measure in which a genuine Christian is inconsistent with regard to relating, rejecting, and receiving in every issue of life, the principle of verse five applies. Christ says, "Without me ye can do nothing." This is totally true of an unsaved person, for to the absolute degree his life amounts to nothing of true spiritual value in the estimation of Christ. But the same principle also applies to the saved person whose characteristic is to abide. To the degree that he is abiding in a given hour of life, to that degree he bears the fruit of the vine. Christ lives His quality of life in and out of him. But to the degree that his abiding is marked by inconsistency or elements of his self-life rather than true Christlikeness by grace, to that degree the fruit of his thoughts, words, and actions is either "nothing" or of lesser value, consequence, or significance than it might have had in God's scale of appraisal.

As we come to verse six, Christ tells us about the person who does not abide. Nonabiding is the pattern of his life. He is unsaved. His life is altogether one that accomplishes "nothing" in terms of verse five, for the quality of Christ being lived in and through him is not there genuinely in any measure at all. This man's life is conceived to be in direct contrast to the life of one who does abide. Our Lord is evidently referring to an unsaved person (even though he may have made some kind of profession), for every phrase in verse six points consistently to this conclusion when it is related to its more likely connections in Scripture. This study has devoted an entire chapter to developing these associations.

What we have said does not mean that we discount the elements of *truth* found in certain other views, even though they wrongly explain verse six as speaking of a saved person. For example, when some make the verse refer to a saved man whose poor testimony is a mockery spurned by others, there is the truth that this kind of phoniness does occur in saved people sometimes. We may recall, for instance, that David gave "great occasion to the enemies of the Lord to blaspheme" (2 Sam. 12:14). But although this does happen, it does not mean that Christ is speaking of a saved man *in this verse*. Also very true in other Scripture (though again wrongly pressed into verse six) is the idea that a saved man must face the fires of the judgment seat of Christ, where rewards will be given. That is the teaching of 1 Corinthians 3:11-15, but it is not what Christ is talking about in John 15:6, where the subject is an unsaved person.

• • •

So this is the meaning of our Lord's vivid picture of the vine and the branches. Now as we come to the end of the study, let us keep before us the main point that Christ was seeking to emphasize. Our heavenly Father is looking every day for fruit in those who are true branches in Christ. This is possible when we are abiding in Christ, and, as Adam Philip has said so aptly, "The fruit is the tree's success." [2] Let us prosper in this true success of abiding in Christ and bearing fruit!

[2] Adam Philiip, *Lingering in the Sanctuary, Notes on John, Chapters XIV-XVII* (London: James Clarke & Co., 1936), p. 88.

Made in the USA
Lexington, KY
27 October 2017